DORÉ.

BY

A STROLLER IN EUROPE.

My dress is splendid, you behold,
Blazing with the ruddy gold.
FAUST.

Je commençai ma réforme par ma parure ; je quittai la dorure.
JEAN JACQUES ROUSSEAU.

NEW YORK:
HARPER & BROTHERS, PUBLISHERS,
FRANKLIN SQUARE.
1857.

PREFACE.

Gentle Buyer! the following Letters were written during a year's residence in Europe.

As they were written on a third visit to that country, they will be like a man selecting his third wife, not caught by glare nor dazzled by show.

They will endeavor to call every thing by its proper name, and nothing by an improper one. Therefore, when they meet Mephistophiles dressed like a lord, and "blazing with the ruddy gold," glancing at his club foot, they will not hesitate to say, "Sir, you are the devil!"

Doré means simply the difference between the inside and outside of things, and as this difference has always struck the author more than any thing else in Europe, he has adopted that title more as a fit emblem of the position of the Old World than as a representation of the general tone of this work, which is merely a book of travels, as little in the style of the guide-books as possible. The comfortable and orderly appearance of things in Europe, as compared with America, has often been remarked upon; but, as the author of the *Con-*

trat Social says, "there is a comfortable and orderly appearance of things about a dungeon." That is no indication of happiness. The bayonet can make every thing look orderly up to the very day when an unhappy and oppressed people break out in revolution. If any American be alarmed at the noisiness and boisterousness of his own country, which must, of necessity, always show the worst side to the world, just let him rub off the gilding a little in Europe, and he will find no cause for dissatisfaction with Republicanism.

Having assumed a letter-writer's privilege of neither re-reading nor rewriting these pages, they are expected to share a letter's fate—the fire!

Hoping the Gentle Buyer's vengeance (if he be disappointed) may descend with the Letters into the fire instead of upon the writer's head, he remains, with respect,

A STROLLER IN EUROPE.

NEW YORK, *October*, 1856.

CONTENTS.

DORÉ.

SEA HOTELS AND LAND HOTELS.

Paris, November, 1855.

I AWOKE this morning in Paris, having gone to bed, or to sleep rather, at a pace of forty miles an hour somewhere between this and Calais. This is fast sleeping, and might be called a long nap; but it does not equal that of some of my fellow-passengers in the steamer Africa, who got into their berths at Boston to get out again only at Liverpool. I can not tell if they slept all that time; if they did, certain noises in their state-rooms assure me that they had very strange dreams.

I took just eleven naps on the passage across the Atlantic, ate eleven dinners, and as many breakfasts, lunches, and suppers. I made no inscriptions on the waves, and the waves made none on me, although this amiable reciprocity was freely indulged in by many, who came below with wet backs as the reward of that ambition which induces so many travelers to leave their *marks* where they can not leave their names. If columns and monuments had the ocean's wit, there would soon be an end of such cheaply-purchased fame.

That man was a poor judge who said a ship is the best place to betray one's true character. The only things that can be seen better at sea than on land are salt water and baked potatoes. A baked potato, at sea, has more character than a dozen inanimate passengers. It is really lovable, and seems to have as much affinity for a landsman as a pea-jacket for a midshipman. But more characterless things than a steamer full of passengers are not to be found except in James' novels: they differ only by nationalities. Frenchmen talk all day, and do nothing; Englishmen eat all day, and say nothing; Spaniards eat nothing, and say nothing; they are the atrabilious favorites of Neptune; Americans drink and smoke all day.

But for the wonderful things of the sea, its storms and its waves, the drunken boots and the dancing looking-glasses, the musical crockery and quiet babies, are they not written in the chronicles of a thousand travelers?

I staid in Liverpool just long enough to make a herring of myself, which was just the time necessary to get out of it. I, however, had an opportunity of seeing the advancement made in that city toward increasing the comforts of travelers. I had the same room I occupied five years before at the "Adelphi" hotel, the same bed, the same furniture, and the same curtains; perhaps beds and rooms are like pipes and fiddles, all vastly improved by smoke and age. The coffee-room, too, that spot

"for contemplation formed,"

is still the same quiet, solemn retreat as formerly. One would suppose men slunk in there to perform some secret, disgraceful act, instead of to indulge in a social, rational repast. The most awful stillness prevails;

you hear the rapid ticking of your watch, and even the pulsations of your heart; you shuffle your feet, knock your knife and fork against your plate, and bustle about in your chair, as if to produce some animation about you, but it only seems to render the succeeding quiet more intense, while the leaden eyes of the lonely eaters are raised to see the cause of the clatter, and lowered again, as slowly, upon the smoking dishes before them. The spectre waiter—spectre only in act, for he is plump as a Southdown mutton in appearance—glides noiselessly to your side, and suddenly startles you by placing a dish under your nose while you believed him at the other end of the room; he inquires seriously, as if asking of your spiritual concerns or about a cancer in your chest, what you will take next; impressed by his manner and the pervading silence, you reply solemnly, *plum-pudding!* "Plum-pudding!" he repeats, majestically, adjusting his white cravat, elevating his chin, and gliding away noiselessly as he came. What with the solidity of the diet and the atmosphere of the place in which it is taken, your ears soon begin to ring, a film grows over your eyes, and, to prevent worse consequences, you rush out of doors for relief into the open—smoke! Mem.: Infallible recipe for stupidity—roast beef, plum-pudding, and silence, taken conjointly.

Five years! Five years of the nineteenth century, equal to the whole of an old-fashioned century! Five years of steam, and of railways, and of telegraphs, and of peace and war, and peace again, during which travel has increased five fold, and yet I am to awake in my room in the same musty bed, in that ill-arranged *first class* hotel, and find every thing in exactly the same position as if I had gone to sleep there five hours instead of five years ago! Conservatism with a vengeance! In that time the Metropolitans, the St. Nicholases, and the Grand Louvres have sprung up, and palatial hotels even dot the stormy waves of two oceans, and yet all that Liverpool, one of the first commercial cities of the world, can offer her guests is this same old Rip Van Winkle hotel! I ventured to suggest that some improvements might be made in the hotel system in England, and was answered, "Oh! *we* like it as it is." It certainly was preposterous to suppose that old nations like England and China could learn any thing new: have they not the accumulated wisdom of centuries handed down by forefathers' forefathers? I paid pretty dearly in pounds, shillings, and pence of 1855 for this wisdom of centuries as displayed in the hotel-keeper's bill, and was glad to get away from Liverpool.

I felt snappish all the way to Calais Custom-house, where the officer put me in a better humor by first putting me in a worse one. Counting too much on the mutual friendship of France and England, I had forgotten to bestow a becoming appearance of usage on a certain article bought in London; but custom-houses know no allies, and the offending object was laid on the appraisement table. I put my hand in my pocket, and happened to rattle my *keys* at the same instant, when, suddenly, the officer, probably thinking the article of too small value to notice, politely returned it to me.

THE TOWER OF BABEL.

WHETHER a confusion of vision as well as of tongues was part of the punishment inflicted on mankind for their vanity in building the Tower of Babel, I can not say; but certain it is that every nation seems to see every other nation standing on its head; the houses are upside down, or there are a dozen houses in one, as in Paris; the people write, beginning at the right-hand side of the page instead of the left, as in China, or they wear their tails on their heads instead of where our horses see fit to wear them; or even if we discover men with tails in the right place, as in Africa, we find fault with that; in New England and Germany, they call the 12 o'clock meal dinner; in Paris, breakfast; and the supper of one place is the dinner of another. In France they eat roast horse; in China, roast rat; in Nova Zembla, roast man; in England, roast beef. Which is right? I leave it to some future congress of all nations to decide, and also to devise means of establishing a universal language, which will place us all *as we were.* How simple and easy to decree that all infants born after 1860 shall speak but one and the same tongue! I am sure it would be a matter of entire indifference to the little innocents whether they were taught to lisp English, French, or Latin; and the only obstacle to the plan I can think of would come from that large class of conscientious persons who allege, as the reason of their not having learned any language besides their own, that it would be thwarting the designs of the Almighty as exhibited at the Tower of Babel!

Owing to this confusion of sight, travelers are apt to divide themselves into two classes, namely, those who see every thing upside down because it is different from what they see at home, and those who start out determined to be so very liberal that they out-France France in what is French, and out-Turkey Turkey in what is Turkish. These last will have their mistress in France and their three wives in Constantinople. They worship at the Greek Church in Russia, and are good Catholics in Spain. Pipes, mysticism, and beer are their ideals of life in Germany, and during their *dolce far niente* in Italy they believe that, after all, the true end of life is to study the beautiful. Of all travelers, the American most readily assimilates with the customs and habits of other nations. In Paris you may know an American at a glance, he is so very *Frenchy:* the cut of his hair, beard, and coat are all French; he has on his person all the "*hautes nouveautés*" of the season, a *haute nouveauté* around his neck, another on his back, and another on his feet; he is like those modern walking advertisements seen promenading the streets with long placards on their backs, only that he carries the *article* advertised instead of a description of it. In Germany he becomes all négligé again, and sits by the hour smoking and talking, and imbibing German habits and German beer all at the same time; and so, into whatever country he goes, he becomes for the time being a part of that country, adopting its usages, comparing them with his own, and improving on what he has seen after his return to America.

The Englishman, on the other hand, is just the reverse. Held in the tenacious grasp of habit, he is slow to receive new impressions, and, indeed, thinks every thing foreign so inferior to every thing English, that he is apt to condemn, with proud disdain and without examination, whatever differs from the insular style of the foggy isle. On this account he is not spared by his witty neighbors, who, for years, have made him their butt: they have laughed him into and out of a thousand follies, because, in Paris, being determined to enjoy himself if he can, he lays himself fairly open to them. Conscious that he is ridiculed for his taciturnity and sobriety, he tries to be gay and lively, but he has indulged his *noli-me-tangere* humors too long, and the Parisians, instead of laughing with him, laugh at him. He then intrenches himself behind his British dignity, which is no better protection, for his lively little tormentors surround him, some taunting him with cries of "*il s'en ira! il s'en ira!*" while others pique his vanity by crying "*il ne s'en ira pas! il ne s'en ira pas!*" Finally, he assumes his national character, and becomes paymaster-general, in which capacity he always succeeds. The Parisians dance, and he pays the fiddler; and many a grisette and common actress await the summer to sell the smiles which may be picked up in the street by Frenchmen for the trouble of stooping, to "Milor Anglais," or "Mon Gros Anglais," for rouleaus of British sovereigns. One thing, however, the English have learned by all this, and that is to bear ridicule. The lesson has been taught them entirely by the French; it has been beaten into them; their skins have become so toughened that they are entirely insensible to it.

But the Americans are impatient of the slightest criticism; our vanity must be fed on sugar-plums and sweetmeats! we are an *enfant gaté;* thin-skinned and sensitive as women; so successful in most things, we are unwilling to be found faulty in any.

We whine a good deal when told by an Englishman that, while traveling in one of our railway carriages, he thought there was a snow-storm, but afterward discovered it was only the people spitting; we get very angry because a European lady tells us that she sat a whole hour reading, while an American gentleman, with his feet cocked up on the back of her chair, had a boot against each of her ears! At the same time, the lessons have taken effect, and it is now considered very vulgar to spit snow-storms, or to rub the ears of European ladies with one's boots; still, there is room for much farther improvement in these matters, and we shall cordially welcome every year as many English and French as have no objection to making Trollopes of themselves, and who, while caricaturing, misrepresenting, or delivering partial truths only, may touch the sensibilities of Brother Jonathan, and lead him to repair many things that sadly need mending.

I commenced my Letters by awaking in Paris, but as it was neither in my own room nor bed, nor, indeed, in any bed at all, I must subscribe myself yours till both are found.

CHAMBRE À LOUER.

ROOM hunting! Some years ago, in New Orleans, I thought it fine sport to travel all over the French part of the town and look at the *chambres à louer* (as well as the young Creoles who showed them). I then swallowed all the French politeness so lavishly expended for twenty dollars worth of *expected* rents; but it was one of the follies of youth, for which I have since received due punishment. I verily believe that all young mankind and all lady *room-renters* are sworn enemies from the moment they fail to strike a bargain, and then the question for the former is, how to get out of it. After several day's search up the sunny side of the Boulevards and down the shady, all around the Madeleine, and through the Rue de Rivoli, the fiftieth lady had me finally penned up in the five hundredth room examined, and seemed determined to keep me there! I had exhausted all my excuses on the other forty-nine ladies in finding the other four hundred and ninety-nine rooms too large or too small, too cold or too warm, too cheap or too dear. What on earth to say now I did not know; the perspiration stood on my forehead, as well it might, and it seemed as if my terrible enemy, with her hands planted on her hips in determined attitude, read in my eyes the whole forty-nine excuses which had cost me three day's labor. At last she asked me for how long a time I wished the room. A happy thought flashed across my mind, and I answered, "*For one day*, Madame." She not only *permitted* me to go, but opened for me the door, which slammed to again at the imminent risk of my coat-skirts, and without being ajar long enough to permit the issue of a *bonjour*, which I have no doubt she uttered.

I descended hastily, resolved to take the very next room offered, which I did, being rewarded, too, for my perseverance by getting the best room I had seen at a reasonable price.

Any one of moderate means who has visited Paris, and wished to live comfortably for a few months without being in a hotel, will not accuse me of being hypercritical. The comforts of Paris are made for the wealthy, and it is not at all difficult to get a richly-furnished apartment of two, three, or more rooms. But to find a convenient and pleasant sleeping-room, clean, large, and airy, as in America, is very difficult indeed. And in the matter of excuses, it will appear strange to you not to mention at once the fault one has to find, and go; but that is only the beginning of an argument to which there is no end. As an instance, I was inquiring for a room with a southern exposure; the lady answers, "We have none; but we have a very pleasant room facing the north; come and see it."

"Useless, Madame; it will not suit me."

"But just look at it; Monsieur is not obliged to take it."

Out of politeness, or, rather, because I can't help it, I enter, and say all I can say, viz.,

"Madame, the room is pleasant, but the sun does not enter it."

"Mais pardon, Monsieur, it does—*in the summer.*"

it being now December, and I to remain in Paris three months.

And this is the style of reply all over Paris—in short, in room-renter parlance, black is white and white is black.

Alas! I shall never forget my three days of room searching in Paris; but it was an instructive lesson of patience and perseverance, as well as of street nomenclature and household arrangements.

I lay in bed until a late hour the next morning, and when I awoke the welcome sun was streaming through the windows, and twice gilding the large mirrors which ornament every room in Paris of the least pretension to comfort—in fact, in furnishing a room, a Parisian buys first his rich mirrors, four feet by six in height. "*Orné de glaces*" is his alpha and omega of rich furniture: he will live on bread and wine six months to be enabled, in the seventh, to look at his attenuated form at full length in his own *glace*. After his mirror, if he has any money left, he will perhaps buy a wash-bowl and pitcher, but they will be the smallest and most insignificant things in his whole apartment. I was lying in bed thus, making the acquaintance of one and another article of furniture about my room, and extracting a bit of character out of each, now wondering who first invented wax-polished floors, and what a drubbing he would get from a hundred thousand *frotteurs* if he were alive, and now thinking how much more comfortable the room would look if that shining floor were covered with a good warm carpet, when—tap—tap—tap at the door.

"Entrez."

Enter the "*bonne.*" She was a pretty *bonne* (all the *bonnes* in Paris are not pretty). She was a chatty *bonne* (all the *bonnes* in Paris are not chatty). I felt conscious of deserving a *bonne* uniting the two qualities. Shall a man search Paris three days for nothing?

"Monsieur, veut il prendre son café?"

Ha! ha! it was not in Oregon, some two years since, when, rising from my bed in the sands of Cape Blanco, where, with a pillow of stones, and heaven for a canopy, after a twenty-mile walk on the sea-beach, I had slept soundly, lulled by the music of the waves as they broke on the shores—it was not there that *bonne*, or any one else, demanded if Monsieur wished his coffee. "Monsieur" jumped up (a little stiff certainly), lighted his fire, and made his own coffee.

"Oui, Monsieur veut prendre son café."

Exit *bonne*, Monsieur rolling over in bed as much like a lord as he can.

And, after all, a man with some taste and education, with a red shirt on his back, and waiting on himself, provided he have a few books in his possession, may be as happy in the forests or on the shores of the Pacific as he can be in Paris. Instead of pictures, he admires the rolling waves, the gigantic trees, and clear blue skies, such as can only be seen on the Pacific coast and in Italy; for science and amusement, if he has the taste and perseverance of a Hugh Miller, he can not lack; for food, he may make his selection of venison, quail, snipe, salmon, trout, crabs, etc., etc.; and in lieu of the highly-flavored sauces of the Maison Dorée and Café Anglais, Nature provides him with a hearty appetite—"il n'est sauce que d'appetit." Still,

I must confess that, for the moment, I felt very well contented where I was, and it requires a deuced deal of philosophy and capability of self entertainment to—tap—tap—tap at the door again. Enter *bonne* with a waiter and bowl of smoking-hot coffee, a little thimbleful of salt, porcelain plate strewn with *scintillations* of butter, which look as if they had been petrified and struck off with a hammer, and, lastly, a delicious roll, all of which she places on a table at my side, meanwhile chatting furiously, and, finally, with a "*voilà*," darting out of the room, leaving me a little stupefied at her volubility. Now I do not know how many times I have been through this same operation in Mexico, New Orleans, and Cuba, but it is certain that our well-trained quadroon slaves (no bad specimens of grace), or even the Cuban señorita, with her "*Quiere Vmd. su café?*" can not equal in style and grace the French "*bonne.*" She is unapproachable, so clean and fresh-looking, always lively and in good spirits; innocent-looking as a lamb, yet cunning and wise as a serpent; she is not at all squeamish, and enters your room freely at all hours; and if you have a *cool head* yourself, she will hand you a towel while you are taking your bath with the same nonchalance with which she would hand you the bread at the dinner-table; but if you are one of those nervous individuals that, at sight of a petticoat entering, rushes out of his bath, covering the floor with water, and hiding under the bed, she will give a shriek, and dart out of the room with an "*Oh! ce Monsieur là, est il affreux?*"

THE GOTHS AND VANDALS IN PARIS.

Paris is no longer the Paris of 1851, but Paris more beautiful and more expensive, though perhaps less gay and agreeable.

Consider that one hundred thousand foreigners, *Parisianicé barbarians*, have, during the past summer, invaded the place, and ravaged it, like the swarms of locusts in Egypt. They have not carried off the Tuileries, nor stolen the statues of the Louvre; they have knocked no *chips* off the obelisk of Luxor, nor pocketed any "rare old editions" in the Bibliothèque Royale; but they have damaged the hotels, ruined the garçons in the cafés, stimulated the avarice (already in excess) of the shop-keepers, and, worst of all, nearly destroyed that hospitable deference toward strangers which abounds more or less in all countries, but which particularly distinguished Paris.

Formerly, the proprietor, attended by half a dozen waiters, received you at the hotel of your selection; you chose your room, your luggage was instantly brought in and opened; the *bonne* flew about, supplying you with water, towels, etc., etc.; and last of all appeared the *blanchisseuse* to receive your soiled linen. Now, although the Exhibition is over and every body gone away, yet the vicious habits learned remain; ten to one if you see the proprietor of your hotel at all. A servant, without any "*by your leave*," transfers you to the English, German, or Spanish quarter of the house, as the case may be, where you find a stupid

Irish girl, who prosily *fixes* things for you in *her* way. Nobody unstraps your trunks; nobody comes for your linen; nobody offers to do any thing for you—pah! man, have you not a tongue in your head to ask for what you want? and ought you not to be glad to get a bed at all, and wait on yourself? Last summer, says the girl, people slept on the floor, with three, four, and five in a room. And so they imagine their houses are still full, and that they have neither time to attend to nor room to accommodate all their guests.

After such a reception, you are fully prepared for a poor dinner; but, nevertheless, I was surprised to find so great a change for the worse in the *table d'hôte* of the Hotel des Princes, formerly celebrated for its good table.

To crown all, I picked out of my bill errors enough to reduce it nearly one half! Not at all strange; "so many bills to make out, and so many items!" and then these Turks, Russians, Spaniards, etc., all they want to know is the total; they do not care for items, and can not read them if they did.

When a stranger enters a café, the garçon begins making signs at him, taking it for granted he does not understand a word of French; if he lays down the newspaper a moment, the waiter snatches it without asking permission: it is not his fault; he has asked a thousand times during the last ten weeks, and has been answered by an empty stare! He no longer says *merci* for three or four sous gratuity: it requires silver for that; and to bring forth a *merci bien*, which in 1851 cost only three sous, now costs a franc. He is not to blame, poor fellow! Have not rich nabobs, who were here for a week at the Exposition, glorified themselves in tossing him two and five franc pieces?

Such was the state of things at the time of my arrival (a month since), but it is surprising what an improvement is already taking place. Paris is again assuming its agreeable, polite demeanor. The cafés are again becoming the gay and social saloons they once were, and the garçons, under the renewed training of the Parisians, rival one another in amenities. The best waiters in the world are some of those well-trained mulattoes of the southern part of the United States, who have all their lives waited on gentlemen; but for a large class of waiters, the Parisian *garçon de café* is matchless; he is polite without being officious (a fault waiters easily fall into); he is of agreeable appearance, dresses neatly, and has an excellent memory; and none better than he can guess character at a glance. If you do not know what is good, he will read you in an instant, and be assured he is not going to waste delicate tit-bits on you, but will satisfy you according to your taste; you shall be as gustatorially pleased as you are capable of being: Mohammed's Paradise could do no more.

The people, too, are beginning to flatter the little vanities of travelers (all travelers are vain), and to look upon them as guests; in short, in a few months Paris will be itself again, and then those other changes, which have made the city more beautiful physically, will be enhanced in value.

Louis Napoleon will probably be mentioned in history as having done more for the city of Paris than any other single ruler of France. The finishing of the

Louvre alone would be glory enough; but, besides that, he has lengthened the Rue de Rivoli, and made it one of the finest streets in the world; he is adding, at enormous expense, another boulevard to the long line now existing, which is to be named the "Boulevard de Sebastopol;" he has cut away many of those ugly angles that were to be found all over Paris, and left in their stead either open spaces or handsome buildings. All these things have been going on while the war and the Exhibition have been absorbing his time and attention, and may be said to have served as his amusements. Happy the people whose kings indulge in *such* amusements!

Fillibuster emperors are not likely to remain idle. If they are of the right stuff, as Napoleon III. seems to be, they are a blessing to the class from whence they spring, however disagreeable to an elegant but effeminate aristocracy. Louis Napoleon courts the army and the people, and if he can keep the reins, will improve both. But he has a difficult game to play. France is still on the crater of a volcano.

But I am determined not to write politics and pictures more than I can help, though both are always under my eyes; the first in the newspapers, and the second in the Louvre; and from the newspapers, Vasari and the guide-books, you will learn of both more than I can tell you.

FILLIBUSTERS.

SPEAKING of fillibuster emperors in my last, I must explain the meaning of this term, lest his majesty Napoleon III. take umbrage, and, following the example of his uncle in the case of Madame de Staël, inform me quietly that he understands, on the most *undoubted authority*, that I intend quitting Paris to-morrow!

The word fillibuster, then, although it has hitherto been applied only to Americans, is a word of the most extensive signification, and hereafter will take its place in the dictionary, and rank in importance in the world with the words steam, electricity, and other powers of that ilk which have existed since the world began, but have only developed themselves fully in the nineteenth century.

The first fillibusters of whom we have any notice were the Children of Israel, who took away the beautiful land of Canaan from its inhabitants because they were unworthy to possess it. I can not *understand* the justice of that; but of one thing we are assured, namely, that it was not for any goodness in themselves that these fillibusters were permitted to revel in the milk and honey of Canaan.

England is the greatest fillibuster the world has ever produced. The grand scene of her operations has been in India, just out of reach of the spectacles and spy-glasses of her *conscientious* citizens, but within rupee distance of all. This territorial aggrandizement goes in England by the name of *Can't-help-it-ism;* but it is only another name for the same thing. A few degrees of latitude and longitude change heat into cold, and *vice versa;* a few centuries change theft from a virtue to a vice. Well, it is the destiny of England to overrun all India, and, taking it away from its wretched occupants, benefit that country as well as the whole world. I can see the benefits of it, and rejoice at them, but can not understand the *justice* of the act. Perhaps, if the Old Testament were being written now, nearly the same language would be used with regard to England and India as was used in relation to Israel and Canaan.

Napoleon Bonaparte was a fillibuster, but afterward turned robber. If he had remained at home on the throne of France, and concentrated his energies in improving and elevating her, he would have then remained a fillibuster.

William the Conqueror was a fillibuster.

Cromwell was a fillibuster.

Napoleon III. is a fillibuster.

The English House of Lords is descended from Norman fillibusters.

Maternal Rome was fillibustered.

Colonel Walker, of Nicaragua, is a fillibuster; it remains to be seen if he will continue so, or become something worse. The government of the United States is not a fillibuster. If it had kept California without paying for it, it would then be classed in that category; but as it paid $15,000,000 for that barren land, or about twice what it was worth in the market at that time, it has so far preserved its escutcheon spotless.

A fillibuster, then, is merely an agent, representative,

or instrument of "manifest destiny:" it is a strong, healthy, *common sense-y* man, people, or nation, which goes and saves, or relieves a land just as it is tumbling into decay and ruin through the effeminacy and vices of its occupants or rulers.

The fillibuster has not a nice conscience; he believes that the owner of all the earth has a right to destroy all nations who, neglecting the trust confided to them, live in effeminacy and ease; and, without scruple, he constitutes himself the agent of that destruction or renovation.

According to all principles of justice that I know of, the fillibuster should be hanged unless he can "show his papers."

The next lands converted by fillibusterism will be China and Japan: they will be washed out, cleansed, and renovated, and then be of service to the whole world, instead of cumberers of the earth; but it is sad to think that so much good must spring from blood and crime! Such results have been and will be, but they do not justify the means.

Having sufficiently explained the meaning of this word, and apologizing if I have trodden on any corns belonging to crowned heads, I shall now relate a little history.

In the days of Victoria, Queen of England, there lived a mighty ruler, and his name was Jonathan, and he lived in the West.

And Jonathan was exceeding wealthy and powerful. His flocks were many, and spread abroad over the land, so that no man could number them; and his cattle grazed on a thousand hills.

And while he was yet young, Jonathan took unto himself thirteen wives and many concubines.

And he, and his wives, and his concubines increased in wealth daily.

But his concubines waxed jealous, and they entreated him, saying, Take us unto thyself also, that we too may be thy wives, and equal in power with these our sisters.

And in the course of time he took unto himself eighteen other wives from among his concubines; and he had thirty-one wives.

And his fame went abroad throughout all the world, for there was none so mighty as he; and all the nations stood in awe of him.

Now it happened one day, while it was yet summer, and in the middle of the day, that Jonathan looked out of his casement.

And lo and behold! but a little way off there was a maiden bathing in the sea, in the blue sea that washed the shores of his kingdom.

And the maiden was fair and exceeding beautiful, in so much that Jonathan remembered no more his thirty-one wives and his concubines.

So he sent Lopez, his chief officer, to inquire after the damsel.

And Lopez returned forthwith, saying the maiden's name is Cubanita, and her father is called Spaniola, a mighty ruler of the East.

And Jonathan said, Go fetch her; I have need of her. But he charged Lopez that he should tell no man that it was by his command he did thus.

And Lopez went away, and the servants of the damsel's father caught him and slew him.

Now when Spaniola heard of these things, he was exceeding wroth; and he sent a spy unto Jonathan to entrap him.

And the spy said unto him, "O king, thy power is known in all the earth, and thy justice is a terror to all evil doers!

"There was a rich man of the East who had many daughters, but as he waxed old in years his daughters died off, one by one, until there remained unto him one only.

"But she was more lovely than them all, and she was her father's delight, and his comfort in his old age.

"But it happened that a wicked man passed that way, and, casting his eyes on the damsel, loved her, and tried to carry her away from her aged father, with all her jewels and her riches, which were great.

"What shall be done unto this man, O king?"

And the king could scarcely restrain the indignation that was in him, and he said, "Let him die the death!"

And the spy answered and said, "O king, thou art the man!"

And Jonathan's knees shaked greatly, and smote one another.

And the spy returned unto his own land, and told his king all that had happened.

And Spaniola straightway gathered together his mighty men, and his warriors, and his footmen, and his horsemen, and all his vessels.

And he sent word unto Vic, Queen of the Saxonites, and unto Nap, King of the Gallites, saying, "Let us smite and punish this rising ruler of the West while we are yet strong, lest when we be aged, and our infirmities multiply, he fall upon us and rob us of our wives and our daughters, and lead them into captivity in a strange land."

And Nap and Vic took counsel together, and agreed unto all that Spaniola had said.

And they assembled all their hosts, and sent them in many strong ships, with swords, and spears, and instruments of fire, over unto the coasts of Jonathan.

And Jonathan raised his eyes, and when he beheld the mighty fleet he trembled in his boots so that he did shake the earth.

And he sent out presents unto the captains of the fleets, and to all the chief officers.

And he stoutly denied all that Lopez had done, saying that he was a wicked man, and had acted contrary to his commands. "What! shall thy servant, with his thirty-one wives and many concubines, take unto himself yet another? Mammon forbid!" (for Jonathan was a worshiper of Mammon.)

And the speech of Jonathan was pleasing unto the captains and officers, and they made a great feast of bullocks and fatted lambs; and at the feast they all made a treaty together, and agreed to protect Cubanita from any who would carry her off without her father's consent.

And the vessels returned into their own waters; and Jonathan entered his house, determined henceforth to have no more to do with strange women — *unless forced to it by "manifest destiny!"*

HOUSE-TOPS AND JOURNEY THITHER.

Did it never occur to you that the day will come when books of travel must cease? To be sure, it is difficult to make the world stay described; and the New Zealander, who describes the beauties of London to his countrymen to-day, after passing through the cycle of books in which the Londoner shall reciprocate and describe to his decrepit countrymen the palaces of New Zealand, will at least realize the prophecy of Macaulay, and sketch the ruins of Saint Paul's from a broken arch of London Bridge.

The last book of travels will no doubt emanate from some Yankee, who will write with an iceberg for a table and the north pole for a footstool; or perhaps it will issue from the sources of the Nile, which reminds me of a remark of Dr. Johnson's in Rasselas, I think, viz., that a man can not drink at the source and the mouth of the Nile at the same time. As it will probably be a very long time before he will take a sip at the source alone, the worthy doctor's aphorism is likely to remain true for some ages.

More than twenty years ago, Heine thought the best way to write a book of travels in Italy was to say as little about Italy as possible. Pens and travelers have not been idle for twenty years, and positively there is not a stone in Europe left for description, unless we take the house-tops, and even there Bulwer has been prowling about, and devoted a whole chapter to the roofs of London.

The house-tops of Paris are the ugliest parts of the city. They remind one of a handsomely-dressed man crowned with a bad hat. Positively there is a chance for some young architect to make name and fortune by inventing a new and comely style of chimney, roof, and rafter. We should show our best side to heaven instead of our worst.

A journey to these house-tops (for it is a long journey) is a description of Parisian life. Few have a whole house to themselves. Five, ten, and twenty families live in one house, and their histories and position, like the history of the earth, are written in strata. The lowest strata contain the oldest families generally, though modern volcanic eruptions have tossed up the elements considerably, and given this place to gold.

The Parisians attach the greatest importance to this arrangement, and a family of stratum No. 1 will turn up its nose at stratum No. 4; while, in revenge, stratum No. 4 invariably *looks down* on stratum No. 1. But the vanity of No. 4 was piqued nevertheless. So, one day, he locked himself in his room, and, chagrined, determined to devise means of living in stratum No. 1 without additional expense. After a month'ss tudy he sent for his engraver, and ordered five hundred cards with his address, "Rue de Faubourg St. Honoré, No. —, *au premier.*"

"But, my dear sir," says the engraver, "you make a mistake. You are in the fourth story."

"Not a bit of it. First comes the sous sol, eh?"

"Yes."

"Then the Rez de Chaussée?"

"Certainly."

"Then the entresol, and afterward the *first* story. Do as I bid you."

The cards were engraved and circulated, the vanity of all Paris (Nos. 2 to 6 inclusive) was cheated and flattered, and the fashion spread soon after all over France; so that now a fat countess of ruined fortunes, after reaching breathless the fourth story, congratulates herself on living *au premier.*

Seriously, this arrangement is a continual annoyance, and also belongs to a part of that *doré* system which pervades all Europe, from the crown to the clown; a system in which truth, in little things as well as in big things, is constantly sacrificed to vanity and show.

You will hear the Parisians themselves constantly giving roundabout explanations on this subject. If you inquire a person's residence, he tells you in the third (story) above the entresol. The Concierge, in his turn, on being asked, tells you the fourth (story), meaning the same thing. Sometimes there is no entresol, or it is so nearly like a *story* that you would hardly observe it. The time the Parisians lose every year in all these explanations would equal all the working hours of a hundred men for a month—time enough to build a fine house. Do away with this vanity, my friends.

But we were on our way to the house-tops. The servants live next to the roofs; but all the pretty grisettes live, as *they* say, *au deuxième—en descendant du ciel!* where I have also taken my lodgings, so as to be nearer heaven, never fancying for a moment, however, that the grisettes are the angels thereof, although they may impart a heavenly character to an earthly paradise.

Here we have the purest air, the brightest light, the best view, and most freedom from noise, whether it proceed from the incessant roll of carriages in the streets, which lasts from eve till morn, or the almost as incessant trampling of feet within the house, which continues all night, as the various members of the household return—some from the theatres, some from the cafés, some from parties, and sóme from the gay ball-rooms or gambling saloons that are closed only with the dawn.

Yet it is a trying thing for the inhabitant of the *cinquième* to enter his splendid dwelling on the Boulevard or the Rue de Rivoli at the usual dinner-hour. He then passes through layers of gustatory odors, as nicely defined as are the social positions of those occupying the strata whence they issue. At floor No. 1 he is sorely tempted by the high perfume of a *faisan truffé*, which he sees smoking in the midst of a gay company who are assembled in a magnificent saloon where every thing is doré, even to the conventionalisms of conversation! At floor No. 2 the odor of a haunch of venison salutes his nostrils; a fine roast turkey, *au marrons*, is being served as he passes No. 3, by which time his appetite is so sharpened that he rushes through and past the other successions of roast beef, corned beef, simple bouilli, and so on, descending in the scale of quality as he ascends in height, until he arrives at the humble *pot au feu* of the grisette quarter, where, the first cravings of appetite satisfied, he probably enjoys his simple dinner and *simple* society as much as the most delicate palate in the most *doré salon* of the building he occupies.

But it will not be surprising if he sometimes exchanges his *pot au feu* for the silver service of the Café de Paris, as I expect to do to-day, the very mention of such delicacies being a temptation too strong to resist!

MI-CARÊME.

YESTERDAY was mi-carême, that oasis in the desert of Lent where the weary faster halts and refreshes the animal, in order that the spirit may be better enabled to endure the remaining twenty days of privation to which it is called.

Lent is a terrible ordeal to the Parisians; and the worldly wisdom of "*the Church*," with that prescience for which it is distinguished, as if to enhance the value of the victories over the flesh to be gained in future ages, forbid, centuries ago, only one of the least annoying enemies to man's spiritual interests, viz., meat. Roast beef, proud and haughty as the nation of which it is the representative, immediately took umbrage, and fled hastily and forever from France and all Catholic countries, and installed itself with the generous Saxon, where it receives due honor.

But the Parisians, with their accustomed finesse, consulted the chemists and the doctors, and from certain knowledge obtained, which was mostly unknown to the ancients, though probably long since discovered by "*the Church*," they fell with might and main upon fish, eggs, and truffles, a diet they now stick to with such pertinacity that they generally run from ten to twenty days past Lent before they discover it is over. However, the deprivation of a certain class of amusements for forty days is certainly wearisome, and the faithful sigh for their balls and parties. The unfaithful never stop them at all; they are heathen, and never enjoy any thing because they want to enjoy it all the time.

You may imagine the delight with which all Paris arises on mi-carême; the flesh, dried and wrinkled by twenty days' privation (*from meat*), assumes plumpness at the thought! The messengers of Potel and Chabot may be seen at an early hour hurrying from door to door, and leaving a truffled turkey here, a ham of Bayonne there, and a leg of venison somewhere else. They are swiftly followed by the confectioners, who distribute from house to house their *fruits glacés*, creams, and bonbons.

Thousands of promenaders crowd the Boulevards, and carriage-loads of masks amuse themselves by driving from the Madeleine to the *column of July* and back again. They are mostly low people, however, and one wonders how they find any sport in such drives, as they all look very sober, and seem to say and do nothing.

Their amusement undoubtedly consists in having 100,000 people stare at them; it is a part of the universal vanity of human nature, which is displayed, too, by the first minds in Europe, when they trick themselves out in fantastic costume, and show themselves to the vulgar gaze. Fantastic is only a relative expression, and to Socrates, a modern court dress and a butcher's masquerade dress would be equally fantastic! So let us not blame the butcher and the baker for finding delight in that which can entertain and tickle the vanity of European potentates.

It is certainly a pitiful sight to see wise men tricking themselves out in travesty, and wearing every thing worn by the clown at a mask ball except the mask, and wearing that, even, over their hearts! All this gold, and pomp, and false show of courts is intended to dazzle the eyes of men, and blind them to the faults of the system under which they live, and which has been for centuries reducing them gradually to a worse and worse servitude, until they have been brought to a point beyond which they can scarcely go, and are now crying out every where over Europe for their rights. But it is partly their own fault. Mankind naturally tend toward toadyism; they must worship somebody, and they will willingly pay their labor, and their money, and their independence to place the object of their worship (often no better than a heathen idol) in a position they can not hope to approach themselves. He must be doré, his court must be doré, and he must doré the chains of his slaves. And thus Europe has gone on with a system of splendor covering deceit till she is in the saddest position imaginable, both as a community of nations and of individuals. As nations, distrust reigns every where; not a single nation in Europe but what feels afraid of its neighbor; not a diplomatist that dare come forth and utter the truth about things; hardly a single alliance is formed from motives of justice and truth. Every thing rests on a fictitious basis; suspicion and distrust prevail every where. Such is the condition to which the avarice and injustice of the few have reduced the masses in this quarter of the globe.

But, instead of mi-carême, I am getting on to politics again; and as they are rather an exciting subject at present, I may change my mind in relation to them, and recur to them frequently before finishing what I have to write of Europe.

But *revenons à nos moutons.* Toward six o'clock in the evening the throng tire of walking, and looking, and gazing, and direct their steps by thousands toward the restaurants and cafés, which now begin to fill with a hungry crowd who are supposed to have fasted during twenty days. The garçons fly about with unaccustomed activity, and the guests do as all guests do at dinner, and, besides that, lay their plans for the night, and select out of the five hundred private and public balls to take place that night the one they will honor with their attendance.

There are six hours' time to kill before the grand ball at the Opera commences; and the theatres, and the cafés, and promenades, and a thousand nothings are all called to assist in the murder of these six hours.

Finally, the witching hour of midnight arrives, and the doors of every house pour forth a motley crowd of masks and dominos—of kings, counts, marquises, gamins, pierrots, &c., dressed in all colors and styles, and tumbling out pell mell, like the variegated *dragées* from a Christmas-box. The side-walks swarm with humanity; nobody is distinguished, because every body is so much distinguished. The rights of the real king, even, would be disputed by the tailor's son, who is decked as a king. Such is the effect of dress! The streets rattle with the continuous roll of carriages, moving in long double lines as far as the eye can reach, and kept in order by numbers of mounted policemen. We are soon borne along with the mass to the front of the Grand Opera House, which blazes with festoons of gas; and while admiring, amid the crush of silks, and satins, and powdered wigs, the outside of the building, we will defer the description of the splendor of the inside till our next.

BAL À L'OPERA.

As the last sound of the twelfth stroke of that hour which summons ghosts and witches died away, the doors of the Grand Opera House opened, and the over-crowded ante-chambers poured into the vast theatre a cornucopia of pretty things, representing the outside of every thing great under the sun, and as unlike ghosts as suppers, silks, and satins could make them. Not less beautiful to the eye was the theatre, with its countless chandeliers sparkling with gas, its decorations, its wide sweep of floor inviting the dance, and, most of all, its *Strauss* with his hundred musicians! I was swept along by the gentle bosoms, not of the breeze, but of the sweet *Parisiennes*, who pressed behind and wafted me (and it is pleasanter than being wind wafted) right up to the orchestra.

And here I must obtrude a bit of advice. No boys

under thirty should go to the mask balls of the Opera, and no men over sixty. The periods comprised between these two ages, and which Professor Flourens calls the second youth and first manhood, are the only ones in which Saxon blood should expose itself to the dangers which will there beset it. As Gallic blood loses its inflammable particles, and becomes thin at twelve to fifteen, owing to precocious education, no rules need be prescribed for it. Men past sixty, however, are always liable to do silly things.

But the archet of Strauss, quivering with latent harmony, and the cynosure of a thousand eyes, suddenly moves through the air, and summons countless tinkling feet into motion, while it delights the ears of those who are merely spectators by the bewitching music which it frees from the thraldom of its hundred masters.

A lame man could hardly help dancing to such music, but the French shouted and danced; they danced with their feet; they danced with their legs; they danced with their arms; and their eyes danced most of all. Now the locks of a marquis brush your face, and now the toe of a countess comes within an inch of your nose, though you be taller than she! A *Pierrette* whirls you completely round and out of your philosophy, while perhaps a real danseuse from the Opera, in performing one of her *entrechats*, carried away by her enthusiasm, falls into your arms.

The scene was indeed brilliant, for no lady is allowed to enter unless masked and dominoed, or in travesty, and no gentleman unless in travesty or full dress; so, whatever might have been the character and standing of the individuals of the assembly, their exteriors were certainly always elegant and often splendid.

Among the ladies in travesty I noticed a decided majority preferred the pantaloons (this is true all over the world). Some of these were of velvet embroidered with gold, and others of blue satin fringed with lace, and reaching just below the knee; in short (the pants were short too), they were of all shapes, colors, and qualities, as dictated by taste, or required by the characters represented. Nothing more bewitching than these *manmaids*, who unsex themselves by your side as if to show how much superior to you they are in grace and elegance, whether in the garb of females or males.

As the night wears on and the blood grows warm, the excitement and noise increase: every body talks with every body, *tutoyers* every body, and ridicules every body. They laugh at one another, and tread on each other's toes, or kiss those they had never seen, and yet all with the best nature in the world. One man has an enormous hat covered with raw cotton, loosely fastened on, which he manages to rub against the new dress-coats of a score of gentlemen, leaving his white marks every where, and followed by bursts of laughter. Another collects a crowd around a hapless Englishman, who is standing fixedly firm in one spot without moving a muscle: "Oh, quelle vache tu es!" says he, "What a cow you are! how tame you look!" and he dwelt on his salient points with such wit that I at last fancied I could see a brindle cow wagging its tail and chewing its cud. The poor Englishman, with his red hair, peculiar cast of countenance, and ignorance of French, did look uncommonly tame and quiet, but probably had more sound sense than fifty like his persecutor. But no one gets vexed; indeed, a man at a mask ball in Paris who would get vexed would be thought a fool.

At three o'clock in the morning the excitement reaches its height; the musicians have caught the general spirit, and play with redoubled energy; the demand is for noise as well as for music. One of them seems occasionally to strike a barrel, another a tin pan, and another a gong, which certainly gives a wildness to the instrumentation in perfect keeping with the whole scene. A fine dust arises and fills the whole theatre; it is just enough to dim a little the blaze of light, and impart a hazy look to the splendid array of beauty spread out on all sides. The noise is deafening; shouts of laughter in every key of the diapason rise from five hundred voices at once; a blaze of wit and repartee, stale enough in Paris when one knows it, but brilliant to the stranger, flies about one's ears like the popping of squibs. The third sex (for a grisette must belong to that sex, as she can hardly be ranked as masculine or feminine) is now all animation; she claps her little hands and dashes in, performing all the most approved evolutions with surprising dexterity. Having put a cigar right into the policeman's mouth, she feels at full liberty to put her toe right under his nose; and though he ought to be hardened enough to correct and reduce the wonderful angles she forms with her legs, he can not resist the double compliment, and even blushes. He is her prisoner instead of her being his. And now what a clatter of feet, and flashing of eyes, and tossing of heads! How the tall plumes wave in the air, and how the snowy white locks of the marquise dance to the music, and what a shaking of gaudy dresses, and laces, and spangles, and epaulets! What beautiful white shoulders and bosoms flit under your eye! What taper forms are continually bounding about you, and rivaling all the positions of the graces! Surely they are all intoxicated with pleasure, and perhaps a few thimblesfull of Cognac.

I was standing near one of the most beautiful of those *manmaids*, and gazing upon her joyous features and marble white shoulders, which her loose garb fully displayed. She seemed to be the centre of attraction, for there were not only a large number of gentlemen standing around her, but there were several young ladies in one of the boxes above that seemed perfectly fascinated as they watched her with riveted eyes. She had thrown off her mask, and displayed a lovely countenance, with one of the most pleasure-loving expressions imaginable. Her whole soul seemed to be absorbed with delight as she gave herself up with entire abandon to the mirth of the moment; and I could not but notice with what a triumphant yet kind look she kept glancing up to her more virtuous sisters in the boxes, as if to say, See how *we* enjoy ourselves, while you are cooped up there within the narrow limits of decorum. I trembled for the young ladies in the boxes; I should tremble for any one, man or woman, upon whom that lovely being should cast her fascinating glance. But just at this moment I observed a gentleman in black approach and touch her on the shoulder. He was tall and well made, and had a long, straight feather in his cap, but I noticed he had a club foot. She turned around suddenly at the touch, while a momentary paleness passed over her flushed face; but, seeing nothing, she thought it was only the plume of her partner that had brushed across her shoulder. Again the gentleman in black touched her as before, whispering in her ear, "Thou devotest thy life to pleasure; science shall profit by thy death. Thine end the dissecting table!"

I expected to have seen her fall away in a swoon, but at that instant Strauss and his hundred (ah! who can resist Strauss and his hundred?) burst forth with one of his choicest morceaux, and the fair one, with a smile, dashed into the dance. The music must have drowned his words, but they made such an impression on me that, although his person now seemed disagreeable, I could not resist following him to hear what he would say to others. So, threading his way through the motley throng, he whispered to one, "*Fosse commune;*" and of another he asked, "Where will you get food for yourself and sick mother to-morrow?"

I began to feel outraged at such extreme and heartless liberties; but observing that all those addressed laughed louder and danced with more life even than before, I concluded that no one had heard the gentleman's voice, nor had seen him, but myself, for in an instant, and I can scarcely tell how, he disappeared from my view.

At this moment the French gentleman who accompanied me, and who had been dancing, rejoined me with his partner, and desiring to show me every thing, proposed that I should follow them to the *buffet*, which was situated in the lower part of the building.

Here a scene presented itself such as can never be witnessed elsewhere. The tables were strewn with Champagne bottles, smoking hot punches, bavaroises, cigar stumps, broken cigarettes, coffee-cups, liqueur glasses, and, in short, every imaginable drink or utensil that could be serviceable in a Bacchanalian rout; while around the table, and on the table sometimes, were closely grouped a hundred fantastical forms and shapes of every color, twisted into every possible position, and all talking, or rather shouting, at the same time. The air was filled with a dense smoke from the cigarettes of fifty pretty lips and the cigars of their companions, and if there was any thing they did harder than drinking and smoking, it was the jingling of glasses, banging of chairs, and general efforts to see who could make most noise.

My companion and myself edged our way with difficulty to chairs, now bumping against the rushing garçons, and now treading on some satin slipper, and in return receiving very pretty compliments for our stupidity, which my friend was not slow in returning in voluble volleys, among other things desiring to know why people had such long, awkward feet.

Seated at last, he gave his partner a cigarette, in the management of which she left nothing to be desired by the most skillful señorita of Cuba; she puffed and sipped punch, and sipped punch and puffed, and chatted, all at the same time.

Rattle went the glasses, prattle went the tongues, as only French tongues can; dancing went the tables, and whirling went the chairs, as the new drinkers poured in and the old drinkers *fell out:* it was a real orgie. The smoke alone rose solemnly and thoughtfully to the ceiling, and seemed philosophizing on the scene, except when the music of Strauss and his hundred (ah! *what* can resist Strauss and his hundred?) appeared to break through its thick columns, and send it whirling in rapid pirouettes, just like any other dancer.

For an instant I was completely lost in reflections. Never had I been present at a scene of greater apparent gayety—never were appearances more deceptive. Nearly all of these gaudy, gilded exteriors concealed hearts that were, or ought to have been, miserable; but a short life and a merry one seemed to be the universal aim, and so they danced themselves into misery and death—danced themselves as far away from true happiness as the quiet of a family fireside is removed from the boisterous mirth of a mask ball.

But these thoughts were suddenly interrupted by hearing the gentleman next me, in a violent altercation with a young lady about her mask: he was trying to induce her to take it off, which she positively refused to do.

It was one of those half masks which nearly every one wears at these balls, and which, by leaving the mouth alone exposed, converts nineteen women out of twenty into frights. Who has a pretty mouth? who has a mouth that, deprived of the *dress* of the other features, is even tolerable? A half mask is murder to a pretty face. The mouth is the slave of all the other features, indeed of the whole body; it labors incessantly to support our lives; it is our constant medium of communication; it is an indispensable requisite of lovers, when they wish to express mutually what the tongue and eye are incapable of doing; and not only that, but it is called upon to represent our passions, our feelings of delight, laughter, etc. For all these things the eye twinkles a little, the nostril dilates perhaps, the forehead gives a slight wrinkle, and the ear remains in sluggish inactivity, not even beautifully pricking, as with the horse; but the mouth performs downright physical labor, now doubling its natural size, and now shrinking up like the closed top of a lady's reticule (the inanimate representation of one half of a kiss); next rolled up in wrinkles of laughter, and now compressed with anger, and sometimes called upon to do all at once, until the poor feature, wearied and distorted by the multiplicity of its duties, has settled down into a sort of abject melancholy, which has made but a sorry-looking ornament of it.

I should have devoted a whole letter to mouths, and think a chapter should be added to Lavater, who probably never attended mask balls, which brings me back to my mask.

All his efforts to see behind it were unavailing; punch and entreaties were alike ineffectual; and just in proportion as the difficulties increased, his curiosity became greater, and he felt more certain that so beautiful a form must be the possessor of a beautiful face. At last, desperate by opposition, with the rashness of an Alexander, he cut the Gordian knot which restrained his curiosity, and the mask dropped in her lap, and his heart into his boots, to judge by his crestfallen face! It was cruel! it was rude! She comprehended at a glance the length, breadth, and depth of the disaster (for she was positively *ugly* at the first view), but with that tact which belongs to the sex, and particularly to the French portion of it, after administering to him a smart box on the ear, she burst out laughing, and added the remainder of the moral by saying, "*There! never snatch the mask from the face of pleasure!* Allons."

We threaded our way again toward the ball-room, and in five minutes I thought her pretty, and comprehended instantly the remark of the ugliest gentleman ever born, that, give him half an hour, and he would make any lady forget his ugliness.

Beauty attracts, but it is only our qualities that can retain. In passing the *foyer*, he was obliged to drop his lively companion, the foyer being the sanctuary of dominos and dress-coats; it is forbidden ground to all travesty; it is the grand scene of intrigue; and if the dancing-hall is gay and noisy, this is sombre and quiet, but not less crowded. Every class of woman is here concealed, from the countess to the shirt-maker, and they parade about in their solemn black costumes like the Misericordia of Florence.

Taking the seat of a mere looker-on, I overheard my neighbor say to a gentleman, after considerable talk, "Give me a franc, now, to buy a bottle of wine!" He gave her the money, at which she left, promising to return in an instant. He was a German, and asked me if I knew the lady.

"Not a bit of it," said I; "but if I can only see the tail of a fox, I can tell you something of his color, and, depend upon it, you have caught a very small animal, and one that drinks very bad wine!" He fully coincided, and started off with me in order to dodge her; but she caught him, and led him back with that facility with which a petticoat always conducts men about by their noses!

It was now between five and six o'clock; the last quadrille was finishing. The broad stair-cases were crowded by the descending masses, and in an instant we were again in presence of the cold realities of life. It was a clear, cool morning, and the animation of midday prevailed outside the theatre and along the Boulevards, but a few steps down the Rue Vivienne led into the darkness preceding dawn, and into the quietest hour of Paris—for Paris never sleeps. Here were half a dozen poor women sweeping the streets: they too, perhaps, had, many years ago, attended mask balls, and intrigued, and danced themselves into misery; now they worked like Southern slaves; but, unlike Southern slaves, they could not sing with a light heart, assured of a good dinner and a good rest at night. Farther on were women drawing hand-carts, or driving huge market-carts. Poor creatures! had they no little babes at home to take care of, and to rear into men? Had they no husbands or brothers to do this work, while they attended to household duties? But it was shiveringly cold, and I hurried on, now meeting the slowly-marching policeman, and now some last mask or domino, and now, perhaps, a reeling debauchee finishing his last hour of Carnival.

The gray dawn was just spreading over the east as I closed my eyes in my own bed, pretty well fatigued with twenty-four hours of mi-carême

BANKERS' WIVES IN PARIS.

When I woke, the bright sun of a spring morning was streaming in through the windows; the air was cool and delightful; the birds were hopping about my balcony, and chirping their twentieth song, wondering, perhaps, why they did not receive their accustomed breakfast of crumbs at the usual hour; or, perhaps, sensible enough to fast with good grace, like man, in order to better relish an orgie afterward. The busy hum below showed that at least a portion of Paris had enjoyed a good night's rest, and were abroad betimes; but it must have been a very small portion indeed of the city who were in their beds at 1 o'clock on mi-carême night.

To an American, nevertheless, who is taught from childhood to strain every nerve (for what end not stated) from morning till night, and who is looked upon as wasting time if he pay too much attention to books even, the thought of being a little behind the sun and the day always conveys reproof; but, not doubting I might overtake them at another time, *if necessary*, and that aristocratic American king, custom, being three thousand miles distant, I resolved to resign myself to the inviting indulgence of that pleasing languor which was stealing over me, and which always follows the occasional loss of a night's sleep, provided excesses of eating and drinking have not been committed.

Marie was already bestirring herself in laying the

white table-cloth for a twelve o'clock breakfast. A bottle of rosy wine, a neat French service, and a *dejeuner succulent* formed not an unpleasant finale to the entertainments of mi-carême!

These balls at the Opera were commenced in the days of the Régence; they were then attended by the aristocracy of France; there was no dancing and no travesty; dominos, dress-coats, music, and intrigue alone had the entrée: all that is now changed; every body attends the ball, from the millionaire to the man who goes without his dinner for a week to raise the ten francs required. No lady can enter unless masked, and she is not permitted to take her mask off; but toward the close, the handsome women, by thrusting cigars into the mouths of the policemen, or administering a few words of flattery, generally slip off their ugly encumbrances.

I shall close this account of balls by a very Frenchy story which I translated from a book lately published.

Toward the end of the last Carnival, Madame X——, wife of a rich banker, took a strange freak into her head.

She wished to indulge in the pleasures of a ball at the Opera not buried in a *loge* with her husband, but to go the whole figure (*au grand complet*), without husband, and with supper, Champagne—and accompaniment of lorette. Hearing constantly repeated, in all places and on all occasions, this name of lorette, Madame X——, by one of those thousand fantasies which sometimes enter the brain of a young Parisian lady, rich, handsome, and little occupied, had at last conceived a violent desire to see by her side, and to know one of those happy creatures of whom the men talked so much, and whose rivalry had even excited the jealousy of their more correct sisters.

She confided her project to Mr. N——, an intimate friend of the family, and begged his assistance to put it in execution.

After some observations, which he might have spared himself, for they were not even listened to, Mr. N—— resigned himself, with a good grace, to serve the caprice of the willful young wife.

To deceive the husband, and make him believe she was a little indisposed, while she was promenading at the Opera ball, was a simple thing for Madame X——.

All that remained was to have the supper prepared and to procure a lorette. This duty was confided to Mr. N——. Once interested in the matter, Mr. N——'s pride was piqued, and he determined to do the thing well. He accordingly chose among the indulgent beauties of the ball the most lively, the most piquante, and the most roguish one he could find, so as to offer for the study of Madame X—— the very prototype of the lorette.

Engaged for the supper by Mr. N——, the *tigre* (that is the *nom de guerre* of the petulant Phryné) refused at first, though with regret—her protector was at the ball! She would give any thing, but did not dare to take the liberty—

"Ah bah! *sème-le*," said N——, "and don't fret yourself about the result."

"*Passe pour semé*," said the lorette; "mais encore faut il récolter!"

This sally of wit delighted Madame X——, who

joined her entreaties to those of N——, and succeeded at last in enticing the young *tigre.*

As the classic clock of the foyer denoted half past three, the trio, re-enforced by a young blood, a friend of N—— and the tigre, left the ball-room and entered the restaurant, where they placed themselves at table in one of those luxurious little saloons where comfort and elegance can not be surpassed.

Nothing more gay than the supper. Animated by the frozen Champagne, the inexhaustible wit of the tigre burst forth in repeated flashes and *bon mots*, of which the quality was rather free, in spite of the efforts of Madame X—— to restrain her. By degrees, however, she became accustomed to it, and acted well enough her part as provincial lorette, who had come to try Paris, but was not yet well broken in to the *gay* manners of the capital, but who, with time and the counsels of the *tigre*, bid fair to become speedily an adept.

Every thing was going on finely, and already the *vertes boutades* of the real lorette had ceased to shock her false comrade, who burst into fits of laughter at each new sally, and had ceased to regret the imprudence of the step taken, when a well-known voice was heard at the door of the room where they were supping.

This voice, trembling with anger, was that of Mr. X——, who demanded entrance with a kind of phrensy, threatening to burst open the door unless it was instantly opened.

It is well to say here that the banker had himself left the ball-room, where his wife, believing him some where else, had seen him, but, sure of her incognito, had felt no uneasiness about discovery. To her the voice of Mr. X—— was like the handwriting on the wall.

"It is my husband! I am ruined!" she cried, a prey to the extremest terror.

In spite of his well-known courage, Mr. N—— himself looked very uneasy. The *tigre* alone remained imperturbable, and continued quietly peeling a pear, interrupting this operation only to cast an occasional quiet glance on the couple, whose fright seemed to amuse her amazingly.

"Ah! ah! So Madame is a married woman!" said the lorette, scrutinizing Madame X—— with a sly look out of the corner of her eye. "You have played a trick on me. Never mind; we shall have a good laugh."

Saying which, she got up and advanced toward the door. "Good heavens! what are you going to do?" cried the afflicted wife.

"Open the door for your husband," said the *tigre*, very coolly. "Don't you hear how he raps? Do you wish to wait till he bursts the door in on our heads?"

"Ah! have pity on me and do nothing," said Madame X——, with stifled voice. "Do you wish to ruin me?"

"Heaven forbid!" said the lorette, whose finger was already on the small bolt which alone restrained the vengeance of the angry Othello. "Put on your mask and be at your ease; it is not you your husband seeks."

At these words the *tigre* drew the bolt, opened the door, and the banker stood at the entrance of the room pale with rage.

At sight of him Madame X—— felt herself sinking, dumb with terror, and hiding her face in her hands (for she had forgotten having replaced her mask). She wished herself buried a thousand feet under the earth. Momentarily she awaited the fatal blow which she had invited by her conduct. But what was her surprise, and perhaps her pique, when this torrent of imprecations and reproaches fell upon the head of her new friend, the *tigre*, who did nothing but laugh, as usual.

The truth was then patent. Mr. X—— was the protector of the lorette. Deserted at the ball by his fickle companion, he started in pursuit, and from one inquiry and another at last traced her to her refuge. Angry at having been tricked in this way, and more so by the air of assurance which his unfaithful lorette assumed, he cried, stormed, and made a real *scene* in spite of the presence of Mr. N——, with whom he was well acquainted. But nothing could shake the coolness of the *tigre*, who permitted him to storm at his ease; and finally taking his arm, said, as her sole justification,

"You have finished, haven't you? I hope you will now be good enough to conduct me to my house."

Weak, like all protectors, Mr. X—— felt his anger dissolve at these words, and suffered himself to be led away.

"But, for Heaven's sake, Mr. N——," said he, as he was leaving with the *tigre*, "*not a word of all this to my wife!*"

"Be perfectly at your ease, my dear sir," replied the latter, as he touched gently the arm of Madame X——. "Your secret is inviolable."

LA LAYETTE IMPÉRIALE.

HAVING seen the Parisians in their wildest dancing mood, I had an opportunity of seeing them yesterday in one of their curious moods.

More than a century ago Montesquieu said of them, "Les habitants de Paris sont d'une curiosité qui va jusqu'à l'extravagance," which, freely translated, means that the Parisians would jump into a volcano if they thought they could see any thing on the inside which was not on the outside.

Four generations of inherited virtues have not in the least diminished this wonderful curiosity, as any one may see who will pass, or attempt to pass, through the Rue Vivieme on this 10th day of March, 1856.

A double *queue* was already forming when I arrived on the spot, and was assuming proportions too frightful for American ideas of patience to allow joining it. This *queue*, which is peculiarly an institution of Paris, is a long *tail* whose joints are formed of human beings. It's the noisiest tail you ever saw, excepting a rattlesnake's; and it's the queerest tail you ever saw, not being ring-streaked like a raccoon's, but motley, like — what ever had a *motley* tail but a Parisian queue, with its blue, red, white, black, green, and *dirty* colors, if there be such a color as the last? This queer tail, too, is mended at one end as fast as it is cut off at the other; and, altogether, a riddle-maker could make a very good conundrum out of it. Its origin was Parisian curiosity. You may see it on almost any day, wet or fine, sticking out of some small hole in front of a theatre, and winding along the asphalte, where it coils, and writhes, and twists for five hours at a time! No fox is ever so careless of his tail, and exposes it so much to the inclemency of the weather as these Parisians. But a fox has only one tail; the Parisians have many, like a Pacha.

But, while I have been writing these few lines the *tail* has lengthened a quarter of a mile. The crowd increases rapidly, I grow alarmed, and rush into the centre of the throng.

"For Heaven's sake, what's the matter?" says one and another of the last arrivals. "Is peace signed? Has the Emperor of Russia arrived? Louis Napoleon shot?" "Non, non; c'est la la—" but on rushed the obliging informers for fear of losing their chance, and leaving the sentence half finished. "La la—" I thought of all the la's I could conjure up—Lapin, laquais, lama, etc., but they were all masculine, and I did not believe the arrival of the Grand Lama himself could produce such an excitement. At last, going to a policeman, I was informed that I was in front of Mlle. Felicie's millinery establishment, and that "*La Layette Impériale*" was on exhibition.

Now, as Macaulay would say when he is leisurely plucking the feathers out of some (unfortunate writer—Macaulay-ce) goose, every schoolboy knows what "La Layette Impériale" is; but as four fifths of the human race, including infants, girls, and grown men and women, are not schoolboys, I shall take the liberty, without umbrage to the latter, to inform them that La Layette Impériale means the royal baby-linen and all thereto appertaining.

Catching the prevailing mania, and wishing to see how the imperial infants of parvenu emperors are received into the world, I elbowed my way to the outer door, where were four policemen drawn up in policeman-array—that is to say, looking very consequential, and seeing every thing themselves, while they kept every body else from seeing any thing. Back of them, at the inner door, were four more, and how many inside I know not, all guarding the imperial baby-linen!

I saw that I must, very properly, take my turn; but, alas! that *queue!* it extended both ways as far as the eye could reach.

There were grave men, and gray-haired matrons, and young virgins, and nursery-maids, and every idler of all classes that could spare *four or five hours* from pleasure or business. Added to this, a long line of carriages was continually depositing its load of visitors, who poured into the already crowded halls as if they were afraid the baby would be born before they could get a view of its imperial baby-highness' linen!

Not wishing to add to the rapidly-lengthening tail, I entered a café, and did the next best thing, viz., read through two long columns of the Moniteur, describing what was to be done on the occasion of the birth of a prince of the Napoleonic fillibuster dynasty.

It commences thus:

"When the Empress shall feel the first pains, denoting that she is about to be delivered, the grand mistress of her household shall go to her majesty."

Then follows a list of persons to be admitted to the

chamber of the Empress during the advent of the fourth Napoleon, and also a list of those to occupy the adjoining apartments—the prince and princesses, and great officers of the crown, the marshals and admirals, the Senate, etc., etc. What they are to do, and how they are to do it, all described with a littleness of detail consistent with the littleness of the object of them.

Then (probably about sixteen minutes and a half after the birth)

"The Grand Chancellor of the Legion of Honor shall carry to the Prince Imperial the Grand Cordon of that Order and the Military Medal"—(in reward, perhaps, for his newly-born royal highness' sixteen minutes and a half services—of the lungs).

Then follows the ceremony for baptism, which is detailed in the same manner, and the whole signed Cambacères, "Grand Master of the Ceremonies."

After reading the whole through, with the most perfect absent-mindedness I took out my watch *to see what century it was!*

The document reads just like a chapter in Deuteronomy, or a manifesto of Souloque—for there is only a step between the sublime and the ridiculous.

Perhaps his royal infantile highness will have a *brêvet d'affaire* appointed, like Louis XIV.

His royal highness' baby-rattle (costing 600 francs) is already on exhibition with the Layette Impériale, of which I might give you a description, only it would tire you to read over the list of articles of silk, and satin, and costly lace, and of wonderfully-made gaiters, and cradles, and amber necklaces, archbishop-blessed, and *corbeilles de baptême*, lined with satin and covered with Alençon lace, and bearing the imperial cipher and arms.

It is all beautiful, wonderful, costly—costly enough to supply all the babies that will be born in France on that eventful day with baby-linen—good, honest, warm baby-linen—for a whole year! But the kind-hearted people prefer to deny themselves, and out of their poverty administer to the royal profusion.

The people *will* have a king, although Samuel told them ages ago that he would make servants of their children, and that he would take away their vineyards and their olive-orchards, and give them to his own household.

The French are modern troglodytes, who desire the advantages without choosing to exercise the virtues of self-government. After their spasmodic efforts at Republicanism, they have sunk back into lethargy and sloth, and now hail with delight a successor to the elect of 7,000,000, whose only title to be their ruler shall be *one vote*—that of his father!

How much more time the people of France are to lose over this baby-linen, and the baby itself, in illuminations, gun-firings, fêtes, etc., it is difficult to say; but the only Parisians who will say, with Alexander, "I have lost a day," will be those who *failed* to see La Layette Impériale!

MÉLANGE.

Paris is *succulent* with delight and amusement. It is not alone the budding spring, with its warm sun, which always brings happiness; nor is it that the Parisians have again got possession of their own home, together with the wealth left by a hundred thousand foreigners. These are ingredients, but, besides them, they have many novelties not often united.

First, there is the Peace Congress now in session, which keeps the Bourse and the quidnuncs in a continual state of fever, while it enlivens the court by the dinners, balls, concerts, etc., of which it is the object. Then Louis Napoleon, who seems to have not one guiding star, but whole constellations in his favor—who seems to derive benefit from the very combinations of circumstances which have proved disastrous to other nations—whose gala-days even the elements have always conspired to render bright and clear, is preparing a rare fête for the Parisians in giving them a prince, perhaps just at the time the treaty of peace will be signed! What eclat! it must have all been planned with Napoleonic foresight and knowledge of French character.

The people are already filled with the glory of their late achievements; their one armed and crutched heroes walk the streets of their splendid capital with eyes glittering fire, and their breasts sparkling with medals won at Sebastopol! and their powerful enemy, instead of meeting them in conference on neutral ground, comes to their doors to sue for peace! The theatres contribute more than their share to the general hilarity—never was such a combination of talent present. Ristori has returned, and makes us shudder before the tragedies of Alfieri; Grisi, after eight years' absence, is again upon the scene of her old conquests in Norma, Semiramide, etc.; Marie Cabel is drawing all Paris to the Opera Comique, to see her representation of Manon Lescaut, the plot of which, however, has been a good deal changed by Scribe. Rachel, too, escaped from the perils of the sea, and the climate, people, and railroads of the United States, has arrived, but is not yet performing.

Here we have diversion for every age, taste, and condition, and a happy issue of the *labors* of the Empress and Peace Congress in giving at the same time a prince and a peace to France, would be the very climax of glory as well as of amusement to the people by the public fêtes which would follow.

Count Orlof is treated with the most marked kindness and attention; nothing is allowed to disturb his equanimity; the most delicate viands and finest wines regale his palate, and private concerts and theatricals refresh his mind after the labors of the session. The fate of Europe perhaps hangs on an ill-selected truffle, on a false note at a concert, on a tight boot, or the admission of a bottle-fly into his sleeping apartment! So the prince is delicately cared for; the wind, even, is not permitted to salute him roughly. But still, if on some cloudy day the *corns* of the prince give him a twitch, which not even a Napoleon could foresee, and this *sub-table* influence communicate with the top of the conference table, a dispatch is immediately sent to the Emperor, "*The prince is obstreperous!*" Forthwith ten thousand French troops are marched past the windows, with infernal din of drums, trumpets, hautboys, etc., which generally smooths away any little difficulties existing; but if that is ineffectual, a dispatch goes to London, and next day comes the London Times with a thundering review of the fleet, and the enormous preparations making for the ensuing campaign! This is an end of argument, and the prince forgets his corns!

While you are still shivering under chilling winds and late snow-storms, Paris has shaken off its icicles, and is basking under as lovely spring weather as you ever felt on the sunniest day of sunny May. After all, it is a pleasure to have such a thing as winter. Until the one just past, it is fifteen years since I have seen a winter, and I never before knew how to appreciate spring. Perhaps, by analogy, our sicknesses, our misfortunes, our rainy days, and our gloomy days, all serve to give us a greater sum of happiness in life than we should enjoy without them.

The people of warm countries only live half their days. They have no time-marks of the seasons to tell them how far on they are in the journey of life. How they miss this annual resurrection of man and nature!

In these first days of spring the lungs expand with renewed life; they are avaricious of the air. The world becomes beautiful even to the misanthrope and cynic; the fruitful soil buds with promise of the coming harvest—promise more beautiful and more glorious even than the bow in the cloud.

"La terre frisonne de plaisir! Les fleurs sont des

hymnes que, dans son enthousiasme, elle chante au soleil."

Invited by the lovely weather, I spent a strolling day, now passing the Boulevards, where hundreds of nurses were sunning their infants in front of the Café Anglais; and now taking a seat in the garden of the Palais Royal, animated by troops of children playing under the trees, around the grass and flower-pots, and near the ever-musical fountain; and finally rambling away through the large gardens of the Tuileries — those *geometrical* gardens, where the French have extracted, and display for our admiration, all the beauty contained in a straight line—where every grain of sand has been more manipulated than the handsomest statue in the garden, and where the trees, after having exhausted the wisdom of the Creator, have been subjected to the training of generations of men. What sights those trees have seen! What kings and queens have walked under their shades! What noble minds have sought recreation among them! They once formed an irregular park (till the reign of Louis XIV.); now they stand ranged like gens d'armes in fearfully straight rows, their very branches and leaves partaking of the general straightness; and if some bold shoot dare to sprout out of column, he is immediately cut off like a deserter. All the rose-bushes grow in lines, and the thorns that are upon them. The fish in the ponds have caught the lineal fashion, and swim in lines. The rows of box-plant are agonizingly straight, and laid with such care and so finely that at a little distance they look like long green marks drawn with the brush of a painter.

And it is all beautiful. What at once is more curious and charming than those arches of shade, dense as if hewn from the solid rock? What prettier than the little plots of grass and flowers, or the statues and ponds abounding on all sides? What more inviting than the coup d'œil of the whole? Still, I do not wish to see many of these geometrical gardens in the world. I prefer nature, and like better, for example, the style of the Royal Gardens of Boboli in Florence, with their hill, and dale, and winding paths.

I purchased two sous worth of pleasure (the cheapest I know in the world) in the shape of a chair, and watched the children, and the nurses, and the birds, and the gardeners, and wondered why we could not have such things in America. Is it childish? Is it trivial? Is it wasting time to have parks, and gardens, and statues, and pictures?

The United States are now looked upon as a wealthy nation, as they certainly are, and they have a very great many wealthy citizens, who have both inherited and made money, but who toil just as hard to hoard up more as they did when they or their fathers were poor. They have no object in gaining more unless it is to lose it by speculation, or leave it to their children to lose. They must work night and day because they enjoy it, and because they have been brought up to believe that there is no work under the sun commendable but that of making money.

If I were a teacher in America, I would whisper such heresies in the ears of rich men's sons that they would (if they possessed any ambition) surprise their mercantile papas some fine morning by being caught with a chisel or pallet in hand instead of pen and ledger; or they should pass a life of study, and write if they had any thing new to say, so that another generation at least might take a little different color than that reflected by ships and cotton-bales. Rich men's sons, however, are rarely those who excel in any thing else than spending money.

As it grew later and warmer, the crowds of children doubled; they swarmed about like bees, and were of all ages, from a few months to eight or ten years old. French children are pretty and well-behaved, but they are not children. All these little things about me act like little ladies and gentlemen; they have even a fineness, and what I may call a perceptiveness of expression that belong to maturer years. Here is a little black-eyed beauty of five or six summers, who looks the intelligence of seventeen. She seems to notice, and be conscious of the fit of her *robes*, and I am sure would perceive an impropriety in conduct or taste about ordinary matters nearly as soon as a grown person.

And those schoolboys a little farther off, how quietly and *genteelly* they play! and they are just at the noisy age too! They are marched two by two to their play-ground, and they play pretty much as they march. In America, from Dan to Beersheba, from Boston to San Juan, all the boys are every where noisy. See them rush out of school! what shouting, and dancing, and boisterous fun! But fifteen years later the positions of both are changed. The French become noisy and talkative, or, rather, talkatively noisy, while the boisterousness of the American is centred in earnest, continuous, quiet action.

The French, I think, change very much in the course of their lives. The girls are prettier than the young ladies; the boys are more sensible than the young men; the married ladies are far more interesting and entertaining than the young ladies. They are very apt to get too fleshy after the age of thirty-five or forty. The men improve much after thirty, and there is not a more agreeable person in the world than an *old* French gentleman: he unites the experience of age with the gayety and animation of youth.

The most insipid and meaningless person on earth is a young French lady of seventeen. Her body is bound up in corsets, and stays, and crinoline; her feet cramped in tight shoes; and her hair strained either very far back, or very far forward, or very far up, as the fashion may direct; and, last of all, her soul is shut up in the strong iron box of *virtue*, of which her mother keeps the key, just as if the poor child would jump out of the box the moment her mother left the key on the mantel-piece! In this constrained position, tied hand and foot, cramped soul and body, just at that age of life when she ought to be most free (for it is the age that gives tone and color to the future of a woman), like a poor dove she is offered for sale in the market. She is denied access even to her own heart; she is not supposed to have a heart; and, indeed, it is to be feared that, in this way, the heart has been completely crushed out of the French nation. She grows thin, pale, and dejected at that lovely season—the spring-season of the soul—designed by nature to be the brightest portion of our lives. The market opens; the stock for sale is examined—oh! how coldly and superciliously! just as the Turk examines the Circassian; as the Southern slave-dealer examines the black he is about to purchase. A price is offered; mothers are consulted: it is not enough; the article will fetch more. Other purchasers appear, and now and then, perhaps, the poor girl sees some one she would almost be willing to be sold to, if she must be the object of a bargain; but this is rare, for her constrained situation checks the feelings of her own heart. Finally, Mr. So-many-thousands-of-francs-rent offers himself; the mother concludes the bargain; the proper papers are drawn up; and the timid maiden is united in body to one, while her soul soon becomes the property of another; and the sequel (which really happened only a few days since in the South of France) is that Mr. So-many-francs comes home some day, and finds the gentleman who has the affections also in possession of the person of his wife; and suspecting, perhaps, a crime where there is none, immediately shoots him. The uncle and guardian of the lady entering immediately, her only exclamation, as she points to her dead lover, is, "*Ah! why did you not let me marry him?*"

So long as this system of buying and selling wives continues—so long as young girls are locked up to make them virtuous—and so long as men—men who have mothers and sisters—continue to look upon women as only so much prey, so long will France be celebrated as one of the most licentious of civilized nations.

I am sorry to say such things, but it is truth; and, indeed, their own writers have said a great deal more.

I have known many unmarried French ladies in different parts of America, and all I have known, who were brought up there, were not excelled by any for their virtue and charms. So I conclude it is the system of education that produces the difference. The young women of America may be too free in their manners; it is bad style, but it is the freedom of innocence. There is a beauty, and freshness, and naturalness about our women that I have seen nowhere equaled. They carry about with them the charm of unsuspecting, *unconscious* virtue. They have a great fault, however—the fault of the whole race of Americans—and what do you think it is? *They are too thin!* which can only be remedied by correcting the habits of the whole race. I am confident the Americans wear the flesh off their bones merely by *racing* through life as they do! It surely is not climate, for there is every variety of climate in the country. The French ladies of New Orleans are not lacking in embonpoint (which, translated, means are not flat as pancakes), yet their fathers, for two or three generations, have lived in America; but they have led quiet, easy lives. On the other hand, the American ladies there, although born in the place, are like their sisters all over the country, pretty in face, but *thin* in person.

I have seen merchants in New Orleans light their candles before daylight in the morning, and commence work. The hour for commencing business in the United States is every where early, and, once begun, it is hardly ever left off; for the merchant eats without knowing what he is doing; he eats as if he were sampling cotton or rice, while his features are coruscated with the figures of a hundred accounts current; his head is at once journal and ledger, as well as principal of "the *concern*." He sleeps as he eats, dreaming of business; and at thirty-five he wonders how he ever got the dyspepsy—such a temperate man in his diet!

Fifteen hundred miles off from this mercantile specimen, I have seen farmers in New England who arise during the whole year at three o'clock in the morning, and I have breakfasted with them before daylight! The same restless activity pervades the whole country. No time is idled—a great deal wasted.

And so the country has quadrupled in growth any other country that ever existed; not alone because every man felt a perfect freedom to embark in what pursuit he would, and without the trammels of a meddlesome government, but also because every man has really equaled an average of more than four Europeans. This statement will not appear exaggerated to any who have seen how time is idled on the Continent, or who have watched the stupid labors of bungling peasantry, or who consider the millions who do nothing, the millions engaged about royalty in empty employ, and the millions (in 1855 it was over 4,000,000) of men whose sole duty is to march and countermarch, and polish their bayonets!

Well, then, the country has grown rapidly. I will not ask what is the use of it. What's the use? is one of the most frightful, hand-binding monsters in existence. It is an ogre that shall alarm the merchant in his office, the farmer in his field, and the philosopher in his study! Never ask what's the use; it will make the stoutest heart quake!

What, then, have we gained by this rapid growth? We dwarf trees and plants if they grow too fast; we try to do the same for boys and girls. Is there no danger that nations, also, may weaken themselves by growing too fast?

But I have rambled away from the young French ladies before making them the apology I intended. It is evidently not their fault, the awkward position they occupy in the sweetest part of life, and whoever knows them well will not need to be convinced that they are not the demure, stupid beings they look; no nation could at all compare with them for grace, tact, elegance, and conversation, if they were but permitted to act their natural characters. How long are they to be kept in strait-jackets?

The boys are manly-looking young fellows, and spirited. But from that you can hardly judge the future. Montesquieu, speaking of Louis XV. in his youth, says he is amiable, etc., etc., but that one can never know the character of Continental kings till they have passed through the grand ordeals of mistress and confessor. So of French boys generally, you can know nothing till they have passed the age of boyhood. They are passionate, but at an early age destroy all the illusions of youth, and then become cold and heartless till after thirty, when I think they improve greatly in character.

But while taking notes and reading here in the garden I am left nearly alone. The children and boys have dropped off gradually; the gardeners have gone home, and hardly a *flaneur* remains in the place but myself; the gray of twilight is creeping over the sky, and a solemn stillness has taken the place of the laughing children and the chatting nurses. It is so quiet that the waving tricolor on the top of the Tuileries, hardly seen, can almost be heard flapping in the light breeze; the night steals on apace and grows cool, and I arise to walk about as long as the gates remain open.

I would wish to remain for hours at this quiet time, walking about under the thick shades or admiring the beauty of the heavens, but gens d'armes and dinner-bells brook no delay, and the first were already prowling about for stragglers previous to shutting the gates, while the second, viz., the Tuileries clock, had long since sounded *six*, the most stirring hour in Paris.

AMUSEMENTS.

It is fashionable in Paris at present to rave about Ristori; the Sunday papers are all filled with long criticisms upon her gestures, voice, shape, face, and dress. The French language is tortured—as all languages are by critics—to find some unnatural way of expressing common things, or to point out niceties where none exist. More than half the criticisms on music, painting, and the drama are sickening bits of lack-sensical composition, intended rather to convey an idea of their author's wonderful acuteness of perception and powers of language than any accurate and intelligible description of the object in question. But out of all these criticisms you may have gleaned enough of truth and accuracy, comparing one with another, to infer that Ristori is perhaps the greatest tragedian alive, not excepting even Rachel. I heard her last evening, and have certainly never before seen man or woman that seemed to me to be the very impersonation of Tragedy. Many of her postures, suddenly petrified, would have made even Angelo weep at the inefficiency of his chisel!

I hope she will go to America, and take a better company with her than she has had in Paris. She is not supported by them at all, so that the listener is continually chilled as often as the lips of Ristori are closed. They measure off monotonously the Italian as if they were afraid that by speaking naturally they would not be understood. As the majority of the audience can not understand in either case, it would be better, perhaps, not to spoil their words for the few, with the little hope they can have of benefiting thereby the many. If Ristori does go to America, pray do not let a few persons connect her with the humbug that greets nearly every great artist going to that country. The lessons of the past should teach the American public to greet coldly every *Barnumized* artist, and the evil will cease. These lessons, too, should check that spontaneity and cordiality with which the American people have been accustomed to welcome every great name, whether in literature or art. You are laughed at for it both by the objects of it as well as by the people of other countries. Don't make fools of yourselves by drawing Elslers in carriages, carrying Dickens on your shoulders, or paying for a chair near a Rachel as many dollars as can be placed on it at one time without falling off. No one admires you for it; on the contrary, the beneficiaries of it all laugh at you over their wine on your own soil, and ridicule you before the world on their return to their homes.

The latest instance of this kind is that of Monsieur Beauvalet, who is amusing himself and the Parisians amazingly at your expense in the Figaro, a bi-weekly journal published here. Poor Monsieur Beauvalet is evidently very much piqued about something—probably his genius was not duly appreciated in America. He belonged to Rachel's company, and while you were listening to *his* tragedy, he was laughing in his coat-sleeves at your expense. He rehearses the story of some New York editor (passing it off for his own wit) about the rustling of the leaves as the audience turned to a new page. But if Monsieur Beauvalet has ever heard Ristori in Paris—Paris, the arbiter of elegance, fashion, taste, universal knowledge, etc., etc.—he has seen exactly the same thing with all those who were not too avaricious to buy a book, or too vain to use one though required, and that for a language spoken at their doors, and by a people more distinguished for fine arts than themselves (if it be possible to excel Paris in any thing). From the listless appearance of many, the newspaper reading of others, and using of one book by a group of three or four, it was easy to see that the Italian was not more popular than any other foreign language in Paris.

Monsieur Beauvalet infers that, because Rachel did not "take in" over 26,000 francs the first night of her performance, in a country more than three thousand miles distant from the language in which she performed, therefore the people of America do not like tragedy! He is piqued at Jenny Lind's success, and evidently thought the first ticket for *tragedy* would sell for 5000 francs at least! and that he would ride in a carriage drawn by Americans—"those silly Americans! those barbarian nabobs!"

I do not think the majority of the Americans appreciate tragedy.

Legouré says, " Si la comédie, et le drame représentent dans leurs tableaux le vraie, et le réel, la tragédie se propose un autre objet, qui ne nous est pas moins nécessaire, *l'idéal.* La terre est le domaine de la comédie, et du drame; mais la tragédie, elle, a toujours besoin d'un coin de ciel."

No one will pretend that there exists in America much of the *ideal;* all there is real and practical. Nevertheless, there is not a city in the union of 50,000 people where a good tragedian would fail to have an audience, and that, too, when a large part of those people who are well educated and of good taste never go into a theatre at all!

The truth is, America labors under the disadvantage of having her *masses* compared continually with the *aristocracy* of other countries. The aristocracies of old countries are always foremost to hide the defects of the people. The majorities of no countries like tragedy. Take France, for example; half of her people do not even know, probably, what tragedy means. France has 36,000,000 of people. But Parisians, and ourselves even, when we speak of France, mean the Boulevards, the Champs Elysées, the Louvre, the Tuileries, the Rues de Rivoli, de la Paix, de la Chaussée d'Antin, and one or two others—this is France; and the court and royal family, and the élite of Paris—these are the French. The brilliance of the sun hides its spots, and the glory of Paris is so dazzling as to blind the eye to the defects of the whole empire. The masses in France are no more to be compared with those in the United States in intelligence, education, or any thing else, than an Oregon squaw with the Empress Eugénie. I think any one who has traveled over the two countries will acknowledge this.

American travelers come to Europe, and look at and describe only its fair side; European travelers go to America, and see nothing but its dark side, and where it is not dark they paint it so. I hope it may continue so, as the Americans are not slow to learn, and will gradually benefit by their caricatures.

It is not yet known if Rachel will share the honors of Ristori this season. There is no notice of her future appearance on the stage.

In music, the great furore at present is Marie Cabel, who is singing at the Opera Comique in a new opera of Auber, the plot of which is taken from the Abbé Prevost's novel of Manon Lescaut. I do not know if this novel is translated into English. I have never seen it, and must confess I do not wish to see it read in America. We can very well dispense with that class of books. It belongs to the "Dame aux Camélias" and "demi monde" literature. It is well written and affecting, for which reason it is the more dangerous. For many nights it was impossible to get a seat at all in the theatre. The box-office was not even opened, every place in the house having been taken days beforehand.

The opera of Manon Lescaut owes its success more

to the interest taken in every thing touching Manon than to the talents even of Marie Cabel, who is a rising artiste of great merit and beauty. Not a man, woman, or child in Paris that has not wept over Manon Lescaut, a lewd, abandoned woman of the lowest class, but beautiful, and with some fine traits of character. I shed my share of tears over this base, lovely woman—this outrageous, generous thief! No one can resist the contending emotions excited by the abbé's skillfully-written novel.

This opera will have a "great run." All pieces that are indecent and lewd, such as those mentioned, and others of the same style, fairly saturate the whole Parisian public. They have a far greater success than any other class of plays; they are performed hundreds of nights to crowded audiences; they are printed in cheap form, and permeate every avenue and corner of the city; and the effects, partly of this depraved taste, are but too visible in the sad state of French society at present.

How fathers and mothers can lead their daughters nightly to see scenes in the lives of prostitutes, graced off with the attractions of music, and beauty, and lights—how they can sit with them through five-act dramas of the intrigues of countesses and other court ladies, all represented in a style to make vice appear lovely, even through the thin varnish of morality with which they are sometimes washed over, and expect them to remain virtuous, is indeed wonderful. It is true that

> "Vice is a monster of so frightful mien
> As to be hated needs but to be seen."

But vice represented and punished on the stage is not vice in its true appearance.

It is one thing to look at vice sitting in a comfortable *loge*, surrounded by beauty, and fashion, and brilliancy, and the ear filled with melody, and another to see it naked in the every-day world.

An ordinary pebble becomes a jewel when handsomely set. Spartan youths were taught sobriety by seeing drunken helots; they were taught virtue by seeing the gymnastics of nude women. And I could understand, perhaps, how virtue now might be inculcated by seeing the whole downward course of vice; but all that I can understand from the present tone of the French stage and of French books is why the young ladies of France fear to look at a man.

So I trust none of our publishers will translate any of the thousand indecent plays and books that are now flooding Paris. Let us have theatres and amusements in abundance, but of the right kind and at the right time. This continual referring to the gayety and amusements of the people on the Continent, which has lately been observable even in the British Parliament, is a most fallacious mode of inferring happiness.

The thousands we see amusing themselves in and about Paris, for instance, on the Sabbath, how small a portion are they of the whole population! How much misery are their fellows that are out of sight enduring? Yet every thing looks gay and lively; and nine persons out of ten, viewing London, New York, and Paris on a given Sabbath, would say the latter was the happiest city. But statistics, which look beneath the surface, show us what a miserable city Paris really is—miserable with all its gayety and laughter, which drown its cries of distress. A city can not be considered happy where two thirds of its population can not afford the expense of burial, where in every three births one is illegitimate, and where one out of every 3000 persons commit suicide. It is said, too, that in Paris there are 30,000 persons, besides those assisted by regular charities, who arise every morning without knowing how they will get a dinner. This is only supposition, of course, but it is commonly believed.

I state these things from no ill-will, but simply because I do not wish to see America relax in two important things, viz., her respect for women and the Sabbath. Nothing can be more certain than that, in just so far as these two are cherished, loved, and respected (the same terms apply to both), just so far will a nation be prosperous and happy. I speak neither of Puritanism nor prudery.

In Paris there is no such word as home, and the want of it is another great cause of vice. A Parisian, on entering a house where a family, as happy as families can be on earth, is quietly enjoying its domestic comfort in conversation or books, would exclaim, "Oh, how stupid!" And so the men rush to the theatres, cafés, etc.; and the ladies, if they must stay at home, are miserable, but the probabilities are that they will be at some ball, play, or other entertainment.

In the matter of Sunday amusements for the people now agitating the English Parliament, it is to be hoped that government will not open public places and force some of the people to work for others on the only day that all ought to be free. It is opening a very big principle for a very little purpose, and would finally open the theatres and shops on the same day. Let the people ramble the fields, and gardens, and streets if they will, as in France or Germany; let them find all the amusements they can without setting a quarter of the population to work for them. But there's the rub, you say. They can not get to the fields, etc., and they prefer to drink gin in the grog-shops or at home. Well, then, the matter simply resolves itself into the old one of *condition*, and the way to alleviate that condition is not to begin by opening Sunday entertainments. Why is it not better to endeavor to give them Saturday afternoon? It is more difficult, true, but will cost less in the end. By the first plan a fictitious appearance of happiness is created, which only serves to hide misery and make it the more neglected.

The people problem is a hard one for Europe, and as it grows daily in importance by the growth of population, the sooner it be grappled with the better. Sacrifices must be made to them, and the sooner they are commenced the lighter they will be. But do not mistake gayety for happiness. Every body will give a different definition of the word happiness. Contentment is, for a people, perhaps its principal ingredient.

I will tell you what I consider a happy people, and I will draw from nature.

There is a town in the United States containing five thousand people. Theft was never heard of there; suicide and murder are unknown; there is no law against prostitutes, because a prostitute had never lived in the town; there has never been a jail in the town; nearly every family has its small farm, and its little white house, and garden, and big barns stored with hay and grain; the people are all well educated in their public schools, and many of them have classical educations; there are no persons there *very* rich, none *very* poor; the young men are as virtuous and modest as the young girls, and would nearly as soon think of committing murder as to attempt seduction; there, every body reads the newspapers, and they all have pretty good ideas of what is going on in the world. That village is over two hundred years old, and nearly all their principal families can trace their genealogies back more than two centuries to the parent stock in England. Their crests are the virtues of their ancestors cherished by children's children. That village is in New England, and is only one of many in that contented land.

Now in that spot the Sabbath is almost kept Puritanically, and it is a scandal to be seen walking for pleasure on Sunday through its green meadows or under its quiet elms. That I think an absurd strictness, and yet I have no doubt that the jealousy with which that people regard the Sabbath is one great cause of their long-continued happiness and prosperity.

But to get back to European people; the first step toward their regeneration is to wash them. Cleanliliness is next to godliness. I never saw a bad man in a bath-tub. I never knew a bad man that could take a daily bath. Hydrophobia and vice hate water. The want of baths and clean shirts was the cause of the French Revolution. The bath killed Marat; it has killed many a tyrant (aided a little by daggers, it is true). It will kill or cure many more. The Seine kills hundreds every year, most of whom, by their own confessions, are not fit to live. A dirty soul will not live in a clean body.

THE SON OF AUSTERLITZ.

THE prince is born. On the 16th of March, on Palm Sunday, at the dawn of a European peace, and in the twilight of the days of Prince Jerome, this happy-starred youth makes his appearance on earth.

The hopes of hundreds of thousands of Revolutionists died that day.

Paris is filled with rejoicing, and for a week has displayed the outward evidences of it by its illuminations and flags. Political exiles have been invited back; many prisoners freed; small objects redeemed from the pawnbrokers', and many other acts of kindness and charity performed. The Emperor and Empress have also declared themselves godfather and mother to all the legitimate children born in France on the 16th of March. And the poor little illegitimate innocents, what is to become of them? just as if it was their fault! But it is the universal law, the sins of the father, etc.

The London Times, with a blunt stupidity which is incomprehensible, appears this week in a long article to show how unlucky late princes have been in France: all the late French princes born have had untimely ends, or been unhappy, or some other such dark-colored stuff. There is no purpose under the sun, political, domestic, or any other, to warrant such an article at such a time. It is not only a rudeness toward a whole nation, but a cruelty toward two persons who are none the less human because imperial. And if the Emperor and Empress of the French have gained the respect of the world for their positions, certainly none have better earned than they the love of their countrymen and others as individuals.

It was when looking into the cradle of the young prince Louis XV. that Montesquieu remarked on the struggle that would ensue between mistress and confessor for possession of the future king.

Fortunately, after the example of the present Emperor, there is but little danger from either.

There are now no brilliant Aspasias and Phrynes, powerful as queens, to tarnish court morals and vitiate the principles of the future Emperor. There are no Gabrielle d'Estrées, La Vallières, and Pompadours to eclipse virtue even by their splendor and good qualities, and to debase a nation so prone to admire whatever is grand or glorious, whether in virtue or vice. The prince has a good mother, whose amiable and charitable character has endeared her to the hearts of the people. Good mothers are the soul of a nation. And he has a father, who, unlike Francis I., Henry IV., Louis XIV., and other less conspicuous examples of great nobility of character allied to great licentiousness, seems now, at least, determined to set a notable example of purity to France as well as to the young prince.

As for the confessors, there is not much to be apprehended from them. They are far behind the age, and I doubt if a Napoleon will wait for them to come up. Grandpapa at Rome, that poor, dear, good gentleman, is sad in the present, and sad for the prospects of the future. They say he sits all day long with his eyes fixed on the ruins of the Coliseum, and weeps to think that its departed greatness is but an emblem of the fleeting power of *Rome.*

I fear neither women nor priests for the Napoleon dynasty. The only thing to be feared is the people —that revolution-loving people. That fear will soon cease if Louis Napoleon will only conduct the *Revolution* himself as he has begun.

France is not ready for Republicanism, but she must have revolutions. England is the only nation that has ever understood how to conduct revolutions. Colonies are the only countries where revolutions can be made by one blow; in old countries, to be beneficial and substantial, they must be gradual. The age has come when mankind all over the world are looking after their rights. The true policy of kings is to conduct them to their rights. If they do not lead, they will not be led, but *trampled* on. Napoleon III. has commenced aright. He has a difficult task to perform, but he seems equal to it. The French are easily satisfied. Give them plenty of *bread* and *glory,* and they will always be content. But it is not solid nourishment, this bread and bonbons, nor always to be had. There is not a Sebastopol to be taken every five years, and the French are not good at colonization projects. What, then, is to be done with the people? What substitute for glory can be found to keep them quiet? Internal improvements, such as railways, telegraphs, canals, steamers, etc. Let them glorify themselves in their country, and commerce, and works of art. It will not cost so much as an army of six hundred thousand men, and will be a better protection. No danger of Austria or Russia annexing a little bit of frontier while the people are brick-making. England will look out for that. She allows no nation to annex but herself.

With all this, open your common schools and scatter broad-sown the Bible. Education, bread, and the Bible will draw any nation out of the mud.

All very fine, you say. Well, it must be commenced, or something worse will follow. It is not so difficult as either to commence a war or a bloody revolution. All revolutions are difficult, but bloody ones are worst. The Revolution of 1789 and its consequences cost France directly and indirectly over 8,000,000 of lives (all lost by violent deaths), and Heaven knows how much property, and the people were not much better off than they were before. I predict a revolution for the present emperor, but a bloodless one, and one that shall leave France far happier than he found it.

The day after the birth of Napoleon IV. all the theatres gave free performances by command of the Emperor, and I was amused to see how thousands of men and women stood for hours in the rain to get a *free ticket* (*!*), when they were paying at that moment the huge sum of $25,000 (equal to the salary of our President) simply for the prince's *baby-linen!* But we must have a king. We will have a king.

THE CHURCH.

THIS is Holy Week, and I have heard some excellent music and preaching, and one sermon, at least, with half a chapter for text instead of one verse. This, I remember, was a recommendation of Voltaire's—a hint to ministers. There is a most pleasing earnestness and simplicity about the more ignorant Catholics of the lower classes in the exercise of their religion. What satisfaction they exhibit after dipping their fingers in the holy water! How unconscious of all the rest of the world they throw themselves on their knees in a large church, and pray as absorbedly as a Protestant could do in his closet, and as he could not do on the stone floors of a church surrounded by loungers, or even by devotionalists! To such persons one can pardon any ceremony, the most ridiculous. But I must confess I can not help smiling when I see hundreds of educated ladies and gentlemen defiling out of the Madeleine, and as they pass a fat, red-faced, unshaven individual, touching a wet paint-brush (such it appears) which he holds in his hand.

I will respect as far as possible the forms of every religion when I see the spirit. A sincere conscience, be it Turk or Mohammedan, is never matter of ridicule. But if you can tell me what are the forms and principles even of this chameleon Catholic Church, you have a finer discernment than I.

In Italy, behold it with intellectual brow and refined tastes, surrounded by works of art and genius, now moving with state and pomp on some great occasions, and now dreaming its *dolce far niente* in Sybaritic elegance. In America it walks with quick, vigorous step, dressed in a decent black coat and hat just like any other citizen. It rises early and reads the newspapers, talks stocks and cotton, and very rarely obtrudes itself before the public so as to attract notice. Very dégagé in the streets, it performs Herculean labors in secret. In Cuba and Mexico, on the other hand, it is lazy and sensual, and permits and does every thing; is not at all superstitious; is afraid of nothing in, above, or under the earth. In fact, it is a *laissez aller* sort of gentleman, who has inherited large estates and intends to enjoy them. In other places it is a superstitious, dark-looking personage, that can call down fire from heaven and consume the wicked. Now what opinion am I to form of it?

I entered a village church once near Toulon, and saw the most wretched daubs of paintings representing miracles performed in the neighborhood by the Virgin and angels, such as snatching a person from drowning who had given so much to the Church, saving another from a burning house who had given so much more, etc., etc. In Cuba I saw the bishop on a Sunday morning at a fair, and in the afternoon at a horse-race. In Mexico I saw the children of the priest, who is not allowed to marry, playing about his house like any other illegitimate children. I could go on citing such barbarities and inconsistencies, and the priests, in their infinite skill and wisdom, could explain them away as fast as cited; but can I respect a Church when I see it every where dragging its robes in the mud? Be assured, railways and steam are ugly things for the Catholic Church. The nineteenth and twentieth centuries (Mr. Macaulay to the contrary notwithstanding) will wipe out that splendid fabric, or at least so change it that its best friend will not know it. So much of it as is built on the Bible will remain forever. The Roman Catholic religion is tyrannical; it has always been so wherever it had the power; it has always forced its opinions at the point of the sword; it would do so again, if possible; but the days of all tyrannies approach their end. No fears of being called illiberal or bigots by this arch-bigot can now prevent men from fighting against this monster for the liberty which she would destroy, and the best bombshells to shoot at it are Bibles. A broadside of Bibles poured into it would send it flying into the Mediterranean, like the herd of swine that rushed down into the Sea of Gennesareth.

It is surprising what a fear of the light this establishment has always exhibited; how fond of getting into the vaults and curious hiding-places of old churches; how she dodged behind thick convent walls till this pert, manly young nineteenth century, whom she hates and fears, insisted on looking over the fence or peeping through the cracks. The infallibility of convents, inquisitions, &c., having failed, it remains to be seen how long the infallible nonsense, gewgawry, genuflexions, incense-swinging youngsters, Latin mummeries, and lewd priests can stand the blaze of knowledge of this age, which is now being poured into every corner of the world from Tahiti to Kamtschatka.

The difference between Roman Catholicism in one country and another is greater by far than that between Mohammedanism and almost any other ism you may choose to select. During a voyage around the world you shall learn and unlearn your religion a dozen times in this one infallible Church, assuming always that man assimilates with the god or idol he worships.

In the United States she is certainly very seemly and respectable, but an inhabitant of South America would not recognize her any more than he would Mephistophiles at a masked ball; and I am not sure even there that the evil is not striking inward, like some temperance reformations we have heard of, which drive drunkenness from the streets to the parlor, and in place of one drunkard substitute a hypocrite and a sot.

In all this I speak not a word against any one's religion, but against the humbugs, and shams, and outrageous weights that have broken the back of the poor thing, so that the majority of men, even in Catholic countries, laugh at the fooleries of their own Church. Some of my best friends in different countries have been devout Catholics, and I would be glad to be as sure of heaven as they.

Being one of those unreasoning animals that believe (like the devils, to be sure, with fear and trembling) pretty much all I see in the Bible as we have it, I like to think that its simple precepts are alone sufficient for man's salvation, without the aid of Latin (why not Greek and Sanscrit too?) services to make it more comprehensible to the ignorant, or of apostolic successions, elderly traditions, forms, ceremonies, etc., etc.

These are the tools the poor sinner has to work with, and by the time he has learned to use them, and begun to shape out his religion, the dark shadow flits across his path and summons him to another world.

A thousand infants, with a thousand Bibles, wrecked on a thousand savage islands, each a thousand miles apart, would build up a thousand churches, all very similar, I fancy; but if a thousand *savants* were wrecked after them, in fifty years the thousand isles would be the seats of a thousand *isms*.

NOT ALL ABOUT MINOR NUISANCES.

PARIS is not altogether Paradise, although the very look of the name seems to suggest the idea. Minor nuisances exist here as elsewhere, and one of the greatest of them is the asphalte—the elegant, classic asphalte, that suggests notions of Boulevard dandies, splendid lorettes, and of whatever belongs to fashion and beauty. You can barely walk a square in any direction without seeing the black fumes arising from a huge black kettle, and spreading on all sides till you are enveloped in a cloud that, from the odor, you would suppose had issued from a volcano, and, indeed, the stuff itself would make a very good substitute for lava, though it seems to me to make a very poor one for good hard paving-stones, not because it is not more agreeable to walk on, for there is a kind of soft elasticity to the tread that is pleasant, but because it seems to need such constant repair. Nor is that the only objection to it, for it keeps one's boots, likewise, in constant need of repair. If flagstones were an invention of washerwomen, asphalte certainly was of bootmakers. You might as well walk on files. Three times in two months I have had my boots heeled after having had them cut down nicely to an angle of forty-five degrees; and as a man's character may be certainly told by looking at the heel of his boot, it becomes a double trouble to keep one's character in proper condition.

A man with high-heeled boots is proud; a broad heel denotes solidity of character and prudence; a very low heel denotes indifference and listlessness. You may be sure that the wearer of a boot run down at the heel is a sloven. There is no exception; and I mention this for the benefit of those foppish Achilles whom I have often seen strutting the streets, every where proof against the fire of criticism except in the heel. Flagstones sometimes syringe one's white pants with an injection of mud and water, which is an evil quickly remedied; but this being constantly filed into slovens, to say nothing of being stifled with bituminous fumes, is a very inelegant nuisance.

Apropos of minor nuisances, no one in Paris whittles, whistles, or spits. That is a great relief, at least to the non-whittling, non-whistling, and non-spitting Americans. But, in exchange, we have to endure something worse. Every body smokes bad cigars. Such dried, hard, decrepit-looking things as our Southern slaves would hardly deign to put in their mouths, the *elégants* of Paris perfume the Boulevards with, and make one pray for a Boston law; and being novices in the art of smoking (an art for which they ridiculed the Americans very much a few years since), every man smokes double the number of these offensive things that he requires. A year or two ago, there were but few cafés that allowed smoking; now they nearly all permit it, and it really makes one sigh to see such *vulgar* smoke licking the gilded walls and enameled panels of these fashionable resorts.

My next-door neighbor is an inveterate smoker of these bad cigars, and as he lies in bed till midday, and keeps his room always shut, and without a fire, the only way for his stale smoke to escape is through the cracks and keyholes communicating with my room; and, owing to my blazing fire, these cracks and key-holes act like a score of high-pressure bellows.

I have tried every way to stop the nuisance without treading on my friend's toes. I called in friends to have a counter smoke; I burned paper and shut my room up tight, but he did not even *grunt!* I am sure a man who smokes such cigars has all his sensibilities blunted, and is capable of any crime! I have at last resigned myself like a philosopher, conscious that there is no state in life free from its "minor nuisances." This is another penalty of batchelordom in Paris, where half a dozen *garçons* are on one floor, every room of which communicates by a (secret-betraying) door.

This arrangement of Parisian houses gave rise to a ludicrous suit a short time since. A rich young man who had just come into his rents, and who was spending them freely, happened to take rooms next to a musician, the trombone of an orchestra. As many young men do in Paris, our rich friend used to pass his nights at the theatres, cafés, and clubs, and retire about five in the morning. This was just the hour that Trombone, who was a hard-working man, began his rehearsal for the evening. The consequence was, that the *Rentier* could not sleep. He protested, and declared the other a nuisance, and even offered to buy him out *of his room*, all without avail; Mr. Trombone simply remarking that if he went to bed at the proper hour he would not be annoyed. There was now no resource left but the law, to which *Rentier* applied, but found no redress, the court deciding that a man had a right to exercise his daily vocations after five in the morning. Finally, becoming desperate, he scratched his head, as all desperate men do when they do not know what else to do; the scratch was effectual, and immediately suggested an idea. He went to an organ-maker, and ordered an organ that would run eight days without stopping, placed it in his chamber close to the door of Trombone, and *touched it off* just at the latter's bedtime, after which he locked the door and went into the country for a week. What torments poor Trombone suffered may be easily imagined, but will never be known; but his vacant room at the return of *Rentier* showed evidences of a hasty departure, while the door communicating with his own showed unmistakable marks of boots, boot-jacks, inkstands, and other missiles, with which the tormented musician had expended his rage.

I had a real prick of the conscience yesterday, Easter Sunday morning. I was just finishing a rather late breakfast when enter a Catholic priest, who seated himself at my table, within a metre of my nose. Verily I trembled in my boots, for the ink I had wasted on the *Establishment* was not yet dry, and it seemed as if punishment, by some mysterious sympathy, had been overlooking my shoulder, and was now about to take revenge. But I was instantly reassured by hearing my friend call out, with an eagerness and firmness of tone that showed the bent of his thoughts, *biftek au pommes.*

I call him my friend, because I always like priests. They are always good companions, intellectual, anecdotical, gastronomical, and possessing a thorough knowledge of the world—a knowledge distilled from thousands of gentle, confiding hearts, when, bruised by repentant consciences, they shed like flowers their sweetest perfumes.

The *biftek au pommes* came, and afforded an example of the perfection of the results of Lent. It was his first *plat gras,* and after forty days of eggs, and oysters, and fish, and truffles, and such light, womanly diet, imagine the new world of delight that is opened by the view of that first smoking red steak, as it peeps through the nut-brown strips of potatoes. My friend was not by any means thin and lantern-jawed; indeed, how forty days of eggs and oysters (or perhaps dry bread) could produce such jowls (it's the very word I want, and I'll have it) would be puzzling, if we did not remember that great eaters are nearly always thin. Yes, his mouth was bad, eminently sensual, without even a good sensual expression, and it had forced into its service all the lower muscles of the face, and had distorted them by over-labor and hereditary deformities till they were but a sorry accompaniment to the intellectual brow and fine eyes which commanded them; in short, that one face brought Hyperion and Satyr nearer together than I have ever seen those celebrated gentlemen before, and I have no doubt they have made that poor priest's life such a battle-ground as those people who are fortunate enough to be born good have no idea of in their lives of negative virtues; and such men, who may be abstractly worse than their neighbors, deserve, for their hard fight and doubtful victory, a crown brilliant with glory. They are the Sebastopol soldiers of life, to whom, while but *half* conquering the place, belongs the fame of the best fighting the world has ever known.

He cut the steak and commenced eating, and the supreme satisfaction with which he expressed its juices gave me such an appetite that, to keep him company and wash it down, I was obliged to order a chop and an extra half bottle.

"Well?"

Well—

"What then?"

How, what then?

"Where's the point?"

The point is, that he ate the steak, and I ate my chop and drank my half bottle of wine.

The Italians have a proverb which runs thus: "If you tell the name, hide the deed; if you tell the deed, hide the name;" which is better translated by the *sub rosa* written on our dining-room walls.

I shall, however, give you just one anecdote, told me by my friend the priest, which will not violate this precious table rule. I have heard a good many Continental jokes about the sons of the foggy isle, and perhaps this is as old as any of them, but it's new to me, and may be to you.

An Englishman, full as a nut of the English phlegm of an Englishman, was traveling on a certain railway, when a sudden halt and loud report informed the passengers that some accident had happened. Every one rushed out, of course, to see what was the matter, except Mr. Phlegm, who sat tranquilly, as if not at all interested in any thing beyond the halo of his own thoughts. Presently a person came up and informed him that the engine had burst its boiler.

"Awe!"

Then came another, saying that there were fifteen persons killed.

The Englishman still sat unmoved, and grunted out another

"Awe!"

But, finally, a third messenger ran up in great haste, and said,

"My dear sir, your valet has been blown into a hundred pieces!"

"A—awe! *Just bring me the piece that contains the key to my portmanteau!*"

Lately, the word phlegm is applied as much to Americans as to Englishmen, but in a different sense: it is represented with the former as volcanic and *earthquakic*, and liable to sudden and violent ebullitions. Some years ago, I never heard the word applied to us in Paris. At the Gymnase they have been playing a piece called Lucie, written by George Sand, and in which the American manner is supposed to be represented. The American is a sandy-haired individual, wearing a cap and gray clothes, and, indeed, looks more like a foggy morning in December than man or American. He moves about to the tick of the clock, or as if he was rheumatic, but, at the same time, does every thing in a business way, until he is smitten by the fair Lucie, and startles her by the violence and sudden intensity of his love—which would propose, be accepted, marry, and off, all in the same hour!

I have seen a good many Americans with this intensely quiet demeanor, smothering a fiery energy and will, but the most noted example is General Walker, the fillibuster of Central America. When I first saw him, he came merely to ask me a question concerning a person who was in Count Raousset's expedition to Sonora, and his manner was so excessively quiet and modest-looking that I thought him a country farmer, and was much surprised afterward to learn that this bashful timidity belonged to the iron-willed Walker.

Men who have endured a great deal of suffering as prisoners or explorers, and who are constantly thrown upon their own resources and invention, are almost invariably silent and thoughtful, except when roused by great occasions; yet but slight scrutiny is required to see the power which reigns within, concealed by impassibility of feature. Such men necessarily abound in America, and particularly on the Pacific coast, where there are tens of thousands who have walked across the Plains, a distance of twelve or fifteen hundred miles, enduring all kinds of privations. This may be seen, too, in the women and children of the West, and they pass through this ordeal with a courage and endurance not inferior to the men. The wife of a Western judge told me that at the age of fifty-five she performed that journey, and when all the men nearly were sick. She drove one of the ox-carts herself, walking along beside it! She was not sick a day. But all her smiles were dried away, although she was kind-hearted and amiable.

PARISIAN MANNERS AND FASHIONS.

I AM going to give you a letter on manners and fashions; for to come to Paris and write nothing about fashion would be like going to Italy without eating maccaroni, or to Russia without tasting caviar, or to Rome without seeing Saint Peter's, or to America without writing scandal.

But do not fancy, for all that, that I intend changing in one day Broadway into a Boulevard des Italiens. You Americans are such an opinionated people, and are so determined not to think every thing beautiful that comes from Paris, or every thing elegant that is practiced in courts, that it would, no doubt, require several months' constant drilling to wash off your barbarities, and make you fit to stand before the most ordinary Parisian.

Paris has for a long time been the supreme arbiter of fashion and elegance for the whole world, *that* every body knows; but every body does not know that the world, by its own fault and toadyism, has at last come to worship a very false idol—a real cheat of an idol, and an idol that plays all sorts of tricks and pranks, because the people like to see all sorts of tricks and pranks. Why Paris got this enviable leadership, and why she keeps it, is because she has had, and would still have if left to herself, more taste than all the world besides; but the mischief is, the world will not leave her to herself; and even if she did, her own citizens will not. There is always a craving for something new, and this is the only city that can satisfy that craving. Any thing is beautiful provided it be stamped Paris, and the most absurd custom requires only to have had its origin in the Faubourg St. Germain to spread like wildfire the world over; and, indeed, what with the different tastes of men, and the force of habit, which soon renders that pleasing which was at first disagreeable, one is almost led to believe that there is no true standard of taste either in fashion or letters, but that we are led about in such matters by chance or by the caprice of a few.

If you doubt this, just put on a hat that two years ago was the admiration of the town, and you will be affrighted at its oddness. Let the young ladies put on a pair of bishops' sleeves, once so much admired, or a gentleman knee-breeches, or try any of the old thrown-off fashions, and you will see that habit has more to do with taste than arithmetic. *Chacun à son gout* merely means that taste is not one of the exact sciences. How few authors are universally admired, and how much admiration of them depends on fashion! Bishops' sleeves and Racine were all the rage at one and the same time; now both are out of fashion. Montaigne has run through a dozen cycles of popularity and oblivion. He was praised by La

Bruyère, and decried by Malebranche and Balzac; exalted to the skies by De Sevigné, and pulled down again by Voltaire, etc. Milton's Paradise Lost was first sold for twelve pounds; to-day its value is measureless. And so on, a thousand examples might be cited of the fickleness of taste. A few degrees of latitude or longitude even often completely change the whole character of a thing. Wealth and position will sometimes make that refined and admired which is in itself low and vulgar. It is thought ill-bred in America for men to sit with their feet elevated as high as their heads, even in their own houses; but what shall be said of the habit of *ladies* in Paris riding through the streets with their feet cocked up on the front seats of their carriages? Yet this may be seen in almost every fashionable carriage that drives through the Champs Elysées. Truly, vulgarity is not confined to one side of the Atlantic, as we shall show in some other cases. And the itching for something new has led men to some very false standards of what is beautiful.

When once the prettiest bonnet or prettiest coat is made that can be made, all successive attempts at improvements will be only abortions. That point has long since been reached, but St. Petersburg still continues to call for a change of furs; the London beauties call for new styles of silks; the pretty faces of New York for a new shape of bonnets, and the dandies of Madrid for a more stylish boot. So the dressmakers, and boot-makers, and milliners pass sleepless nights of invention, drawing diagrams, like Napoleon, or like the president of the Jesuits portioning out the world with crosses of conquest. Here they lengthen a point, there they cut away one (when the cloth is scarce); now they reduce a frill, and then add a lace ruffle (the lace market being overstocked). The week rolls around, their labors are finished, and, presto! all of *last* month's fashions are dispatched after the sun to perform the world's circuit, while the *new* inventions grace the Boulevards and Rue de la Paix windows.

I would try to be eloquent on *crinoline* and *point d'Alençon*—names I have heard ladies use mysteriously a thousand times, but am not yet exactly aware of their nature, whether they are nouns or pronouns, or what purposes they subserve in the feminine economy. I shall therefore, as Wellington advises, "speak of only what I know."

Of the fashions that this thirst for the new and the different from the *hoi polloi* has engendered, there is one of manners (for manners follow the same changes and extremes as dress) so disgusting and dirty that I am almost ashamed to mention it on paper. It is universal, as well in private society as in the restaurants, and has lately been copied to some extent in other parts of the world. It is that of rinsing the mouths and spitting in bowls after dinner and at the table. How such a filthy custom ever got vogue in society is truly puzzling. To see a table of fifteen or thirty ladies and gentlemen, the élite of Paris, sitting in full dress, blazing in silks, laces, and diamonds, stop their elegant conversation, and at a given notice commence gurgling and spitting, is more surprising than the conduct of the Western man at a dinner in New York, who, after drinking all the water in his finger-bowl, where there was a slice of lemon, said that really the dinner was very good, but he did not think much of the lemonade! At a restaurant the evil is worse; for just as you are beginning to take your soup, from certain noises on either side you imagine your neighbors have a sudden attack of sea-sickness.

Charles Dickens conducted the spitting orchestra in his overture to America, and all the little Dickenses, and all the big Dickenses, French and English, chimed in, striking every note of the gamut and inventing others, till we spit snow-storms, spit cotton-fields, and spit rivers of tobacco; and many persons in France now think that spit is a profession in America, followed by a majority of the people, the rest being slave-owners! There *is* more spitting in America than in any country I have seen, but the lowest of them never spit at table. This, however, is only one of a thousand instances of the way America, the best-slandered country on earth, is judged. How many fashions and customs there are that are thought refined in Paris, that if they existed only in America would therefore be thought barbarous and hooted at! Such is the toadyism of men. The use of finger-bowls is not disgusting, because it is absolutely necessary to wipe one's fingers after eating, and whether we wipe them wet or wipe them dry, there is not much difference; it would certainly be very rude to run the risk of soiling a lady's fan, or books, or gloves by neglect of this custom; and so all fashions ought to have, at least, some slight basis of utility in them, and even then not be adopted if involving any thing offensive to others.

The next piece of Parisian refinement I will notice is the polished floors that may be seen every where in mid-winter. The only argument in their favor I can think of is that they are cleanly. So are white pantaloons in mid-December. But cleanliness may be secured without waxed floors as well as with them. We can keep our carpets as clean as our woolen coats, dresses, and shawls, and I do not see why our floors should claim any higher honors than our persons on that score. On the other hand, they are objectionable for a good many reasons. They absorb the time of an immense number of laborers, who are at work polishing from dawn till nine or ten o'clock every day; they give an icy-cold look to a house, as well as an icy-cold feeling; they deprive a room of that snug, finished, and comfortable air which a carpet, even of the plainest kind, imparts; and, lastly, they cause some considerable danger to life and limb. The labor of polishing them is so unnatural that the physicians forbid women to do it at all, serious injury having been often caused by the practice, and, once polished, they are so slippery that one not accustomed to them may easily slide and fall. After a dinner one day with a party of gentlemen in the *Chaussée d'Antin*, I fell flat on the floor while going from the table to the mantelpiece, which highly amused my friends as soon as they found I had neither broken nose nor broken neck. Being all their lives accustomed to walking on the ice, of course they attributed my fall, not to the slipperiness of the floor, but to the empty bottles on the table.

It is only a slide, and a very easy one at that, from

the floor to the fire-place. These are so small that there is no danger of getting burned much, even if you should tumble into one. What they are made for it is impossible to imagine, unless to economize wood, which is sold by the pound, like gold in California. As for warmth, you might as well try to get it out of a twopenny candle. What a cheat those great big chimneys, nearly as large as our houses! To look at them from the street, you would fancy they led down to fire-places large enough to roast an ox!

The wash-basins and pitchers are, like the fire-places, playthings for babies. I astonished my landlady very much by gradually collecting all the stray pitchers and decanters about the house until I had accumulated five. She thought it very funny until she discovered that they were all emptied twice a day. Since then, she thinks this love of water is one of those *idées barbares* of the English and Americans.

Another of the luxurious refinements of Paris is the multiplicity of kitchens in one house. Their number varies from one to three on each floor. In the house in which I live (one of the finest on the Rue de Rivoli) there are twelve! The barbarian of the West, who lives in his house on Fifth Avenue, with only *one* kitchen in the whole dwelling, may readily imagine how far he is behind the civilization of Paris! Here we have the delicious odor of viands in our nostrils from early morn to dewy eve. No. 5 has just done breakfast as No. 4 begins; No. 3 succeeds, and so on till, just as No. 1 is finishing breakfast, No. 5 commences dinner. Thus there is a constant rotation of smells. But there are also some advantages in this gregarious style of life. It enables families to concentrate themselves near the centre of a city, and also to occupy the part of a fine house rather than the whole of an inferior one. These advantages would not be much appreciated by Americans, but gratify two French tastes, love of society and love of show.

Parisian beds are delightful. They are almost the only article of furniture made as much with reference to comfort as to show. French furniture is nearly always fine, often splendid. It is always richer than their table, and generally than their purses. In this they are exactly the opposite of the English, whose table and purse always surpass their furniture, thus displaying the taste and vanity of the one and the sensuality and prudence of the other nation. There is nothing the Parisians are vainer of than this very thing of furniture. Their mirrors, beds, curtains, gildings, palisandre, buhl, mahogany, and, in short, whatever can delight the eye, are a constant source of gratification to them.

The Parisians are naturally very conceited, but it is a good-natured, smiling conceit, that shakes hands with you, and never wounds your feelings; they are desirous of your admiration, but not at the expense of your own humiliation; they seem to guard every one's *amour propre* as much as their own; they are conscious of possessing a beautiful city, and of giving fashion to the world, so their vanity is grounded on something: it is as different from English conceit as a smile from a frown. English conceit marches with upturned nose and drawn down mouth; it passes you as if you were a worm, without deigning notice upon an animal that is, beyond doubt, so much inferior; it belongs to that class which is odious to all mankind.

Vanity is certainly as much a part of all humanity as is the back bone of our bodies. A frank vanity is never very offensive, particularly if accompanied by good nature and some talent. All nations show it continually in one way or another: the Germans, with their never-ending, high-sounding titles; the Spanish, with their grandiose style; the French, with *la gloire de la grande nation;* and the Yankees, with their greatest nation in all creation; but it was reserved for the conceit of England to make her vanity apparent even in her name, Grea-*a-at* Britain! Great is Diana, goddess of the Ephesians!

Conceit, thy name is Englishman!

Another Paris fashion, which is now, however, *de rigueur* all the world over, and which calls for an answer to a *why,* is the requiring a gentleman to appear at a party or dinner in what is called *full dress,* namely, exactly the same dress that the waiter behind your chair wears; and as many waiters, in Paris particularly, look more like gentlemen than some of those they wait upon (for there are waiters here who have the *manners* of a king), it is often easy to make a mistake, and commence a very animated conversation with the butler in a parlor of twenty gentlemen, not one of whom you have seen before. At a dancing-party only is there good reason for wearing a dress-coat (*habit*). Skirts are there in the way of the hands; but for dinners, social visits, and other parties, why should all men make a string of cabbages of themselves? Why must I, with my long legs (pardon the *word,* which is obsolete in America, though the *thing* is not), suffer the martyrdom of seeing Mr. Adonis display admiringly his well-turned calves, while every one is laughing at my lankness? I speak as the representative of the majority of the male race. Our legs are good enough as the Almighty made them, hidden under a frock-coat, but man unmakes them with one of these monkey imitations of a tail. Why not compel all the ladies, blonde, brunette, rouge, and citron, to appear in blue? Expel taste at once, and let uniform be the wear from the soldier and servant down to the ordinary civilian. Brummels and D'Orsays have no sway in evening dress excepting a little latitude of vest and cravat; if they rip a sleeve in their haste in putting on a coat, all they will have to do is to send down to the kitchen and borrow John's coat!

Now for a sensible fashion, namely, taking *French leave.* This was the invention of a wise man, and ought to be a ceremony, or absence of ceremony, observed all the world over. Many an assembly has been prematurely broken up by the interruption caused by some gentleman who goes to take an affectionate farewell of the mistress of the salon just as she is engaged in an earnest conversation on the discovery of a way to propagate truffles, or on the invention of a new dish. The Parisian slips quietly out without disturbing any one, and thus may leave early where he has another engagement, his disappearance being entirely unnoticed.

This brings me to hats—a man can not go without his hat.

Worthy of all praise the custom of carrying your

hat into the parlor, and holding it in your hand during a short visit; it saves you the trouble of putting it down and taking it up in the hall. But at a dinner the habit is not so convenient. The whole company of twelve or fifteen gentlemen stand holding their hats till dinner is announced, at which moment every one searches for a hat depository. Fifteen hats will occupy fifteen chairs, or fifteen corners when there are only four in the room, or fifteen snug little niches of which there may be only half a dozen. Now the niches and corners will always carry the day with any man; he knows his hat will not be mashed there under some bashful man's coat-tails, and that no one will put it on the floor to get a chair; and then it is just so easy to come right to that corner and find it afterward; the consequence is, that fifteen men rush with their hats to one corner; they all bump noses and cry *par-r-rdon*, and the whole fifteen rush away again, leaving the corner vacant. They next attack simultaneously a niche; but, as Locke says that two bodies can not occupy one and the same place at one and the same time, the consequence is, that the fifteen hats, not being acquainted with philosophy, pay the penalty of their ignorance, and are knocked into fifteen cocked hats! another roll of the letter *r*, like the whirring flight of a flock of partridges, follows this last assault, as the fifteen gentlemen again demand par-r-rdon. The combatants now arrange their damaged beavers and form an armistice, standing thoughtfully and considering the best plan to adopt, until finally one gentleman turns quietly around and places his hat on the floor behind him. The other fourteen immediately follow his example, each turning on a pivot to avoid farther clash, and wonder they did not do so at first.

Amid the wine and wit of the dinner-table, of course, hats are entirely forgotten; the consequence is, that, later in the evening, as each one prepares to take his quiet leave, he marches straight to the first corner he had selected as his hat depository, chuckling as he goes with that feeling of knowing what he is about which every man understands who is at all a party-goer, or who has ever lost a hat in a crowd; he puts his hand down involuntarily—"*Tiens!*" the corner is empty. He is sure he left his hat *there*. Scratches his head—Ah! it's in corner No. 2. Empty likewise! Now these two corners have made an indelible impression on every one of the gentlemen, because they had selected those places beforehand, and determined to remember them, forgetting, however, the change they had been compelled to make on the spur of the moment. The consequence is, the whole fifteen have lost their hats, and now go about the room playing "button, button, who's got the button?" peeping into sideboards and behind chairs, under ladies' dresses and on the tops of tables, now "*burning*" as he casts his eye on the well-known mark of so and so, hat-maker, Rue Richelieu, and now "*freezing*" again as he finds the thing won't go on the top of his head. The result is, that, after displacing every lady in the room, the hats are found, and the gentlemen take their French leave in a very noisy manner, returning to their homes sadder but not wiser men, for they know they will do the same thing over again to-morrow, because it is the fashion!

The picture is hardly overdrawn. Is it not more simple, when invited to dinner, to hang one's hat up in the hall?

There are numberless other silly affectations of refinement introduced by those weak-brained persons that fancy every thing elegant that is uncommon, but it would scarcely repay the ink to notice them, particularly as I wish to pay a little homage to wit.

The Parisians have a perfect furore for *esprit*, which is by no means well defined by our term wit, although often including it. Most of their great writers have either remarked on or ridiculed this mania of Paris, which besets alike all classes. Molière, in his "*Femmes Savantes*" and "*Précieuses Ridicules*," is unsparingly sarcastic upon its exhibition in the salon. Montesquieu, in the "*Lettres Persannes*," frequently alludes to it, and Voltaire aimed his satires as successfully at this as at other national peculiarities.

Bel Esprit is the goddess of the Parisians, more devoutly worshiped than beauty, wealth, dress, pictures, music, or any thing else that can please this pleasure-loving people. And wo be unto the Frenchman or woman that enters society sensible of lacking the gift of tongues, or, rather, the gift of a limber tongue. They had better see written over every portal, as over the gates of Dante's hell, "*Lascia ogni esperanza*;" for they may be assured they will be *lashed* in the purgatory of scorpion tongues within.

A stupid person is hailed with delight by a Parisian assembly; he serves as a butt for the wit of the party: he is the stick—the rod that draws the electric spark from the overcharged brains about him; at the same time, he will perhaps be unconscious of the part he is performing; for if there is any thing more curious than this furore for wit, it is the complete satisfaction and confidence with which every one assumes to possess it. Therefore you will hear the most stupid persons continually calling some one else, probably much more witty than themselves, *bête*. There is no word one hears so often in society as this. It seems as if they thought that the moment they could point out somebody else as being *bête*, that moment they secured to themselves a character for *esprit;* and if you could overhear all the remarks of a party during a whole evening, I am sure you would hear nine out of ten of the whole number termed, by some one else of the company, *bête!* and the very stupidest persons of the whole party would have used the expression most frequently.

The love of society, centuries of practice, and study, and natural disposition, have undoubtedly rendered Parisian society the most *spirituelle*, as well as gay, in the world; but, at the same time, there is a great deal of *routine* about it. All this fire of *bon mots* and repartee that at first so startles the stranger in Paris, loses, after a short residence, much of its brilliancy, because of its lack of originality. He finds what he supposed to be the pretty speeches of the moment are often but the closet wit of some comedian as old as Molière. The wit of the stage and the current French plays is all rehashed in the drawing-room, and frequently, where the party is not distinguished for originality, you may almost anticipate the reply to a given sally of words. It becomes tiresome, too, this constant effort at making bright speeches, for it is evident enough by the number of failures that there is often a great deal of effort about it.

Some of the gayest Parisian parties are among the *third sex*. Here joy is unconfined, though Bel Esprit often draggles her robes in the mud. The *third sex* is never at a loss for words; besides her natural tact, she is completely saturated with the fine speeches of the Boulevard theatres, which, after passing through the alembic of her brain, reappear at her dinner-table more funny, if less polished, than before. She is often well supported, too, by some of the first authors of Paris, as well as by the gay *bloods* of do-nothing-dom, who frequent her parties to refresh themselves after the more stately and ceremonious reunions of the Faubourg St. Germain.

At least half of the Parisian wit consists of ridicule. They laugh at one another as much as at every thing else; but their ridicule is thoughtless rather than malicious, and it is amusing to see with what skill and tact they can pick one another to pieces, selecting at a glance the assailable points, and seeming to plant just the right kind of a shot in just the right place. This spirit extends to the very lowest circles of society.

I have been amused by the hour at balls in hearing a grisette launch sarcasm at every girl that passed her, making fun of a shawl, now of a bonnet, and now of a nose; but the attacked took it all in good nature, and were ready with quick replies, so that my companion, playing *mohino*, as the Spaniards expressively say (viz., one against fifty), came out of the fight rather the worse off. I asked her if she was not afraid of giving offense. Oh no, she said; we all do it.

But the Parisian especially laughs at every thing that is not in or of the Paris of to-day. Every thing foreign is barbarian. They would laugh to-day at what they will practice to-morrow. So soon as *they* have embraced a folly, it becomes respectable; so soon as they have laid it aside, vulgar. *Paris c'est le monde.* The world is not any physical distribution of sea, land, rivers, mountains, men, animals, etc. You may know all these; you may have studied art in Italy, or science in England, or metaphysics in Germany; you may have swept the ocean in all directions, and studied character the globe over, from polished Europe to the distant forests of the Pacific coast, where the voice of civilization has never startled the red man that inhabits them, and yet, if you have not been in Paris, you do not know the world. The world is the Faubourg St. Germain.

But I defy you to get vexed at this conceit. It is so amiable, and the denizen of the world takes such delight in showing it to you! he experiences himself all the pleasure you can possibly feel. If he locked and barred all the gates of the world, and went up into his premier to look out of the window and make faces at you, you might justly get angry.

The world could not be thrust into a better place than Paris.

I am every day more pleased with Parisian manners. Manners have but little to do with morals or with heart, and here lies a great source of misunderstanding between Saxon and Gaul. We persist in considering the French hypocritical, because, in looking from our point of view, a certain cordiality of manner is evidence of a certain cordiality of heart, which *they* do not pretend to. On the other hand, the French fall into the same error in regarding English coldness of manner as an evidence of an absence of all feeling. A Frenchman does not take it as any evidence of *friendship* that another Frenchman holds a long conversation with him in a café. He dances into one café and out of another; now to a theatre; now to a ball, talking freely with all, sipping a little honey from a flower here, and another there, and the next day forgets even the faces, perhaps, of those he has talked with. An American would remember the next day every face he had seen, and would go up and *shake hands* if he should meet with them again. He mistakes amenity for friendship.

With the majority of persons we meet in life, the most we can do is to show these pleasing amenities which tend so much to make life agreeable, and it is universal with the French to the very lowest classes. Therefore, on his first arrival at Paris, a stranger is quite deceived unless he is aware of the character of the people. He is astonished at the cordiality with which he is welcomed; he believes he is among the most warm-hearted people in the world; in short, he is delighted and charmed with every body and every thing he sees. When he discovers that he has been deceived, has he a right to accuse the Parisians of hypocrisy? I let Jean Jacques Rousseau answer.

Our eccentric friend, Jean Jacques, had just arrived from his native land, Switzerland, and believed, as he says, that by the cordial manner in which he was received at Paris his fortune was made. He very quickly discovered his mistake, however, and, more generous than most strangers, explains this part of Parisian character thus:

"Let us render the French justice. They are not so prodigal of protestations of friendship as they are said to be, and those which they do make are nearly always sincere; but they have a *manner* of appearing to interest themselves in you which deceives more than words. One fancies they say less than they wish to do, in order to afford you an agreeable surprise. They are not false in their demonstrations; they are naturally officious, humane, benevolent, and even—whatever others may say to the contrary—more true than any other nation, but they are light and fickle. They feel, in effect, the sentiments they express to you, but these sentiments go as they came. While speaking with you they are full of you; out of sight you are out of mind. Nothing is durable in their hearts; the work of the moment is every thing with them."

There is a great deal of truth in that description, and that is what I call having no heart; and if having no heart consists in that, it is certainly a very delightful thing for a traveler and stranger to visit a people having no heart. But would it not be wearying to live there always?

I must close this letter, already too long, by describing the last, latest, and most wonderful fashion, which is an article of dress I discovered only to-day, and it was after a deal of peeping, prying, and bribing that I found it out. (*Gentlemen may skip the rest of this letter.*) In passing through the Rue Vivienne, I have often stopped to admire what I thought to be a new species of life-preserver, so arranged as to provide both warmth and safety. Several air-tubes encircled it, and it was inflated by means of a long, slender tube, provided with a mouth-piece, and made of India-rubber. But what surprised me most was that so many ladies were continually entering, and never any gentlemen, which was the very thing that determined me to enter too. I noticed all the ladies blushing as they came out, and arranging their robes with unusual care (for they are always adjusting their plumage like the birds). Of course, the guard met me at the door with an "On ne passe pas ici, Monsieur," which, at the touch of a two-franc piece, was changed to a lift of the hat. I walked straight to the mistress of the store, telling her I wanted to buy one of those things, having not the slightest idea of what I was to receive. Bless my soul if she didn't bring me a petticoat! It was too late to retreat; the only alternative was to turn red, which I did—red as a lobster. But I examined the thing thoroughly, and received full explanations. Its name is *jupon à tube d'air.* And saying I would send for it, I retired the observed of all observers, but having acquired more practical knowledge of certain female gear than I ever before gained in a whole month.

The uses of this invention are numerous. If a lady sees a gentleman approaching whom *she* does not like, she remains blown up to full sofa size, and he can not come within six feet of her. If he is a friend, she puts her hand in her pocket, and turning the valve attached to the connecting-tube, allows a portion of the air to escape, so that he comes within three feet. For a lover she collapses entirely; he sits on the sofa.

In New York no more terrible accidents on the Hudson. The boats may take fire, but the ladies, gracefully supported by the *jupon à tube d'air*, will float off, bobbing up and down in the water like fancy fishing-corks, and carry, perhaps, their husbands or brothers, who are too stupid to swim, on their backs.

The thing has some disadvantages. A sad accident happened here the other day. A young lady, Mdlle. C——, had blown herself up beyond the usual gauge, and immediately got into her open carriage for a drive to the Bois de Boulogne. While passing through the Champs Elysées, she was observed to rise slowly out of her carriage and ascend gracefully toward heaven. I thought, as I saw her embraced by a fleecy white cloud, that it was one of those Parisian exhibitions representing Leda and the swan, just as I had seen here, some years since, the enlèvement of Europa by the bull. But I have learned that the poor girl has never been heard of since. She is probably now passing through the rings of Saturn, and is given up for lost. It is supposed that the air of the jupon becoming highly *rarefied* was the cause of the accident. The sleepy coachman had driven all the way to the Bois de Boulogne before discovering the absence of his mistress.

SPRING AND A RAMBLE THROUGH THE GARDENS OF THE TUILERIES; IN SHORT, A RAMBLING LETTER.

I THINK I announced once the arrival of spring, but a late snow-storm spoiled it all, and covered up the green grass and budding trees. Now the holy sunshine comes down again, making the heart of man expand with delight, and the very little birds praise God with hymns of joy. All nature, animate and inanimate, swells with happiness. The buds of the gardens of the Tuileries, which seemed to lock their tiny hands with sadness on their bosoms during the late frosts, are to-day clapping their opened little palms in the sunshine and the breeze. They seem to sympathize with the sports of the children as their merry voices resound beneath them. The marble Venuses even, that yesterday sparkled with snow and icicles, to-day look warm as flesh and blood. Every one walks smilingly and with opened mouth, as if some passing breath of the delightful air should escape; the ever-shut palace can not resist the general expansion, and opens its gloomy windows, and the zephyr that touches your brow now, in the next moment kisses the Empress's cheek. The little circular pond is the centre of great animation; it is plowed in all directions by little clippers bearing the flags of all nations, and is every now and then the scene of a grand naval combat between the noble white swan, who considers himself sovereign of the seas, and the little vessels of war that occasionally dart within bill-shot of his long neck. The swan fights admirably, and now and then puts the admiral's ship completely under; but the latter, thanks to her heavy keel, quickly rights herself, and, a favoring "whiff" coming down, darts off with flying pennons, all sails set, pursued by the swan, who drops rapidly aft, because not *clipper built.* This take-to-your-heels victory is celebrated by five hundred partisans of the clipper style of things with loud and continuous shouts; but the swan holds himself proudly, nothing daunted, and, like Charley Napier, he would still sink the whole fleet if you would only give him—what he never can have—a little of the clipper spirit of the age.

It is just midday, the sunny hour when babies, white caps, and invalids begin to appear in the gardens. They swarm in through all the gates, filling the avenues, benches, and chairs. The nurses chat furiously; the children roll hoops and play marbles; and the invalids sit droopingly, doubtless ready to exchange positions with the happy children, or even with the nurses.

But babes, and gens d'armes, and invalids, and *valets d'enfants* (as I call these nurses) are not the only idlers to be seen. Crowds of young men, and old gentlemen, and ladies with their sewing, and students with their books, may be seen seeking recreation, or perhaps doing what they do always—nothing. It always astonishes me to see the immense crowd of people in Paris who have nothing to do, just at the very hour, too, that in America every one is hard at work, from the richest down to the poorest. How do all these people live? It is none of my business, to be sure; but I should very much like to know, for all that.

Here they are grouped about the fountain near the Place Concorde, watching by the hour the leaping crystals, that seem to be more ambitious of rising in the world than the lazy do-nothings about them; now they walk on through the *Place* toward the *Arc de l'Etoile*, stopping sometimes to look at Punch and Judy or the flying horses, and at others hiring a chair, and watching the occupants of the various carriages that pass with incessant roll. As it grows later, the crowd of pedestrians and carriages both increase, until at 4 o'clock the Champs Elysées is a mass of animation, in which every class of society is represented, from the Emperor and his charming bride, who dash by in a pair of carriages, each drawn by four horses mounted by handsome young postillions, down to the dried-up old woman with a face of exactly the same color as the *plaisirs* she offers for sale. And one bound out of all this gayety and happiness brings you into a side street where the most abject misery presents itself to view, within hearing, even, of the aristocratic rumble of the titled coach, and the gay laughter of thousands of happy promenaders. Such is Paris! the world is not very different.

To the invalid spring comes grateful as the dawn after a night of trouble; to the old it is the inspiration of a new youth; to the poor it brings long-coveted warmth and the promise of food when the winter store is beginning to fail; and to all mankind it is the collecting in one bright, joyous month all the out-door enjoyments banished by a winter's snows. It opens the windows of a whole city, and airs dark corners that have not breathed a fresh breath for months; it dries the mouldy, leaking roofs of the sombre habitations of the poor, and many a weeping eye under them. Truly, I like to see the warm spring descend over a large city.

In benefiting every body, it would be strange if I were neglected. The spring has made me acquainted with my opposite neighbors. We are only twenty feet apart, but until lately their curtains, my curtains, and the cold air have as effectually hidden our faces as if we were twenty miles apart. Now our windows are thrown wide open, and I see daily my two *vis-à-vis*. They are two girls of about seventeen or eighteen years of age. They are not stylish-looking, but interesting; they live in a garret, but they wear nice, clean white caps. They sew all day long; in the cold morning, in the gray evening, and at noon; when I go out and when I come in, when I get up and when I lie down, these poor girls are still seated at their window, sewing—sewing as if their lives depended on it, as probably they do. Alas! why *do* men wear shirts? They look resigned, not contented. They talk but little, and never smile, although their large, dark eyes do brighten for an instant as they look across the narrow street and find themselves the object of attention to a young man. A young woman will smile then, if ever. But how pale their faces look underneath their dark hair! They have sewed away their color, they have sewed away their smiles, and they are now sewing away their souls. And it is but a step to the Faubourg St. Germain! And yet hell is not farther from heaven than these poor girls from the Faubourg St. Germain!

O ye blind philanthropists, that talk of abstaining from sugar and coffee to benefit the "poor slave," who is rollicking in fatness, and happy as the day is long, why do ye not think of the starving, suffering poor of your large cities—of those who want for bread, even, not a mile from your own doors? Form your abolition societies for the abolition of city miseries, to help those who are emaciated by sickness, disease, and want, and then, if you have any thing left, *give it* to help the "poor slave," and no more of this endless cant about human suffering which is confined to a race in the main as happy as yourselves, perhaps, whatever may be the crime of those who keep them in slavery.

The houses opposite are clean enough, but old. They look like old clothes repaired and made new. Fortunately, too, they are lower than their aristocratic Rivoli neighbors, which enables us on this side—that is, all the *us-es* that are not too lazy or too vain to live in the fifth story—to have the air pure from heaven before it has washed out the neighboring garrets.

In one of the rooms in front is a fiddler. He plays well, and sells dearly by playing little; but he annoys me by that instinct which seems to belong to all good performers, of commencing half a dozen beautiful snatches of pieces, and then stopping short and wedging in a scrape or two, as if to tune the instrument, to do which he does not turn a key, but merely gives them a slight touch with one finger, or blows a breath upon them, such is the fineness of his ear!

Lower down are people better off in the world—a young man and his mistress, who seem happy in the present, thoughtless for the future. Not a foot from them is a mother and her two daughters. The thickest stone wall is scarcely thick enough to separate such an example as lies within a foot of the pillow of these innocent girls. Still lower down, we come to milliners' shops and fancy shops of all kinds, where may be seen lively-looking young girls and women who are not over-worked. Women seem to swarm every where in Paris. Indeed, it is almost as puzzling to tell what becomes of all the women as to know what to do with all the women. It is not a puzzling question in America, because there woman occupies her true position; but in Europe, where they are knocking about in stables, and in wheat-fields, and meadows, and streets, and garrets, and Heaven knows where, the poor things would seem almost like cats—a creation *de trop*, being of no use to any body—an evil to be endured when once they are grown, but an advantage to society if they were not there. Nobody would drown them off in infancy like young kittens, but every body seems to think it would be better if there were fewer of them born. However, I'll not *bephilosophize* you on the subject, only I am glad to see that in Paris they are opening all kinds of occupations to women suited to their weakness, so that the excuses for a girl's abandoning herself to vice will every day grow fewer. You may nowsee women waiters, women barbers, women shop-keepers, women book-keepers, etc.; but you see, likewise, women street-sweepers, and women employed in many other occupations suitable only for men.

After the women, the most numerous and troublesome persons in Paris are the policemen. I have a republican horror of them. You say no good citizen ought to be afraid of policemen. I would substitute, no good citizen ought to be afraid of *good* policemen. I have always looked upon London policemen as friends; they are the best in the world, and they know their places as *servants* of the people, and not masters; they feel their responsibility, and would suffer death almost before attempting to inflict it in self-defense. But to stumble at every step upon men armed with guns and swords, as in many Continental cities, and to have one at your elbow every time you turn your head, is a nuisance that only slaves could bear. Stop to blow your nose, and one of these fellows immediately says in your ears, "*Avancez donc, Monsieur!*" drop into a side alley, and talk a few moments with two or three friends, and they imagine you are plotting against the government; select a good spot at a show or ball, and straightway an *avancez donc* comes up and takes it himself in order to keep the crowd back. They walk up and down among the *coulissiers* of the Bourse, and if the crowd halts a moment, they lay their dirty hands on the nearest gentleman's shoulder with a "*Circulez, Messieurs, avancez donc; avancez.*" Some nights ago, at the sortie of the theatre, I had a curiosity to see the pretty girls come out into the snow, which had just commenced falling, and as they have a very cute way of saying *tiens* on all and every occasion, I was quietly making the count of how many would use the word as soon as they saw snow, when one of these *avancez doncs* gave me the usual polite invitation to pass on (while *he* looked at the girls). I, however, dodged behind a pillar and finished my count, finding that every one said *tiens* who did not say *tenez*. However, the people of Paris at present need pretty much such policemen as they have, and though they are often consequential in the performance of their duties, and play the master a little too freely, I have never seen them impolite to a stranger; and for one thing they deserve the greatest credit—that is, the complete mastery they have over cabmen. This, and the simple and excellent cab laws, make the Parisian cabmen the best I have seen in any city of the world.

The cabmen are all healthy and pleasant-looking; there is hardly a man among them who has not a rosy face, owing to his easy, unconcerned, and fresh-air life. He is obedient and submissive, and never plots rascality, because it is impossible. I wish we could change all of our extortionate hack villains for such men. The policemen, on the other hand, are universally pale. Now both classes live all the time in the open air, and both are up by day and night; but I think the difference is owing to the different feelings continually cherished by each; the one class are in a continual state of antagonism and watchfulness, while that of the other is mere routine and laziness. I often feel like driving a cab, and recommend it to invalids. Invalids, scholars, and aristocrats are generally pale, and some others, as the grammarians say when too lazy to hunt up exceptions.

The regulation which governs cabs is well worthy of imitation all over the United States; the fare is so much a course, or so much an hour. A course is not any exact distance of India-rubber quarter or half miles, which a hackman may stretch as he pleases, but it is a drive to any given spot you may wish to go to within city limits, be it one, three, or five furlongs. The *cocher*, as he is called, always gives you his number, printed on a very small ticket (half an inch long, perhaps), which you thrust into your pocket and think no more of. The next day your umbrella is missing; you go to the police-office, produce your number, and receive your umbrella.

In Paris, indeed in France generally, it is almost impossible to lose any thing by accident, even your life. If an article be left in a railway carriage, it will afterward almost certainly be found at the station. The smallest object dropped in the street travels directly to the police-office, where, if not claimed, it will be advertised in the weekly list of articles found.

And as for human life, you are not permitted to lose it, so far as police regulations can prevent. A most commendable care exists in this respect. Persons are not permitted to walk on the railway tracks; watchmen are placed in front of houses that are being torn down or built, whose sole duty from morning to night is to warn passers away from danger; and in all cases where any risk is to be apprehended, the police take charge of your life, *relieving you of all responsibility.* The consequence is, however, that people become careless for themselves, and are very apt to get under cart wheels and stumble into pits whenever the policeman has his back turned; in short, they are not *wide awake*, as an American would say. Wherever danger can not be avoided without warning, this fatherly care is all well. It is well under all circumstances in France, where the people are ignorant. But suppose, for instance, in America, the people were forbidden to walk on the railway tracks for fear they should lose their lives, there is not a man but that would answer he had arrived at the age of discretion, and did not require to be led by his mother's apron-string. And among a thousand men brought up in that way, the accidents to life will be fewer than among a thousand who are watched by other eyes than their own. But we are reckless of human life in America in ways which make the greatest individual prudence and foresight of no avail. Our boilers, and bridges, and buildings all lack *back bone*, and destroy thousands of lives annually by their burstings, and breakings, and burnings, to say nothing of railway mismanagement.

In a crowd the police are especially active in preserving order; but beware of a Parisian crowd. A Parisian crowd is the most good-natured and amiable in the world to a certain point, but the nervous sensibility and *mercurialness* of the people carry them away as soon as there is an unusual press. They seem absolutely to lose all reason. Each one accuses his neighbor of pushing; the women begin to cry (and a crowd here is always full of women), and the men begin to whine and recriminate, and perhaps a grand stampede follows. Three hundred persons were killed on the Place Concorde at the marriage fête of Louis XVI. merely by being smothered and trampled on by the crowd, which had become alarmed by the presence of some pickpockets among its numbers. On the return of the troops from the Crimea, I had some evidence of the style of action of a Parisian crowd. It became so dense in some parts of the Boulevards that it was impossible to move right or left, and after making a dozen ineffectual attempts to get out into a side street, I resigned myself to the jaws of the masses. The women became hysterical and cried, imploring the help of the policemen, who stood fixed firm as any of the wedges about them.

Fortunately, no serious accidents happened, though several persons fainted. The men generally had sense enough to keep quiet, without thrusting their fists into the faces of the unfortunate persons who were pushed up next to them, as would have been the case in America; and I certainly think it pleasanter to be run over by a nervous individual who is trying to save himself, than to be battered by an irritable one who is enraged because he has caged himself. The accidents and crimes of a nation show very well the character of its people.

Without speaking of China, India, etc., and going into a long philosophical, philological, categorical history, examination, comparison, etc., just compare France and the United States. In the first country we see daily the perpetration of crimes resulting from sickly, diseased imaginations, the results of idleness, want of work, lack of education, bad education, and poverty; in the latter, the crimes are generally what I may call *healthy* crimes, if you can understand the paradox. In France, murder for money is common; in the United States it is rare. In the latter country the most common mode of taking life is in hot blood on the spur of the moment, and generally on account of liquor. Sometimes, too, it is to revenge the more than murder of a female. In France, on the other hand, life is rarely lost in this way. In France it is a common thing for two men, or a man and woman, to commit a *social* suicide with charcoal or pistols, or they jump out of windows, killing another as they fall. At one time even persons were forbidden to ascend the Column of Vendome, owing to the number who threw themselves off. Now a person blows up his house, another hangs his three children and himself, a third rushes into the streets swearing to sacrifice the first man he meets. Numbers daily abandon their infants, and a few days since a man informed his wife that the goose was roasted. On examination, she was horrified to find that the goose was her own child!

A few days since a physician gave a bottle of medicine to a man for his sick wife, telling him to beat it well before administering it. The next day, the neighbors, hearing the most frightful cries, rushed in and found the man beating his poor sick wife with might and main. On being remonstrated with, he showed the physician's prescription ordering him to beat her, but was informed that the pronoun *la* referred to the medicine and not to his wife. In fact, one don't know what may come next here, and I feel sure that a good citizen who does not frequent bar-rooms and brawls is safer in the United States than in France, in spite of all said to the contrary.

RILED BY THE LONDON TIMES.

THREE things have made me open my eyes with wonder every morning for the last ten years. One is *awaking from sleep;* another is the ready facility with which the Roman Catholic Church can explain away or reasonably account for all her absurdities; and the third is how England, while boasting of her bungling diplomacy, as if her blunt honesty were always overreached by the subtle finesse of other nations, has managed to pull a wool-cap over the eyes of the world, and thus invariably to *steal a march* on all her rivals. With more *latent* sense than any other nation on earth, she is stupid enough on the spur of the moment. Wise as a serpent, she looks simple and meek as a lamb. Among the quick-witted diplomatists of the Continent, she makes but a sorry figure at first. She commences every thing badly, and by her apparent stupidity throws the world off its guard, so that by the time her thoughts have bubbled up through the fatty matter of her brain, she becomes more than a match for the strongest. She has the happy art of inspiring an enemy with contempt of herself, and thus, in the end, secures an easy victory. Guided by her Triune Divinity of pen, sword, and keel, she has made herself virtually political dictator of the globe. She has the skill of evading law without breaking it, and of artfully making treaties with the weak and ignorant, which, with her foresight, she is assured *they* must break. The treaties of the strong with the feeble are but pretexts of seizure. It is the alliance of the earthen and iron pots who are to travel the rapids in company. Japan is the only nation that feels this truth; she has been forced from its active recognition, which will be her ruin and the world's benefit.

The domineering character of England commences at home and in the family. She is a nation of toadies. You have in vain to search the world over to find such prostration before title and place. From the child and schoolboy to the premier, every where, might makes right. The fagging system of the schools is but an illustration of the principle, where some physically weak Cowper is pounded by a brute every way his inferior but in brutishness; and a hundred years later, a judge on the bench, in a parallel case, says, "Let him bear it as others have done," and thus the spirit of cringing on the one hand and of injustice on the other is fostered. This spirit is the stuff that "some" Englishmen and all lackeys are composed of. Next to a toady, the most hateful thing on earth is a tyrant. *Toadyism*, after passing through its chrysalis state of transition to power, becomes *tyranny*.

These thoughts came into my head the other day on reading a short and almost unnoticeable paragraph which appeared in the Times, announcing that the little kingdom of Oude, containing 24,000 square miles (or about half the size of England), and a population of 5,000,000 of souls, with its revenue of a million of pounds sterling (which may be easily doubled), were all annexed and forever to the possessions of the East India Company. Why? Because King Wadjid Ali Shah and his predecessors "had refused, evaded, or neglected to comply with the obligations of the treaty of 1801, by the terms of which they were compelled to establish in the kingdom *a system of administration of a nature to assure the prosperity of its subjects.*" Highly-civilized England has declared that benighted Oude has failed to do this, therefore Oude and its revenues belong to England! How many more such foul plots for robberies are now existing in India? How many more will be made? And when all India has been compelled "to establish an administration of a nature to assure the prosperity of its subjects" by pouring its rupees into English coffers, what country is next to be civilized—China, Japan, or Mexico?

This deed is done, five millions of people are robbed of their country, and not a voice lifted in defense! While a congress of nations is dictating terms of punishment to a barbarian for showing thievish propensities, this hoary hypocrite, who is loudest in that congress, has one hand in his neighbor's pocket under the table! (While the family talk economy, Johnny robs the sugar-bowl.)

At the same moment, and with great ambidexterity, she is robbing men in America in known violation of law; but, able as a Machiavelli and cunning as a Jesuit, for this she has prepared in advance her defense. She opens her mouth, and her lips distill sweet words. She says through Clarendon,

"The English government, desirous of availing themselves of the *offers* of volunteers" (observe, the volunteers have rushed away by thousands from roast-beef and two dollars a day, and stand up to their arm-pits in the water along the whole Atlantic coast of the

United States, imploring England to send them to the Crimea!), "adopted the measures necessary for making generally known" (that is, transport vessels appear in the offing and burn a blue light) "that her majesty's government were ready to do so" (kind-hearted creature), "and for receiving such persons as should present themselves at an appointed place in one of the British possessions" (passage free and at the expense of the English government).

At the same time, she charges her agents not to break any law of the United States. Oh no! Fagin says to Smike, "Go get me that gold watch out of that man's vest pocket, but *be particular* not to break the law against theft." Smike does as he is bid, but is unfortunately caught. But Smike was a gentleman, and made instant apology, which the other, who was a brutish, ill-bred individual, refused to accept, and the consequence is, Smike is sent to prison.

This thieving in India by England is continually going on under ingenious pretexts. Now she quarters large bodies of troops in a province to *protect* it (protecting is her forte), and when the province is unable to pay for the protection never solicited, it is mortgaged, and finally the mortgage is foreclosed, and the province swallowed up by the East India Company. Now she resorts to some other expedient equally culpable, but capable of certain plausible defense, which her pen ever has the power and readiness to produce.

Speak of these crimes to Englishmen, and they tell you, "Oh, my dear sir, we don't know what they are doing away off there in India; it's not my fault." True, they don't know; they are like that ancient sect that were always pulling the *mote* out of their neighbor's eyes. They can easily see three thousand miles away to America, and pick out the smallest peccadilloes. It is truly astonishing, such monstrous hypocrisy! America indeed labors under great disadvantages. She is transparent as a crystal; her thoughts, and motives even, are all known to the world before conceived in action. With frank, straightforward *smartness*, she lacks entirely the finesse of the Continent, and the plotting, smooth-faced hypocrisy of England. She has keel enough, and the spirit of '76 is not so dead but that she would have sword enough, if required, but, since Webster, she absolutely lacks a pen of European reputation. England can make the worse appear the better cause; America can not put the better cause in its true light. Eloquent sophisms are more effectual than ill-told truths. I do not wish to see a Jesuit pen in America, but I wish to see a pen capable of making truth as lovely as it really is. God grant that America may fail in every act of injustice or oppression that she may ever attempt. Such acts may advance a nation for a day; they may procure the means of luxuries and refinements, which shall be, however, the instruments of punishment and decay. There is no future punishment for nations except future oblivion; their hell is on earth, and to them death is eternal sleep.

Now and then the good spirit of the English nation arouses itself, and looks at its own misdeeds; now and then a Hastings is impeached; but, under the pen of a Macaulay, his history glows with such a halo of brilliancy as to hide all vice, and make ambitious men aim at a Hastings's crimes. The nation then sinks again into apathy, as if it had done its duty; oppression and robbery continue; and, to calm their own consciences, they assume the protection of that of America. The microscopic eyes of all the monarchies of earth are fixed on the "Experimental Republic." They delight to detect her blemishes; they feel no gratitude to her for relieving them of their thousands of ignorant paupers and criminals, instruments of disease and revolution on one side of the Atlantic, of health, progress, and happiness on the other. They feel no thankfulness at seeing a whole continent, with its fine rivers, and lakes, and fertile valleys, and splendid forests, explored by hardy pioneers, redeemed from waste, and made to smile with a contentment and happiness which has overflown and benefited the world. They do not appreciate her commerce, and cotton, and sugar, and gold, and her highways across the Isthmus, which cost thousands of the lives of the unfortunate builders. No, they are too refined for all that. The tourists of Europe and America, who meet midway on the Atlantic, go—*these*, freighted with only what was to be admired in Europe; those, with only what was to be censured in America.

So far from any spirit of jealousy of England inspiring these remarks, I would be glad to see her, if she could do it justly, possess all India, and all China too, but not Japan, toward which lovely island I must confess to some tender feelings, perhaps because we yet have no island, though born with *hereditary* love of them, perhaps not to give England the labor of forming all the "systems of administration of a nature to assure the prosperity of the subjects" of all the world. England and the United States are the only two nations on the face of the earth whose interests are exactly identical; who speak the same language, and worship the same God in the same way; who read the same authors and have the same ancestry; who are both commercially great, and fortunately, perhaps, different in the general employments of life—the one being an agricultural nation, and the other a manufacturing one; and yet we are always quarreling like two women in one household, or like a young mother with a grown daughter! and I really think the jealousy is on the part of the mother. The daughter has forgotten, over and over, the cruelties practiced toward her in youth, but the tender spot is continually irritated anew. Whenever there is the slightest chance to say or do something annoying, it is taken advantage of. The beginning of the Mexican war is a signal for the ridicule of the whole English press; yet compare the conduct and management of bodies of raw volunteers with the bungling style of the English army in the present war! Bodies of freebooters and outlaws escaping from the extended seaboard are looked upon as agents of our government. We are told at one time that as soon as England and France are done with Russia, they will look after us. True, it is the Times that says so, which is not the government, but more powerful than the government. And now that the war is finished, and the whole country is on a grand war footing, the same paper is particularly arrogant, writing long, *affectionate-looking articles* with *stings in their tails.*

And, after all, England wonders that Americans do not love her. They do love, and wish to love her, whenever she will permit it. But change positions for an instant, and suppose that we had done toward England all she has done toward us; with the temper of her nation, we should be in continual war; suppose we had done in India all that England has done, we should long ago have had the fleets of all Europe against us.

If Russia had looked toward her eastern frontiers, and been the first to cry out Stop thief! she might have been at this moment allied with France to protect some Mohammedan kingdom in Asia against the ambition of England, and the latter country would be still engaged in decrying and ridiculing Napoleon as it did at first, instead of playing toady to him as it does now.

The alliance between France and England is hollow and insincere; it is merely a "*mariage de convenance*," and, like most marriages of that kind, its unhappy duration, after being passed in mutual suspicions and recriminations, will close in speedy divorce.

The war and that alliance combined fixed Louis Napoleon in his saddle, and gave him the reins, and at the same time enabled England to check for a moment the only power she fears besides the United States—a power whose robberies were extending over the same fields as her own, namely, the field of Asia.

Poland, and Hungary, and Greece, and Italy wept at this display of sympathy for *poor*, *dear*, *Mohammedan Turkey!*

And what has England gained by a war commenced in hypocrisy and ended in shame? She has strengthened the arm of the very nation she wished to humble;

the blow struck has recoiled on her own head. Russia never stood before the world with such proud dimensions as at present. By showing a power she was believed unpossessed of, she has gained a power she never possessed. She has gained an experience worth more to her than the men she has lost (for she cares but little for men); and, lastly, she has gained in moral strength what she has lost in physical, while her physical losses will soon be repaired. *She is not idle.* Russia now stands like a terrible giant, not threatening the liberties of Europe, perhaps, but promising a growth and force which will in future laugh Balance of Power diplomacy to scorn.

But consider your ways, John Bull, and repent. Look at your great body stretched most indecently across the whole earth, your head on England, your left hand on Gibraltar, your elbow on Aden, and your enormous abdomen on India—a spot you had the good sense to select for that portion of your body, partly because it was of a suitable size, and partly because four capacious pockets would be forever agape just where they could be most conveniently filled. Your right arm is stretched toward America, with a thumb on Jamaica and Belize, and four fingers on Canada, thus spanning the United States, and having your hand in a most convenient position to tighten Jonathan's cravat if necessary. Your great feet rest, one on the Falkland Isles and the other on Australia. You feel a twinge of the gout, and all China cracks; you grunt, and all India quakes with fear. The whole world cries "*Quousque tandem*," which means it will not endure much more from you.

I now leave you to your reflections, John, hoping you will get some kind person to throw a sackcloth (not India gunny-bags) and ashes on your head while you repent of your great wickedness on the earth!

MY THIS AND MY THAT DORÉ.

PARISIANS and Budhists are excessively fond of yellow. Quakers and Englishmen like gray. I like the latter color and people best. Indeed, I suspect Virtue has a partiality for gray; it is a safe color; it hides nothing plainer than itself; but all colors are better than yellow, which is the hue of Vice. Saffron faces, saffron fruits, and "sere and yellow leaves" are not beautiful; give us rosy or even pale cheeks, rosy fruits, the flesh-colored melon, the bloody peach, the purple grape, the green gage, and even the orange, which has appropriated a color of its own. A generous fire spurns yellow, and burns candescent; the spirited gas leaps gayly into white and purple flame, leaving the sickly yellow to ignoble tallow; in short, life and spirit have consigned this color to decay and the Parisians!

Gilt is the glory of Paris. On all sides, whether in the apartments of luxurious vice or of virtuous luxury, one hears only of my this and my that doré. Doré is god of Paris! He crushes more souls than the car of Juggernaut! Whether as god or gilt, doré is always more than sham or humbug. None of the felicitously-invented words of modern times at all describe it. It is always a lie—a very blazing lie! It is always a sign of deception, because whatever is doré, from plaster mouldings up to silver spoons, must, of necessity, be inferior to gold, but the extent of the deception can never be known without examination. Swedenborg said that every thing in the physical has its type in the moral world. (If *he* did not say so, I say it.) And so we have doré characters, doré speeches, etc. We have doré books: such are the trashy novels designed for those well-meaning but weak-minded persons whose principles will not allow them to read the masculine, healthy novels of Walter Scott, but who devour eagerly the baby tales, with baby morals, which are besprinkled with such nice-looking words as *piety*, *charity*, *Christian religion*, and so on. We have doré museums, whither simple people who will not go to the theatre to see a good play of Shakspeare's well acted, crowd to hear a namby-pamby dialogue spoken by bunglers.

We have doré plays, where fine words gild lewd ideas.

We have doré society, where tongue and style take the place of heart.

We have doré men, where gold stands instead of ideas.

Doré trials (principally in America), where judge and jury grant criminals certificates of character.

We have doré treaties, as the treaty of 1801 between Great Britain and Oude.

We have doré diplomacy, of which Machiavelli was father.

We have doré pills, and, in fact, there is nothing so bad or disgusting but that it may make quite a respectable appearance when doré.

Doré-ism keeps pace with civilization and luxury; it is the precursor of decay.

The first building that was doré was the Capitol at Rome; the last was the Hotel des Invalides in Paris. The glory of Rome was at its culminating point when her Capitol was covered with gold. There was but little sham about that; the precious metal was not varnished on in our delicate modern style, but laid on in great solid plates, in a way worthy of Romans. France was in the height of her splendor and power when she gilded the "*Invalides;*" but it is a sign of weakness at the best. It is typical of the fig-leaves that hid the shame of Adam. The temples of Lhasha, and hundreds of tottering cities in the East, blaze with the ruddy gold. When cities turn a doré face toward high heaven, their fate is sealed. When their domes glitter like golden pippins ripening in the sun, the barbarian looks on from afar, and smiles grimly as he thinks of the beauty and booty that await him, for he knows that *slaves are being made there!* Tyrant number one is Luxury, who binds men, while tyrant number two is the barbarian or fillibuster who enslaves them. Ripeness is but a prelude to rottenness. The process is slower with nations than with pippins, but equally certain. A nation is ripe when her people begin to repose in the lap of luxury and sloth. Sparta knew this; England knows it, and England is yet a sturdy, growing giant, though she has already far outspanned in age the dozen centuries that linked the birth and death of imperial Rome. She is still in the vigor of early manhood—still despises gewgawry. Were it not for barbarians and fillibusters, most nations would die of apoplexy; war is sometimes a depletion which saves them; the remedy is not pleasant —no medicine is.

We are sometimes irresistibly drawn into the contemplation of what we dislike; so men gaze, fascinated, at serpents; so young Copperfield steals up to the chamber of the sleeping Uriah Heep to stare at the hideous face of a being he loathed; so *Doré* stands as the title of this book!

ART, AND AN ADVENTURE IN THE LOUVRE.

"THERE are four things," says La Bruyère, "in which mediocrity is insupportable—poetry, music, painting, and oratory." But the taste of some is so fine that they discover mediocrity in every thing. They can only see tragedy performed by a Ristori or Rachel, and hear the music of a Lind or Grisi. They can only enjoy the paintings of a Raphael or Titian, and the dancing of a Cerito or Rosati. Nature is never grand but at Chamouni or Niagara; never lovely but in Tempe or Vallambrosa. The passing cloud has no beauty, because it passes every day; the setting sun no glory, because they saw it yesterday, and may see it again to-morrow. Such persons will rave about an ordinary picture, provided they are made to believe it is the work of a great master, while they would never observe the landscape it represents, although spread before them in all the loveliness of nature. We meet continually, in traveling as well as at home, persons who pass indifferently the finest scenery, apparently unconscious of its beauty, yet who will rave about landscape pictures as if they formed the greatest charm of their life; indeed, they will often leave nature to see a very poor miniature of it. I can fancy a man running away pretty rapidly from a real beggar-boy to see Murilo's picture of him, because there is very little of the handiwork of nature about a beggar-boy. I can fancy him rushing out as fast as his legs will carry him from the filth of an Alpine chalet to view some celebrated painter's representation of it, because painters, faithful as they may be, can never convey to canvas the dirt and smells of a Swiss chalet. We hear often of the *speaking*, but never of the *smelling* canvas! But why people will break their necks to get away from natural scenery, with its accompaniments of fresh air and motion, to view copies of it in a musty gallery, I have not taste enough to understand. It seems to me that a man who loves one must love both.

There is nothing about which there is so much humbug and so much twaddle as about this same subject of paintings. I see it in the parlor and in the artist's studio; I have seen it in the galleries of Italy, and I now see it every morning in the Louvre. This picture *doré-ism*, with which many gild their vulgarity, has become so unpleasant to me that I never dare express my opinion about a picture; in the first place, because I can not, as I know nothing about them; and, in the next place, because I see that even artists and amateurs, who have a right to consider themselves knowing, if any one, so generally differ in their opinions, and are so often deceived, while the majority of those pretending to knowledge simply make themselves ridiculous. Every day we read in the newspapers of fabulous prices being paid by rich persons for a picture pronounced by infallible judges to be a Domenichino or a Van Dyck. Crowds rush to see it; a vocabulary of admiring adjectives is exhausted upon it, and the envied possessor becomes celebrated as a man of taste. Afterward it is proved, on undoubted evidence, to be the work of some obscure or entirely unknown artist, not worth as many centimes as it has cost in francs. Is the picture less beautiful than it was before?

And so, in walking through the Louvre every day, I almost congratulate myself on being a man of no taste, thus being at liberty to admire what pleases me without criticising or fear of being criticised. If the general style and subject of a picture please me, I am slow to see minor defects: a leg may be too short, an arm too long, a finger too pointed—I don't see it, and am as ignorant of the laws of foreshortening, and so on, as are the cattle of Normandy of the categories into which they are divided by the laws of Paris.

To criticise, a man must strip off his imagination and look coldly on things. This is the way we are *compelled* to look at most things in life, and it was one of the first lessons of my childhood, when, by reason of certain little incidents happening daily in the school-room, I came at length to regard a tree merely as a vegetable bearing an indefinite number of switches! *Now* I prefer, if possible, to see knights errant in wind-mills.

Notwithstanding all these my heterodox criticisms on critics, I have my enjoyment in the Louvre, which

I visit nearly every day, and have my favorite pictures there, which I sit in front of by the half hour at a time—not always looking at the picture, it is true; not always thinking of it indeed, but spending a good deal of time in looking at the lookers-on; and it occurred to me that the position of guard in the Louvre ought not to be such a disagreeable one as that of guard in a hospital. These men are surrounded from morning till night by beauty; their faces are lighted by rays reflected from Salvator Rosas and Poussins, and darkened by Rembrandts; they walk over polished floors and under painted ceilings, and every inch of the walls that surround them has been touched by the hand of genius; and, as if that were not enough, the handsomest females of two worlds are continually passing before them, and thus they pass their lives in an atmosphere of beauty that should belong only to poets—or make them poets. But they are, for the most part, frowzy-looking dogs for all that.

Apropos of the living beauties in the Louvre: they are sometimes dangerous rivals of their inanimate resemblances that hang on the wall. I was sitting a few days since admiring Veronese's "Wedding at Cana" (there is a very comfortable sofa in front of that picture, which is always filled with admirers) when one of these beautiful women passed, drawing me away from one wedding to thoughts, at least, of another, and past a whole mile of pictures, my favorites as well as others, which might as well at that moment have been mile-stones for all the impression they made in presence of a most charming English girl, who would have made Titian cut the canvas of his first Venus!

Such a woman was enough to make me repent of ever having said a word against the English nation; but, at the same time, she proved the truth of my remarks, that the English are all fillibusters, even to the young girls who steal hearts in the Louvre. Somehow or other I happened, during a whole hour, to be admiring the very picture that she was admiring, until, seeing she noticed this sympathy of tastes on my part, I abstained from its further indulgence for fear of rudeness, seating myself in a corner to await her return, which I knew could not be long, as the hour for closing the Louvre was near at hand. And there I fell asleep. How long I had remained there I know not, but on awaking I found all the halls deserted and the doors locked, with not even a guard left!

Like Alfieri's Mirra, I dropped down before a painting of Venus, and uttered prayers of thanksgiving. The declining rays of the setting sun were glimmering through those western windows over the Seine, and lighting up with a subdued glow the speaking canvas. The buzz of human voices and the shuffling of human feet having died away, I could hear distinctly through the solemn silence the voices of the dead, whose souls come back to the warm canvas in the absence of the living, and which fell upon my ear at intervals only, not in whispers, but like the sound of an Æolian harp, now earnest and stirring, and now plaintive and dying away entirely, as if broken by sobs. There is Æneas relating his adventures to Dido; I hear his voice distinctly, except when the leaves of those trees beneath whose shade he is sitting rustle too loudly, or when the breeze ripples too strongly the beautiful sea at his feet. A tear starts in the queen's eye. How earnestly she listens! What varying expressions of pity, sympathy, and wonder alternate rapidly over her features! But hush! I hear a sigh. It is Mary; she is wiping the Savior's feet with her hair. As her head is bent over toward the ground, a tear falls. Was it a reflection of the sun? No; there is another. None saw it but I; none knew it but herself and her God. The odor of the precious ointment fills the room. I hear the clatter of the dishes as they are removed by Martha, and even the irregular crunching of that bone as the dog strives to tear off its last fibre of meat. But hark! there is a din of arms; 'tis the battle of Fribourg. Behold the great Condé amid his brilliant staff, the dead and dying about him, covered with blood and ghastly wounds! I am in the midst of the fight. A shudder comes over me; the sun has set; the forests of Fribourg seem to throw a gloom around. I can not shake off the chill which seizes me; my hair stands erect; my knees tremble; I am surrounded by spectres; I fell unconscious. Never shall I forget the vivid realities of that swoon. It seemed at first as if a bullet had struck me in the head; but I was still fighting, with my face covered with blood, and suffering extreme anguish. Then I thought I saw the car of Pluto passing, and the Proserpine that he was carrying off was my lovely English girl. Blinded by love, blood, and pain, with my sword I severed his head at one blow from his body, and sprang into the car, tumbling his vile carcass out, and having just time to see (as the Cupids lashed up the fiery horses and darted away) that in its fall it struck the great Condé, knocking off his cocked hat and frightening the staff, who thought a bomb-shell had fallen in their midst!

Oh, sweet dream of love! How the gentle Proserpine bathed my wounds with the dews of the clouds! How she placed my head on her soft white bosom, her long tresses falling over my face and distilling the odors of heaven! The foaming coursers dashed away from the dark earth through myriads of worlds, and past the sun into the light of Paradise! The Cupids laughed and gamboled, now standing upright on their horses, and now leaping into mid ether, and darting about the chariot, or perched behind, and with smiling faces watching the happiness within. In the midst of this fever of bliss, and while the air was resounding with melodies, I felt a violent shock, and for an instant thought our careless Cupids had driven against some planet. But, zounds! I opened my eyes to discover my head *bumping* a door of the Louvre, and bleeding freely. Proserpine had fled, the chariot and Cupids were gone, and the black darkness of earth, and its chilliness too, were about me. That fall from heaven occupied nine seconds, but I suffered all that the wicked angels endured during their nine days' tumble. Besides that, I felt very small, and how do you think I escaped from the Louvre? Bless your soul, through the *key-hole!*

My appetite was very keen, although I had fed plentifully on ambrosia, and the garçons at Vefour's opened their eyes with amazement when, after having freely indulged in all the latest inventions of delicacies, I ordered a beefsteak and potatoes, with a second bottle of nectar (I mean claret), to satisfy my craving hunger. Since that day I am refused permission to enter the Louvre, and, no reason being assigned, I infer that it is on account of the damage done to the great Conde's hat!

OUR CINQUIÈME.

HAVING lost both Proserpine and my English girl in one short evening, and being debarred the Louvre, I shut myself up in my cinquième, and give you a description of it.

Our cinquième is a true republic, and every one in it is a free and independent citizen—perhaps you would think a little too free even for an American atmosphere. Our hostess is a very good woman when you have her once in training, and I must confess she falls as readily into harness as any French hostess I ever met with. She is a little apt at first sight to think she has caught a "*pigeon*" whenever she hears an English accent, and she immediately commences an attack upon your vanity by telling how many suppers Mr. So and So has ordered, and what a fine man was Mr. Such a One, who has just left the house, after having made her several handsome presents. Finding you order no Champagne suppers, she varies her tactics, and informs you that the blonde in the adjoining room thinks you must be a very wealthy man, but wonders you spend so little money. You are almost tempted to invest half a fortune in a grand supper to the whole household, just to be in the good graces of the blonde, but think it better first to inquire frankly of her whether she really does think you avaricious. In fact, you wish very much to know your position. As it is a cold day, the blonde comes in shivering, with rosy cheeks, and, having no fire in her room, it is quite natural she should accept your invitation to warm her feet, which she allows, not to peep forth merely from the bottom of her dress, but displays freely foot and ankle, as if she really wished to warm them. By accident, you have half a dozen of Champagne in your closet which a friend has sent you, and as that sparkling wine always speaks the truth, besides giving courage to ask disagreeable questions, a cork pops, and the blonde and yourself are soon very good friends. "And so you think I am avaricious?" you inquire, suddenly. The blonde opens her eyes, and protests she has never uttered such a thought, which is exactly what you supposed; but she informs you farther that Madame the hostess had said that she knew you were a very rich man, and did not spend in proportion to your wealth. The next day Madame is informed of the conversation; she blushes as the guilty blush. You inquire of her respectfully why you should be expected to make her presents and have such an affection for her at three days' sight! You ask her, too, why she has charged you twenty-five per cent. more than she has charged Frenchmen for the room you occupy, which is another fact you have discovered! She is perfectly dumb with amazement, asks a thousand pardons, and stammers out of the room. Presently you hear a storm next door: she and the blonde are at it! Such a noise of tongues! such recriminations! such heavy tramps across the floor! Finally the racket dies away, but the poor blonde is marked. She can not pay her rent. An Italian count comes to see her occasionally; he is her "*homme d'affaires*," as the Madame says. He promises every day to pay her bill, but neglects it. She must leave the house. Poor thing! she cries all day, and I hear her sobbing half the night. She has no wood; I share mine with her every day, or invite her to my room, where she forgets her sorrows an instant in conversation and smiles. The count has a wife and family. I do not inquire why he is her business man, or why he does not pay her bill, or why, even, he ought to pay it; but I resolve to stand between the poor girl and trouble. The Madame, in the mean time, has redoubled her politeness to me; I am rather cold toward her; and, being now acquainted with some of my neighbors, I have ordered little suppers, but not in the house. The count returns one fine morning; he has his purse full of bright gold; he pays the bill for the blonde, whose blue eyes flash fire through tears; *now she will go;* the Madame can not retain her; they separate without speaking; and the cinquième seems deserted.

I prepare to leave likewise; but the Madame is so kind my heart is moved with pity. She does many little favors for me. She offers me the choice of rooms. I remain, changing my room, and reading her a long lecture on the excessive avarice of the French, and their fondness for plucking English and Americans. She confesses her sins, I pardon, and we now *understand* one another, and I find her an excellent woman. She allows me to do what I like, when I like, and where I like. She always comes to me for advice, and has even consulted me about her second marriage, and insists on having my opinion of her intended before accepting him! She never flatters me any more, because I tell her flattery is humbug, and I do not like it; in short, we now know one another well, and I am as much at home in her house as I could be any where.

Our cinquième consists of six rooms and a kitchen. They are now all occupied, and we are all well acquainted. The student *en droit* lives in one; he is from the Provinces, and does not attend the lectures at the Sorbonne and College de France as regularly as I do even. He is studying the world, or, rather, the Parisian part of it, and has become a very good scholar in that class. He is a gay, happy fellow, always talking except when he is laughing. He has a ready wit, seeming to almost anticipate conversation. Next to my room is Mademoiselle C——, a young lady of the third sex, who commenced her acquaintance with me by coming into my room one night, the second after her arrival, for a light. She is another lively creature, and keeps a continual sunshine in the cinquième, even on the cloudiest days. Then there is the doctor, who is more sedate and dignified than the rest of us. We do not see him often; when he does condescend to show himself, he is always very polite. A young Parisian and his temporary bride occupy the fifth room. His money evidently will not last long, nor himself either, at the rate they travel. He looks very thin and dissipated, but laughs, and sings, and gives gay dinners.

Sometimes a portion of us have a snug little breakfast together at eleven o'clock, at which we appear in our shirt-sleeves if we choose. Sometimes it is a more ceremonious dinner, with one or two invited friends; but we never permit much ceremony. Mademoiselle C—— is decidedly opposed to ceremony. In America the cinquième would have very poor furniture, but ours is filled with mirrors and mahogany, marble-covered wash-stands, large mirrors, and luxurious beds, and of course the floors are daily polished.

In my room are two or three pictures. One of them is an engraving of the Virgin Mary, with a heart, pierced by seven spears, hanging outside of her dress. Underneath is written "1080 days' (why not 1081?) indulgence to any one who will say an Ave Maria before this picture." I might have had thousands of days of indulgence by this time if I had only known how to say an Ave Maria! It is a sad neglect in my education.

In the *cinquième* we never knock for admission into each other's rooms, because we know we are always welcome *chez* one another; indeed, our doors generally remain open during the day; but sometimes this habit gives rise to what would be considered something worse than ludicrous accidents any where but in Paris; here, however, "*honi soit qui mal y pense*" covers every thing. If a band of music is heard on the Rue de Rivoli, our whole party rush to the front balcony to see and listen till it is past; a half hour more is spent in talking it over, or criticising the neighbors above, below, opposite, and around us, who are, no doubt, employed in the same way with reference to ourselves or others. An incident on the back street carries us to the rear balconies; in short, our balconies are used in common; our rooms scarcely know their own owners; our books form one general library, and even the friends who come to visit one are generally taken into partnership by the rest. So much do the French love society, that I am sure they would be glad to have all the partition walls taken down, and make one vast room of the cinquième, where they might lose no time in talking to and seeing one another, but go to sleep with their tongues still wagging, awake at midnight for an interlude, and have a good chat in the morning before rising. They like to do every thing in society, even to saying their prayers and studying law. I have but this moment left the law student in the room of Mademoiselle C——, with his *Code Napoléon* in hand, and two or three of our party talking and laughing around him; and, judging from the noise I hear there now, and his merry laugh, I fancy he is not learning much law.

I might shut myself up hermetically here as elsewhere, but I should then be called that proud, selfish American. I should know very little of what is going on around me, and for all that I would learn of French character, I might as well be on Regent Street, London, or in the Hotel Meurice at Paris, which is an English colony on French soil.

How different is this style of living from what suits the English and American tastes! The French mode is certainly very agreeable, and seems most natural when you are accustomed to it; for, since man is a social being, has the gift of speech, and is made dependent on his fellow, and miserable if deprived of his society for any length of time, it appears contrary to nature that he should isolate himself so much as is the custom in England particularly. It tends to make the character morose, selfish, and sensual, as well as to blunt that facility of speech of which we are all capable by cultivation. On the other hand, the excess to which the French carry their love of society likewise has its objections; it causes great waste of time, and often fickleness and levity of character, and, I think, a great loss of modesty, for people who never care to be alone must often be seen when they ought to be alone. It will be a great benefit for the three nations to mingle together, as they are beginning to do, and as they will do more freely after they have got accustomed to being *ridiculed* one by the other. And the nation that fears that most is the American nation.

I may close this description of our *cinquième* by a short account of two dinners I attended lately, one in a *premier* of the Chaussée d'Antin, and the other in the cinquième of another house in Paris. I cite these two because of the same class in certain respects, though broadly different in others. I do not describe a grand Parisian dinner among people *comme il faut*, because grand dinners, like grand people, are not very different any where in civilized countries; in such things we all take the cue from Paris. And if a Fifth Avenue dinner company in New York will send up stairs to the seamstress and borrow a little red tape to tie in the button-holes of the gentlemen seated around the table, why then, with their gold service, and rich dishes by French cooks, etc., they may see before them, described in a more agreeable manner than I could do, a grand *diner de Paris!*

At 7 o'clock, according to invitation, I made my appearance at the house of my friend in the Chaussée d'Antin. No one has yet arrived, for which I am not sorry, having thus some leisure to examine the appartement. It consists of six or seven saloons: if gold had not become a similitude of slavery to me, my eyes would be dazzled by the profusion of objects *dorés* to be seen wherever there is room for them; but from the king's palace to the home of the luxurious lorette, or the desolate cabin of the gold-digging miner, or the gilded apartments of the wealthy gambler—wherever I see a profusion of gold, I sigh, and say involuntarily, here dwells unhappiness! I am rarely wrong; then my eye is neither dazzled by the shining gold nor by the profusion of pictures which hide the walls, nor by the buhl, nor by the palisandre, nor by the beautifully-embroidered satin-cushioned chairs, nor by the rich curtains which adorn the windows. The floors, composed of curiously inlaid work, are highly polished, but not a carpet is to be seen any where; a richly-furnished room without a carpet looks like a handsomely-dressed woman without gloves, or a man without a shirt collar! Small but cheerful fires burn in several of the rooms. By half past seven the company has all assembled; there may be twelve or fourteen persons present. The ladies are not in full *toilette;* the gentlemen look exceedingly fresh and neat in their low shoes, black dress-coats and pants, fancy vests, and delicate lilac kids; and no gentleman will appear at the smallest dinner in Paris in less toilet than this; on occasions of more importance there is also a *rigueur de cravat* as well as of vest. Dinner is served; the *coup d'œil* of the broad table, with its flowers, and rich service of Sèvres, and crystal glasses all glittering and radiant in the bright gas, is brilliant; the flow of spirits and the flow of wine are lively, but not excessive; there is far less wine drunk at a table of lorettes and young elegants of Paris than at a table of sedate church-going people in London or New York. The *vin ordinaire* is placed on the table for each one to help himself as he wishes; the fine wines, Sherry, Madeira, Chambertin, Bordeaux, Champagne, etc., are passed around continually by the garçons, but not left on the table. One takes whatever he wishes without being pressed to take any, or to drink healths or toasts with every body at the table—a silly custom still common in England. You are never forced to take any thing that you do not want because it is so good, or because the lady of the house saw it made, or because you must appear to have a good appetite. What! Because the lady of the house has descended to the kitchen, seized a pudding-stick, and given two or three furious blows to the batter, is that any reason you should suffer an indigestion, as you are compelled to do in England and America? The dinner passes off pleasantly; conversation never flags; there are no fearful pauses for the clock to intrude its ticking. Of course, all the latest inventions of dishes are represented; but the faithful old truffle, and pheasant with his long tail, like old friends that never tire, are not forgotten for all that.

After dinner other friends drop in; music, dancing, conversation, coffee, liqueurs, cigars, and cigarettes follow; the most perfect ease and freedom prevail; those whirl off in a short *valse à deux temps* who feel disposed; others sit and converse; some walk about in the adjoining saloons; the ladies puff their cigarettes with the rest; the sound of laughter and gayety, of flying wit, repartee, and bons mots never ceases an instant.

An hour later, and most of the party adjourn to the card-table, where they play lansquenet till an advanced hour of the morning. The gentlemen who do not play will frequently give ten or twenty Napoleons to the lady behind whose chair they are standing to play for them on halves.

I left at midnight. I should tremble to see a youth of seventeen or eighteen years of age invited to such dinners, for many a young man has gone home from such dinners ruined for life!

The other dinner is in the Rue Breda, No. — *au cinquième.* The room is of medium size; the furniture is abundant, but not superfluous; not elegant or strong, but good. It consists of the usual number of mirrors, mahogany bedstead, chairs, etc. There is not a single useful article wanting, and there is scarcely an article to be seen that is not useful. Julie, the occupant of the room, is an invalid. The last time I dined there she was in bed, and looked most interesting, with her bright eyes, and pale face, and negligé dress of spotless linen. The table was then placed at her bedside, but she ate nothing but a little soup and bread.

On the present occasion she was up and dressed, and in apparently good health, with a high color even. Our party consisted of herself and another lady, and three gentlemen, five in all; therefore the dinner was perfectly simple and quiet. Besides a glass of absinthe before sitting down to the table, there was nothing drunk but claret—but the *Bordeaux se parle*, as the French say, and therefore conversation was lively. The French drink but very little Champagne; generally they prefer red wines; but when they do drink it, they have a most illogical, *ungastronomical* way of bringing it on for dessert in the midst of sugar things, creams, and sweetmeats, instead of with the solid dishes of the first courses. Fortunately, we had it with neither first nor last course, and therefore none of its maudlin stupidity. The dinner passed off pleasantly, and with quiet gayety, but the most gay of all was Julie herself. I thought her spirits unnatural, and attributed them to that sudden excitation to which invalids seem liable when they have more than their ordinary allowance of that blessing, unprized by those who enjoy it, health. Coffee follows. We have left the dinner-table, and are sitting around a small card-table. Julie sits on two chairs *à l'Américaine*, and smokes her cigarette. She is a match in talking for three gentlemen at a time; and were it not for her laughter, and an occasional sip of coffee or liqueur, one would hardly have a chance to edge in a single word. Suddenly she stops in the midst of her exuberant spirits, and coughs; her face grows instantly pale; she puts her handkerchief to her mouth; on removing it, it is red with her life's blood. She leaves the room coughing, while anxiety is depicted on every face present. I have rarely felt such a sudden revulsion of feeling as seized me at this scene. I had lately seen the Dame aux Camélias acted by Madame Doche herself, one of the most prominent of the thousand types of that heroine in Paris. I confess having been affected by that shameful play, which no lady should ever see; but never before have I been in a position exactly to appreciate the difference between sensations of pity, sorrow, and grief, excited by theatrical representations, and those caused by the real miseries of life. At that moment Paris seemed the darkest spot on earth. All its splendors arose before me as if in the commencement of a grand apotheosis, only to tumble suddenly into a black and frightful chaos; the gold and the gas turned to a dim leaden hue; fine equipages, and fine horses, and all the pride, pomp, and state of life, seemed but like so many snares or igni fatui to lead men away from true happiness to its false and noisy semblance; and in contrast with all this, the humble cottage of the poor, or the quiet dwelling of the intelligent farmer, where extremes of pleasure or sorrow are almost unknown, but where health, simplicity, and contentment reign, appeared for an instant like a palace, so resplendent is virtue when brought in all her glory into the immediate presence of vice and its train of sorrow. Julie presently returned. She had been spitting blood, and looked very feeble; she could scarcely speak, but tried to smile away the gloom cast over the party. Her efforts were seconded by the gentlemen, who made several attempts at gayety and animation; but it was evidently a failure, and they soon retired one by one, while I remained behind, thinking I might be of some service to the poor invalid. We were now all alone, and after she had recovered somewhat her strength, she related to me the history of her life, which I give exactly as she told it.

She said that when she was fifteen years of age her father wished her to marry a wealthy merchant of Paris, who was hump-backed, and whom she did not like. This she respectfully but firmly refused to do, because she had loved a young man with whom she had been brought up, and to whom her hand had long been secretly pledged. This young man was finally refused admission to the house merely because he did not possess wealth. The consequence was, our lovers were more than ever determined to be united; and as love laughs at locksmiths, our heroine, who is a spirited girl, descended from her window one dark night by a rope ladder, one end of which led right into her lover's arms. It is unnecessary to say that two persons who had lately been so anxious to call in the priest against all opposition, were, under the present circumstances, only too anxious to escape from priests, people, and whatever else could retard their flight to a place of safety, which they soon found among the thousands of hiding-places existing in a city like Paris.

Let us not peep through the key-hole of their room, Rue ———, but return to the father, who was in despair. Ten days he searched the city without success, and at last began to fear his daughter had committed suicide. He locked up her room just as she left it, and allowed no one to enter it but himself. Thither he would repair daily, and spend hours in weeping over his own folly—a folly that unfortunately is the fault of too many parents in other places than Paris. Now, to see his daughter again, he would permit her to marry, not only the man she loved, but one much inferior even. It was too late. *Who is to blame for that daughter's ruin?* I put the question to thousands of parents in all countries who are this day trying to sell their daughters to rich men, because they are rich in gold, though lacking in every virtue perhaps, while deserving young men, who are preferable in every respect save that of money, and who are loved by the only one who has a right to dispose of her own person and happiness, are slighted, and perhaps forbidden the house.

The clandestine lovers, however, soon became careless about concealment, and are discovered on account of their own imprudence. The daughter is led back to her father's house—alas! not as she left it. She is ruined! Pride conquers affection in her father's heart. She is forced into a convent; her lover quits Paris; she remains in the convent some months, but at last makes her escape; she seeks her lover; he is not to be found; she hires a secluded room in the outskirts of Paris, and gives herself up to despair; she is on the point of committing suicide, and, in fact, does commence a slow course of poisoning. To drown her sorrow, she drinks every day, at midday, a tumbler filled half with absinthe and half with brandy, and then falls nearly lifeless on her bed. It requires but a few weeks of such habits to summon Death, and Death, even when courted, rarely appears without his terrors. So Julie was not without alarm to find herself, on one fine spring morning, when Time was causing her gradually to forget her chagrin, spitting blood—her heart's blood—in large quantities. The physician was called. She was placed in bed, where she lay many a day, repenting her folly, and has now become a hopeless consumptive! Ordinarily she appears pretty well, but the least excitement and the smallest indulgence in wines, but particularly absinthe, brings on a return of her attacks, after which she is sometimes laid up on a bed of sickness for days and weeks. There are those whom she calls her lovers that come to see her when she is well, but she is indifferent to every one. She goes to see her father occasionally, but will not live with him, because she says she has dishonored him. Her room, however, remains exactly as she left it on that fatal night, seven years ago, which sealed her ruin; the dresses which she wore last hang upon the nails where she left them; the poems of Beranger lie open at the page where she was reading; her work-box, her scissors, scraps of linen, and the work upon which she was sewing, with the needle and half-used thread, just where she stuck it, lie scattered on the table, and even her bed bears the impressions of her last sleepless rest in her father's house while she was awaiting the dead of night to make her escape. The articles of her toilet, her half-soiled towel, the books of her innocent days, her young attempts at poetry, generally in praise of virtuous deeds, or religious or charitable acts, all lie just as they did in the days of her innocence. What anguish wrings her heartas she gazes on that chamber! What changes have taken place in her life in seven years—seven years, that ought to have been the happiest of her days!

It is not twenty-four hours since she related to me the above history, which I give exactly as it was told me, excepting an omission of her troubles and ups and downs during the past five years, which were spent in trying to drown sorrow in gayety when she was well, and in abject misery when she was ill. I have not tried to make an interesting tale of it, but, on the contrary, have told the truth in as few and simple words as possible.

Perhaps, on my first visit to Paris, I have seen this very girl, at Mabille or Valentino, dancing and smiling like the merriest of earth, and, seduced by her apparent gayety and happiness, as well as by that of those about her, whose lives resembled hers, have wished that we were as happy a people as these thoughtless Parisians. But since then I have rubbed off the gilding in many places besides the ball-rooms and feasting-rooms of Paris, and I ask myself, even if all this were true happiness, is it worth the price paid for it?

If I were relating an account of these two dinners for the purpose of proving any dogma, or for any other purpose than merely to relate the actual experience of a traveler, and the impressions drawn from it, it would be very easy to tell a true tale, and yet relate much more startling examples of gay vice and its consequences as seen daily in Paris. But as my design is only to tell those things

"Quorum magna pars fui,"

and never having been anxious to plunge too deep into the abodes of misery on the one hand, nor to venture too near the fascinating vortex on the other, I have selected instances of such ordinary occurrence all over Paris as to be considered entirely unnoticeable here. And yet such things in the United States are almost unheard of, even in the largest cities; indeed, it is impossible for such a class as Grisette and Lorette to exist in England or America. In those countries, one slip seals the ruin of a woman. She may reform and be *tolerated*, but it is impossible for her to exist in a course of easy vice. She must either be pure, or cast out as a devil! There is no intermediate position. It is the judgment of her own sex, and, though severe, I believe it is full of wisdom, and one of the greatest safeguards of woman.

A LETTER TO THE NATION WITHOUT A FAULT.

MY DEAR, VAIN, SENSITIVE, THIN-SKINNED PEOPLE,— Do you wish to know what they say of you in France? Do you wish to see yourselves at full length in a French mirror? You are very proud as well as very vain. You think you are a great people. You flatter yourselves that you are a free people. You swagger before the nations of the earth as if you thought they were admiring your fine airs instead of despising you for them. If any of these nations tell you you are not so fine a gentleman as you fancy, you feel insulted, and immediately feel your pockets for your revolver. You mistake noise and braggadocio for independence —license for liberty. You have been stumbling about and treading on people's corns till they are tired of you. You once had some friends who thought you, with your grand ways, a very gentlemanly, nice individual; they were proud to know so important a personage; but now they have found you out. Did you ever see a gentleman marching very pompously through the saloons at a state ball, who, on looking suddenly into a mirror, discovers his shirt sticking out through a hole in his coat? You can imagine what he would do. Look into this French glass, and prepare to do likewise. Or, rather, take off your coat, for I am about to lay nine-and-thirty lashes on your bare back, Jonathan, that will make you dance, and perhaps toughen a little that tender skin of yours. You never heard of a cat-o'nine-tails to flog nations with. It is rather a broad figure of speech to devote Trollopes, Fontenays, Dickenses (I'm sorry, Charles, to see you in such company), Beauvalets, Janins, etc., to such uses; but a good deal of latitude is allowable in dealing with persons who have shown themselves so fond of latitude in their writings.

I am not a cruel man, and Heaven forbid that I should make you screech at the first blow, Jonathan! I shall begin gently, and go on *crescendo*—something after the style in which you flog your slaves, wicked man!

Let us hear, first, Brillat Savarin—a name more associated with turkeys and truffles than with politics and people.

This gentleman was in the United States shortly after her independence was declared, and if he never said any thing good, I certainly have never heard of his *saying* any thing bad of the country where he found a home. In his work entitled "Physiologie du Goût," that much-prized repertoire of culinary arts, is a page of *majestic silence* on America.

Smothered in sauces stands a chapter on our unhappy country, thus:

"Séjour en Amérique.

"— — — — — — — — — —
— — — — — — — — — — —
— — — — — — — — — — —
— — — — — — — — — — —
— — — — — — — — — — —
— — — — — — — — — — —
— — — — — — — — — — —."

Gentle Thin-skin, there is not another word in the chapter. Whether Mr. Savarin's heart was too full for utterance, whether he wished to leave all to the imagination, and make our country Utopia to European minds, or whether the burning of a *Perigord* caused him suddenly to drop his pen and attend to more important concerns, I will not pretend to decide, but will prove that, whatever was the reason, he did exactly right, because Mr. D'Almbert, in a book entitled Flanerie Parisienne aux Etats Unis, published only a month since, is exactly of the same opinion.

On page 145 of that work is the following interesting chapter:

"Les beaux arts en Amérique.

"— — — — — — — — — —
— — — — — — — — — — —
— — — — — — — — — — —
— — — — — — — — — — —
— — — — — — — — — — —
— — — — — — — — — — —
— — — — — — — — — — —
— — — — — — — — — — —
— — — — — — — — — — —
— — — — — — — — — — —
— — — — — — — — — — —
— — — — — — — — — — —."

"The fine arts in America" occupy three pages of

majestic blanks in D'Almbert's book. An ill-natured individual at my elbow says it is a very good way to write books. The genius who discovered that Bulwer has stolen one of his late novels from an "obscure work" called Tristram Shandy would call it plagiary; but, for my part, I think it only an instance of the harmony of great minds. And America is more honored in her absence than by her presence.

But it is a poor rule that won't work both ways. I like that style of writing; it fills up a book amazingly. We may answer it by the following quotation from the *Reisebilder* of Henri Heine; see article "Tambour le Grand." One word only is changed.

"Les censeurs" *Americains.* "— — — —
— — — — — — — — — — —
— — — — — — — — — — —
— — — — — — — — — — —
— — — — — — — — — — —
— — — — — — *imbeciles* — — —
— — — — — — — — — — —
— — — — — — — — — — —
— — — — — — — — — — —
— — — — — — — — — — —
— — — — — — — — — — —
— — — — — — — — — — —."

I hope you are now prepared for Marie Fontenay (Madame de Grandfort). I shall divide her remarks into chapters, so as to give them more prominence, but take the liberty of heading the chapters, in order to let you know what is coming.

I quote from her work called "*L'Autre Monde.*"

CHAPTER I.

Wherein Marie disdaineth Prefaces, and taketh the Poker instead.

"Three citations, which will say more than the longest preface.

"TO PHILOSOPHERS AND STATESMEN.

"1st. The authorities have ceased their action against the vagabond, the fraudulent bankrupt, the thief, the forger, the murderer, or the seditious, of whom we spoke some time since. It is now known that he has fled to the United States. (Daily observation in all the gazettes of Europe for the last fifty years.)

"2d. Most of the public offices in the United States are filled by naturalized Europeans, come from no one knows where. (Political statistics of the Union.)

"3d. The Americans are A GREAT PEOPLE!!! (Opinion of a number of eminent French, Germans, and Englishmen.)"

CHAPTER II.

Marie showeth that the Americans are not a great People.

"The exact opposite of the French is the American character."

"Certainly, when one has traveled for a long time through the grand Union, that model republic where assassins are protected, and where thieves are not pursued by justice; where, under pretext of liberty, an ignorant multitude oppress the more generous parties, and where the most cultivated persons are compelled to become the slaves of popular passion, it is sweet to arrive and seat one's self amid this industrious and peaceable Canadian population, more free and more happy under the shade of royal institutions than their proud neighbors, who, *to secure their own individuality*, are obliged constantly to walk with a pistol or a poniard in their pockets."—P. 247.

In Canada, "instead of those hard, cloudy, cooked (*cuits*) faces which the Americans generally have, are to be seen open and frank countenances, radiant especially with an affectionate cordiality."—P. 247.

"The American people represent an act, not a principle. Now acts pass away; it is only principles which remain and build up strong and glorious institutions."—P. 257.

"Ten years will not pass before a revolution breaks out in the United States."—P. 243.

"Democracy in the United States is the greatest lie of this century. In fifty years, the country that will have become the centre of a *monarchism* the most ardent and most passionate on earth, will be the United States."—P. 200. (Now, saffron-faced race, your fate is settled!)

"Public opinion in France is generally in favor of the United States. This is because they have taken seriously the dreams of certain men of talent who have written on America."—P. 201. (Ah! Marie, it's naughty to call Chateaubriand, De Tocqueville, Ampère, etc., dreamers!)

"All those sensations which among us are the signal of prolonged reveries, of ardent aspirations, and of indescribable ecstasies, are to them completely unknown."—P. 198. (The barbarians!)

"The father treats his son like a stranger; if the latter make money, he will make him pay for his seat at the table and his corner of the fireside."—P. 208. (Oh, cruel fathers!)

"Read the history of this people. Have they ever been devoted to any great principle of humanity? Have they ever sacrificed their material interests to the triumph of greater interests? Their independence was born of a question of money. The war of 1812 was a war for the profit of moneyed interests. If France had not paid twenty-five millions, they would, without scruple and without remorse, have attacked France."

"And yet they would force me to say that this people, because they have several thousand leagues of electric telegraph and railway, extensive commerce, and immense resources, are a great people! that it has a wonderful future and splendid destiny! No, no! Where there is no family there is no society; where there is no enthusiasm, no pride, no disinterestedness, no spirit of justice, THERE IS NO FUTURE!"—P. 234. (*No*, gentle Marie!)

CHAPTER III.

Wherein Marie proveth the Americans to be Heathens and Infidels.

"Under whatever form it presents itself, death is for the Americans only an accident, which they regard with indifference and coldness, and which does not more predispose their souls to the glorious hope of resurrection than to the fear of an eternal sleep."—P. 127.

"Love, ambition (!), regrets, souvenirs, *infinite in-*

spirations, immortal hopes—all these things they call idealities, that is to say, chimeras, dreams prejudicial to labor and rectitude of mind."

"A purchase and sale followed by a profit, a heavy dinner, a show composed of animals, a boxing-match—these are the things suited to their understandings. They either mock at or are unconscious of the existence of any thing better than this."—P. 140.

"Protestantism, the prevailing form of religion in America, is incapable of satisfying the heart of man. It can not give him a certainty in regard to his future. This one quits one sect to follow another; that one discovers a new belief; the majority run after what is new, in the hope of finding the support which is lacking in their faith. All in vain; darkness continues to envelop them forever."—P. 204. (Alas! Marie.)

"The moral sense is wanting among the American people on account of the absence of all principles. Protestantism, under the pretext of free examination, has torn down every thing. Religion of fancy and not of sentiment, it lends itself to all the caprices of the individual, flatters his passions, and advances his interests. The dogma comes afterward. And what dogma? Something cold and dry, which leaves the soul more anxious and uncertain than before."—P. 234.

"*The American entertains the greatest indifference for every thing touching morals or religion.*"—P. 256.

"A deplorable tone exists in society; perfidy of man to his neighbor is universal; and on this point the Yankees are but little behind the Italians."

"The man ENRICHED by the firing of his own house, or by three or four failures, is treated every where as an *honorable*, and has a right to call the conscientious shop-keeper whose fortune he has devoured a rascal!" (Marie! spare, oh spare!)

"During the time of the yellow fever and cholera" (on the Mississippi River), "*they left the poor sick creatures whom they suspected of disease, without mattress or provisions, on the banks of the river, in a complete wilderness.* The passengers, far from opposing this base abandonment, often forced it with all their endeavors." And when a burial took place, "They brought the body" (to the hole dug for it), "*while the passengers saw in this spectacle only an occasion for raillery and bitter sarcasms!*"—P. 127. Nevertheless, sweet Marie, if you should ever go to New Orleans during a yellow-fever season, you will see a whole population rising en masse, and giving not only their money to buy medicines, and shelter, and attendance for the sick, but forming large associations, who are drilled into nurses by years of practice, and who spend night after night in watching by the bedside of the sufferer. You will see the wealthy merchant, who has been attending to his business all day in the hot sun, instead of reposing in his dwelling during the cool evening, going into the close, infectious atmosphere to pass the night, watching, perhaps, one of your unfortunate countrymen. He wets his parched lips; he puts the ice on his burning forehead; he soothes him in delirium; with his own hand he administers the frequent foot-bath. At the return of day he leaves the poor sufferer in other hands as gentle; he must return to his business. I confess he will be very likely to take a *cocktail* as he passes *Hewlett's ;* and then you, Marie, who are taking your cool morning walk after a refreshing night's sleep, see him coming out of a bar-room at that early hour, and then you hasten home to make a note of it; and you write—ah! what don't you write?—about these swaggering bar-room Americans, with their heartlessness and irreligion! And when the sick man recovers, he never has a chance even to thank one of his dozen benefactors; he never sees their faces again; they are off attending some one else. And the majority of sick men thus attended by these heartless, commercial, barbarian Americans are Europeans, Marie; but that makes no difference. For a man who is able to pay in New Orleans, and who, being an entire stranger, has no friends there, a yellow fever attack will cost from two thousand to even five thousand francs, according to the duration and severity of the disease. It actually cost a friend of mine three thousand five hundred francs. But the poor immigrant will be well attended without even his thanks.

I shall never forget the sympathy and kindness of that people when, years ago, I lay with a burning fever, an object of solicitude to five physicians. Neighbors, whose names I had never heard even, sent in, morning and night, to inquire after my health; and when I was recovering, one would send me a nice broiled snipe, another fresh eggs and butter just from the country, another a tender young chicken; and finally, when I could leave the house, the kind family of Judge P—— took me to their plantation up the river. And at least one of these families who were so kind was French, notwithstanding that the amiable Marie thinks her countrymen have so degenerated by coming to America. *Ex uno omnes disce.*

CHAPTER IV.

Wherein Marie tilteth at her own countrymen.

"What a Frenchman seeks most to avoid in the United States, as soon as he can manage for himself, is another Frenchman."—P. 235.

"There are no strangers who Americanize themselves so quickly as Frenchmen."—P. 235.

"The Frenchman not only lives apart from the men and things of his country, but is even hostile to every thing recalling his nationality."—P. 235.

"The most ardent Americans of the United States are the French who have fixed their residence there." —P. 11. (That shows their good taste, Marie!)

"It is surely only their excessive love of *ham, tobacco,* and *free women* which can lead to an act so extravagant."—P. 12 (viz., act of becoming Americans).

But it is at the women of America that the burden of the book is launched; and she is so anxious to get at them, that before her vessel has left Europe, even, she has a New York belle at the head of her chapter. This young lady is the beautiful and accomplished Miss Sarah Cardwell, belonging to one of the wealthiest and most respectable families of New York. She serves as a type of her class.

CHAPTER V.

Wherein the gentle Marie leisurely picketh to pieces Miss Sarah Cardwell in the following letter she causeth her to write to a gentleman she has seen but once or twice. Quelle mouche te pique, Marie?

"MY DEAR JULIEN,—You are a charming and witty young man. You talk as they write in France—that is to say, with spirit, grace, and imagination. If you had some hundreds of thousands of dollars you would be a *gentleman*, accomplished and sought after by our ladies. But, alas! America is not France, and your *esprit*, however brilliant it may be, will not assist you in finding an heiress. We Americans do not inquire in respect of a man we would marry if he is amiable, if he is a poet, if he is an orator. No, indeed; we simply ask, *How much is he worth?* and decide according to the number of figures contained in the answer. A heart and cottage seem to us very insipid things, and we think one of about as much consequence as the other. A husband is not for us a lover; he is a man who pays our debts, takes care of household matters, and gives us wealth and luxury. In return, we present him with an infant regularly every two years. We are cold and positive, because all our passions are dissipated in flirting. . . . .

"Jealousy, so common in France, is unknown to us. We allow our husbands the same liberty we demand from them. In a word, marriage, instead of being for us a heavy chain on unsubmissive shoulders, is simply a cord we hardly feel, and which never incommodes us."

There, fair Lady Fontenay, we leave thee for the present.

I now come to Monsieur Alfred D'Almbert, who, like Monsieur Beauvalet, is not a bad-humored gentleman by any means. He shows no malice in what he writes, but a great fondness for raillery, such as all the French have, and such as they display equally in writing of Great Britain or of Paris.

He commences with a Mr. Smith, to whom he has shown great attentions in Paris. Smith is a West-End man—Fifth Avenue, of course. He has used Monsieur D'Almbert terribly at Paris, causing him to make a guide of himself, and trot him to Mabille, etc., etc. But Smith forgot certain little accounts at Paris with the tailors, boot-makers, etc., to whom he had been introduced by his friend. These accounts Monsieur D'Almbert has very kindly paid for him, and therefore expects a very warm reception on his arrival at New York. He meets Smith in the street, and flies into his arms; but imagine his surprise at a cold "How do you do?" from the latter. In the author's words,

"Smith has re-Americanized himself, and changed to a cold, rigid, straight-cravated man! Bon Dieu! . . . When I spoke of Paris, he smiled with an air of superiority and disdain. When I made a modest allusion to Mabille, the fire of *indignation and chastity* sparkled in his eyes. Finally, I ventured to say to him,

"'My dear friend, I introduced you to my furnishers in Paris, and in the hurry of departure you have forgotten to pay two or three of them; and as I made myself responsible for you, I have settled with them. Be good enough to reimburse the sums I have paid your boot-maker, tailor, glove and shirt makers—'

"'Who told you, sir,' replies Smith, 'to take this charge upon yourself? How dare you meddle in my affairs?'" And so on.

Who is this scoundrel Smith? Perhaps he is the brother of Miss Sarah Cardwell! Mr. D'A—— continues:

"America seems like an immense shop, where every thing is bought and sold, and where the highest bidder wins."

"They calculate their sentiments as they do their business; they measure their duties (not Custom-house duties) like calico."

"The dollar is more than king; it is God."

"The dollar weakens their understanding, extinguishes their patriotism, and causes them to mistake their true interests, because among nations, as among individuals, moral questions ought to rule material preoccupations. In political as well as in private life, one only becomes powerful and respectable by the strict fulfillment of duty and the constant practice of justice" (precepts worthy to be found in the Bible, even if not existing in America).

"They say the Quakers start their sons forth into the world, saying, 'Go, make plenty of dollars . . . honestly if you can . . . but make plenty of dollars.'"

"Temperance, it is not a virtue; it is a law.

"In England and Holland a man must drink to preserve health; in Italy, Spain, and Africa, it is often death to do so. In the United States they have *Anglo-Dutch* throats; they are always thirsty."

"The Americans, supple, pliant, and indulgent amid our easy civilization, are haughty, intolerant, and headstrong in their individualisms at home."

"There is only one country where the Americans do not enjoy themselves—that is England. It is true that they are not much liked there. We have for a long time thought that this mutual antipathy proceeded from an old national antagonism, that the citizens of the United States hated their ancient tyrants, and that the English detested those whom they regarded as revolted slaves.

"We were in error. The disagreement proceeds from a cause more logical and human: they know one another; they resemble one another; they appreciate one another." (Jonathan, *you are found out!*)

The Pleasure-grounds of America.

"If the aspect of the cities is wanting in gayety; if the houses, carefully closed, seem so many sanctuaries where it is forbidden the profane to enter; if the shops are melancholy; if the streets are mournful; if the public squares have a desolate air in spite of the little trees which serve to ornament them, or rather because they are humiliated in having a youthful vegetation in a country where ancient forests are expected; if the churches (and how many churches!) seem to reflect the Apocalypse; if, in a word, all that you see renders the heart heavy and gives you a desire to draw your handkerchief from your pocket to wipe away your tears, the fault is not with the Americans, who certainly have not forgotten the important part of all *édilité*, well understood—the promenades."

"They have nothing, it is true, to compare with Hyde Park, the Champs Elysées, the Prado, or even the Candiere; but at the end of every street, at the side of each church, you see a pretty *little cemetery*, neat, clean, laid out with bricks like all the rural paths in fashionable America, and where all the most ancient inhabitants of the country—those who found a race, and are destined to become the foundation of a future aristocracy—have *the pleasure of seeing their ancestors rot!* (pourrir).

"The rural cemeteries of America are a place of promenade much frequented. There people have *rendezvous;* there they conduct the ladies; there lovers whisper tender thoughts; there the children play at hide-and-go-seek, concealing themselves maliciously behind the tombstones. Ah! how gay it is, Mon Dieu!"

"This singular mania is carried to a greater or less extent according to the country one visits."

In visiting one of our large cemeteries, Monsieur D'A—— saw "a great number of equipages filing along, and keeping to the right, as at Longchamps. Their occupants were gayly dressed, smiling, and amiable; they exchanged a friendly word or pleasantry in passing. The dead served evidently only as a pretext for the visit; the promenade was the motive."

"Every body did not remain seated in the carriages; many families were within the iron railings surrounding their family burial-places. The horses ate peaceably their oats, while their masters, seated on the stone monuments, *snuffed up* (*humaient*) *the air under the shade of trees enriched by the bodies of their ancestors;* and as the evening was warm, I remarked that many gentlemen had taken off their coats in order to *smoke their cigars more at their ease!* The young girls gathered flowers from the tombstones, with which they crowned their pure foreheads."

John Smith is the gentleman who accompanies Mons. D'A—— through the cemetery. This gentleman, after walking some distance, suddenly *points with his whip* to a newly-cleaned tombstone, and, *winking his eye*, says,

"'Mr. John Smith, my father.'

"I remained perfectly dumb at such an unexpected introduction, and did not know how to reply; he did not notice my embarrassment, and, ten steps farther on, said to me, with the same gesture, but with an *air of satisfaction* more marked,

"'Madame Smith, my mother.'

"I did not know what expression to wear. I sought a phrase appropriate for the occasion. I should have thought myself the toy of some mystification if my guide, his face radiant with pride, puffed up with importance and the high opinion he had of himself, had not at length exclaimed, in showing me other monuments, and thus allowing the vain plenitude of his heart to overflow,

"'Mr. William Smith, my grandfather, and his wife by the side of him!'

"Then turning around quickly, he led me toward the exit of the grounds at a brisk trot. For him the promenade was finished, and offered no farther interest. He had showed me what he was anxious to show me, namely, that he was not a man of straw; that he had two generations well established, and buried in America; that the Smiths had founded a race of which he was one of the finest scions."—Page 177.

In America "they attach no more importance to death than to an excursion by railway; only, as the road is a little longer, they take a little more pains about the preparations.

"There is in New York, in Broadway, the most animated and commercial street, just in front of the St. Nicholas Hotel—that is to say, at one of the most frequented spots—a very handsome coffin store, the objects of which trade are displayed between a drinking-saloon on the one side and a fancy store upon the other. They drink much at New York; but biers (beer) are highly relished" (the *tasteful* pun translates very well into English—bières, in French, means coffins and beer).

"The drinking-saloon sells great quantities of spirits, and the fancy store does a fine business in nouveautés, but the coffin-maker does at least as good a business as his neighbor. Every moment may be seen entering his store gentlemen and ladies, who compare, measure, and debate the prices of various coffins, purchasing after having made their choice. Do not believe these are sickly, half-cracked people, who have armed themselves with a stern resolution for the work in view of a foreseen end. Not a bit of it. The gentlemen are strong and healthy-looking; the ladies are fresh and rosy; but they live in the provinces—the West, perhaps—where the last style of coat is made with less care and taste than in New York, the great metropolis, and before returning home they purchase a coffin, which they carry with the toys for their children and the literary novelties destined to conduce to the amusements of their winter evenings!"

Mons. D'A—— closes with some advice to his countrymen, part of which I reproduce here, that it may be made still more generally known, and that people may not be inveigled into an emigration which will render them miserable. The millions who have already emigrated from Europe to America have every one of them acted like the fox who lost his tail in a trap—they have lured all their friends and relations into the same snare. But now, silly people! the trick is discovered. It required the sagacity of a Fontenay, a D'Almbert, etc., to lay open the whole plot. Hear!

"It is far from Havre to New York!" (Yes, and we hope no whining babes will undertake it. We want men in America!)

"In that charming country the climate is insupportable; it is too hot in summer, but too cold in winter."

"Make your will before leaving Europe" (unfortunately, the majority of you have nothing to put in your wills), "and congratulate yourself if you return with a whole skin."

"Content yourselves with five per cent. at home, and do not go to a distance to trade in the hope of a doubtful profit."

"Oh, you happy mortals who are accustomed to the protecting rules of the Code Napoléon, submit not yourselves to the blows of a different legislation!"

"Our brown bread, eaten at home, is better than their roast beef." (Soaked in milk, it is still better adapted to infantile tastes.)

"Go ahead! and arms and legs break, and fortunes smash!"

"The United States are absolutely worth nothing as a residence for Europeans." (! ! !) (A late discovery.)

"Nothing resembles the French less than the Americans."

"Consider each railway as a pistol destined to blow your brains out." (*Quite true.*)

"What we do to the right, they do to the left; what we see white, they see black."

"If you are determined to go to America, go, and make your fortune there, but return and spend it in France." (But be careful, after your return, not to tell any untruths, by which some of your countrymen might also be seduced to do as you have done.)

The next gentleman to whom we deliver you over for a while is Monsieur Beauvalet, with whom you are better acquainted than with the preceding persons. This gentleman was kept in a continual dance while in New York by the fleas, just as I am at present in Paris, but just as he would not have been in New York if he had asked my advice about hotels. He went to a certain hotel or boarding-house Mondon because it was French and cheap, and I am afraid that they were some of his own little lively countrymen that made him hop about so in bed by night. But there was another little chagrin that made Mons. Beauvalet hop higher than the fleas. He discovered that the American people do not like tragedy—that is, that they do not like it so much as to suddenly enrich a large French troupe by paying them more in one week than they could earn in a year at home. Monsieur Beauvalet will not forgive that! He had condescended to go to America with Mademoiselle Rachel, and expected all sorts of miracles except the falling of the sun.

"What!" he exclaims, rhapsodically, "Rachel in America! That seemed to us something impossible! splendid! marvelous!"

"It was, to our minds, an event which ought to revolutionize the whole New World!"

"Rachel in America! Why, even the tribes of Indians should have talked of it in their wild forests!"

"Instead of that, they received her as they have received ten, twenty other artists!"

"What do I say? Jenny Lind was welcomed like a queen!"

"And yet, does the talent of Jenny Lind, great as it may be, surpass the talent of Rachel?"

"The receipt of the first evening was 26,334 francs; very good, evidently" (I think so); "but what is that compared with 50,000 or 60,000 francs that we should have received?" (Why should you receive 50,000 francs?)

"What is that, especially when compared with the first receipt of Jenny Lind, which amounted to 93,786 francs!"

"We know very well there is a great difference between the two kinds of entertainment given by these great artistes."

"Jenny Lind sung, and song is a universal language, while Rachel plays tragedy, and it is far from being a universal language, tragedy! Consequently, Rachel can only be comprehended by the understandings of the élite—that is to say, by very few persons."

There is the whole burden of the book. Jenny Lind received 1,765,000 francs in America. The Rachel company expected to do the same. They did not, and were disappointed; and therefore the Americans do not like tragedy! Observe the illiberal manner of comparing Lind and Rachel. He does not mention Rachel's playing in a doubly incomprehensible language; he lays no stress on her playing in *French;* but she differs from Lind only because she plays in *tragedy*—the language of the élite only. And yet, playing in this doubly incomprehensible language, Rachel did better than in her own country even, or than she could do in any country in the world! She received, her first night in America, nearly *three times as much* as she received her first night in London, which Monsieur Beauvalet estimates at 10,000 francs! And her whole receipts in America amounted to 684,000 francs! If she had not been taken sick, they would have been much larger. Where else could she have done as well, aristocracies included? These facts show that if a tragedian of Rachel's talent were playing in America, she would be better appreciated by *greater numbers* than Rachel is even in France.

I am not trying to prove that the mass of Americans are fond of tragedy, but there is no doubt that a greater number of persons read and appreciate it in America than in any other country. A *minority* of other countries may have a *finer* sense of its beauties than the same minority in America.

Having now prepared you for any thing Mr. Beauvalet may say, we quote some of his remarks. Of course, the first fight is with the cabmen. Nine persons, with all their theatrical baggage, pay 46¾ francs to go to the hotel. This is called

"A charming sample of American life!"

Afterward it is found quite natural to *receive* 17 francs from one man for his seat at the tragedy, "ça n'est vraiment pas la mort d'un homme!" But our hackmen are great rascals, and it is a pity we do not govern them better.

At the Hotel Mondon, our friend drank "*chocolat à la graisse,* and milk *à la cervelle de mouton.*" He then throws himself on his back, kicking furiously, and cries, "O Desiré! O Verdiér! O Vachette!" and I must add, Oh *vache!* why did you not take a "'bus" and go down to Delmonico's? He could do as much for you as Desiré or Bonvalet of Paris. That first night at the Hotel Mondon is an awful one—"a Walpurgis night of insects." He swells up like a plum-pudding; he has a horrible nightmare, etc. "Oh! then I curse America, and Christopher Columbus, who invented it, and Raphael Felix, who came to *work* it." But, finally, remembering that it is the 284th anniversary of St. Bartholomew, and that the insects are, of course, all Protestants, and taking their revenge on a poor Catholic, he consoles himself like a man, and acknowledges the justice of the punishment.

After his first appearance before an audience, he says,

"One thing is certain, and we all observed it, that tragedy is not at all the taste of the Americans."

"It is too serious, too stately, and especially too cold for them."

"It did not appear at all funny to them to see the actors always coming on the stage two by two, with legs too naked and robes too short, and *spouting* long rigmaroles by the hour."

"But what stultified them most was being obliged to follow the piece in those infernal translations. Sometimes they turned over two leaves instead of one, so that it was then impossible to understand a single word, and the result was, they all went away half cracked!"

"Dieu! what monstrous success, what frantic bravos would have greeted the actor who, in the midst of a scene of tragedy, had marched in on his head, cut a pigeon-wing, and swallowed his sword!"

That is quite amusing, at least; but Mons. Beauvalet proves himself, nevertheless, to have long ears, like most men who hear well. He says,

"None of the grand tragic scenes moved them much, and the proof is, that as soon as an act was finished, they did not speak to one another of what they had seen and heard. No, without waiting a minute, they began talking of the dollar."

And Mr. B——, who was on the stage, and who did not understand a word of English!!

"One gentleman followed the whole piece of Angelo on a translation of Marie Stuart."

Another mistakes a piece called *Le Mari de la Veuve*, for the first act of Bajazet; and consequently, when this latter piece commences, he supposes the change of costume a mask ball, perhaps, and reads on his second act while the first is being played; and the second during the third; the third during the fourth; and the fourth during the fifth; "so well that, when we commenced the last act, he had entirely finished his translation.

"Oh! then he completely lost his head! He regarded us a few seconds with bewildered eyes; then seizing his hat, he started off at full speed, awaking a whole row of sleepers in his passage."

They are really exceedingly amusing, these descriptions, and all made in perfect good nature, just as the Frenchmen ridicule every thing at home, and one can not get vexed at it. At the same time, in continually ridiculing this ignorance of French in the masses of persons at such a distance from France, Monsieur B—— seems entirely unconscious of the *double* ridicule he is casting on himself and nearly all of his company, who, pretending to refinement, education, and literature, can not even speak a language spoken by 30,000,000 of people within sight of their own land!

Our railways come in for a share of blame, as they ought to do.

"It is inconceivable the little care they take to prevent danger. The rails are laid in the large roads, in the streets, and in the very midst of villages."

"And do not imagine that there are any *garde fous* or barriers whatever. Have the Americans time to think of such trifles?"

"When they pass through a village, they sound a bell—so much the worse for the deaf!"

"Another mania of this country is to have but a single track—a charming idea, because, when two trains clash, one is sure of his affair. But they are in such a hurry, these children of the New World!"

"They only regard one thing—that is, to do every thing they do quickly."

"Therefore, to see these streets, which they have hardly taken time to pave with round stones—these sidewalks, which they were in such a hurry to make that they are the next day broken in fifty different places—these houses, which they throw up in a day—mere card houses, which a strong wind blows over; and, to return to our mutton, to see these railways, built *pour l'amour du diable*, cast across rivers on moving sands, one is tempted to think that this people, who find themselves there by chance after all, has no very strong faith in its own existence, and that it is in haste to live."

Monsieur B—— of course visits the Five Points.

"In order to see this charming spot, it is necessary to go with five or six persons armed to the teeth, and especially to be accompanied by a policeman, who, for the sum of five dollars, never refuses this simple service! Without these important precautions, one is perfectly sure of his affair!" (a favorite expression in France.) "Ah! it is a charming society!"

I was never at the Five Points but once. I then went alone to this worst spot of New York, at nine o'clock at night, and unarmed, and found—a single school there! Perhaps they have retrograded in two years.

"The Americans profess very little admiration for Cooper. They do not even read his works. This is truth. The Americans don't read—they count. They find that more instructive."

The American ladies "are real laths disguised like women, and nothing else."

"Decidedly, America is a *flat* country in every respect."

Finally, Monsieur B—— congratulates himself on his safety in getting upon the *English* Southampton line of steamers to return home. Poor man! he is ignorant that he is on the most unfortunate line of steamers that ever crossed the ocean, the loss of vessels on that one line having been greater in proportion to the number of trips than that of both the Collins and Cunard lines put together!

With an All Rigth (French for all right), he bids adieu to Havana, and will soon be playing dominoes at the Café Riche in Paris.

The article of Jules Janin, published in the *Débats* of Paris, is so insulting as even to disgust the French themselves. I believe it was translated and reprinted in America. He accuses an American of calling out for the Marseillaise during the performance of the tragedy of Cinna. *Rachel never played Cinna in the United States!* He rehashes the slanders of Fontenay. He delights in telling how American ladies take gentlemen on their laps in omnibuses! how they wish to become men! how cold and dead their affections! how they despise the gentle graces which adorn women! Rachel even felt outraged at the article, intended as a compliment to her. Well may she exclaim, "Oh, deliver me from my friends!"

It is really a pity that a foreign artist of talent can not come to America without stirring two worlds with commotion. On the one side, toady sheets must suspend all the news of the day to fill their columns with long puffs, that are now an injury even to a worthy person. A few people, in their enthusiasm, must give grand serenades and concerts, and harness themselves up like asses to draw the object of their admiration. Steamers even are chartered, and military companies go forth to give a welcome to the arriving guest. These last attentions arise from real cordiality and kindness of heart, and ought to be pleasing. Instead of that, they are received generally as barbaric homage to royalty—a right—a due, to be graciously accepted! And for this patronage millions are expected to flow into the coffers of the patron. On the other side of the Atlantic a burst of ridicule breaks forth, fostered by the letters of the very persons receiving so much kindness, and even during the reception of it. The newspapers and reviews amuse their readers with column after column of caricature; and let any one but get up a really amusing lie about America, and he will find the soberest heads eager to swallow it, just in proportion as they are fond of being the slaves of an aristocracy.

To prove that good government, good taste, and religion are impossible in a democracy, is the object of Fontenay's book, if it have any object, and Jules Janin takes up the thread where she leaves off.

Oscar Commettant is now writing articles on America in the Siècle: but you have probably enough. It would be amusing, however, to take a few of these books and compare their contradictions.

For instance, Fontenay says of the American ladies:

"Under their free and forward manner, and frank

and easy air, they *conceal a profound dissimulation, a wonderful egoism.*" Again: "An American lady dines rarely at home. Her husband, occupied with business in the lower part of the city, does not return home before evening, and thus leaves his young wife full liberty—a liberty which she does not fail to profit by. The house is abandoned; the children are sent to college when grown, or stuffed with candy by their nurses while babies. In America they *are entirely ignorant of the sweet relationships of family and of the happiness of the fireside!*"

Now hear D'Almbert on the same subject:

"As soon as a lady is married, she becomes sedate and grave as an old matron; *she hardly ever leaves her dwelling;* her whole time is bestowed upon the education of her children; she never quits the circle of her domestic duties; *she is a devoted wife and an accomplished mother.*"

"Their customs are pure. The precepts instilled into them in infancy inculcate a firmness of spirit which becomes the safeguard of their after life."

And, finally, he invites the ladies of the Old World to imitate their example:

"Let them adopt their habits; let them cultivate, like them, their minds; let them submit themselves to the same labor, and perform their duties with as much perseverance and self-denial, and we shall soon see a renewal of the respect, the care, and attention that ought to surround the weaker sex, and no longer be forced to cross the ocean to find true gallantry."

Of course, people in Europe will believe whichever they choose. We could go on with a pile of books and reviews, out of which the falsehoods and caricatures on America for the year 1855 alone would make a handsome octavo volume, which should be dedicated to—not the aristocracy of Europe; they are too refined and sensible to relish such things—but to their miserable fawners and worshipers.

Jonathan gets well lashed; and is at last so be-criticised, that, bewildered, he sinks on his knees and cries out with little Topsy, "*Oh, I is so wicked!*" Almighty dollar! have mercy upon me, a miserable spitter! a slaveholder! a feeble sucker of mint juleps and brandy cocktails! a lover of cotton and tobacco! (*particularly Mrs. Miller's "fine-cut"*); an amateur of balloon excursions on sections of steam boilers! an advocate of community of tooth-brushes! universal annexer! boarding-house-keeper of all the felons, forçats, and forgers of earth! fast eater! fast liver! fast killer! inventor of two interminable skewers for spitting human beings *à la brochette de Rognons*, called single-track railways! maker but hater of tragedies! Have pity on me, O almighty dollar! Shut me up in prison, and make my Atlantic walls ten times three thousand miles in breadth; pitch my cotton and cocktails, my balloons and boilers, my forgers and felons, all into the sea, and the dice, and the slaves, and the *brochettes*, and the stars (leaving only the stripes, for by them we are healed) after them, and thy servant will take a small farm and a wife, and end his days peacefully in hoeing turnips and potatoes.

JONATHAN CONSOLES HIMSELF.

OH, incomparable beauty of morning! offspring of heaven! how lovely thy daily descent on earth, bringing hope and gladness to man, beast, bird, field, flower, tree, and lake! The little blade of grass hails thee with joy; still plunged in its bath of dew, it lifts up its tiny head at thy approach, and smiles with beaming eyes as it shakes itself dry, like a bird in the bright sunshine. Morning is the infancy of a new life. As many mornings as a man passes on earth, so many lives has he—so many renewed invitations to be good and happy. During the day—*the life of a day*—we grow weary with labor, and the heat of the sun, and the reverses and the cares of the world, and with the workings of our own passions, and we sin through poverty and sheer fatigue, and we lie down at night feebly repentant, and die—in sleep—till the resurrection of a new morning brings us new hope, new energy, and new life.

How fresh the morning air, as it comes through our windows, inviting us forth to the fragrant fields! What forgetfulness of past sorrows and promise of future happiness breathes in that atmosphere! In the very intensity of our enjoyment we experience the need of a purer joy, of which we feel our souls capable, but which we long for here in vain. These feelings are the earnest of our immortality. If our days were measured by years instead of by hours, and we had but seven mornings on earth, we should experience a joy and delight on those seven mornings, compared with which the pleasures of a bridal day would be but trifling. We would sit for hours in mute praise of the magnificence of nature; and all mankind, even to the most savage races, would testify their delight by long-continued festivities.

The burst of a bright morning upon one awaking from sleep is like the floating of sudden harmony upon the ears of misery and distress.

On such a morning, I, Jonathan, awoke from sleep —a sleep into which I had fallen in despair at seeing myself described as such a bad man—a sleep, indeed, which would have been eternal had the River Seine passed through my territory instead of France. The Atlantic was, indeed, near at hand, and was plenty large enough to hold even me; but that pond not being accustomed to such business, and fearing some bungling in the matter, I resolved either to die *secundum artem* by the professor of suicides, or not at all; so, instead of throwing myself into the Atlantic, I threw myself into the arms of Morpheus! I awoke a new man, clean-breasted and fresh-*thoughted.* So might many a man whose body has been covered by the dark waters of the Seine!

> "The darkest day,
> Live but till to-morrow, will have passed away."

Yes, when I first awoke I had forgotten my miseries. It was impossible to be unhappy on such a morning, with the sky so blue, the sun so bright, the meadows so green, and the birds on a tree under my window performing a grand overture to nature. I understood every word they sung. They warbled of the green leaves about them, and of the sunshine dancing on the leaves, and of the willows toppling over with their own elegance; of the waving grass, and of the musical little brook that could scarcely be seen in the luxuriant meadow. The plow-boy interrupted the opera with a pebble, breaking a pane of glass in my window at the same moment, and forcing me out of bed and reverie.

After performing *demi-toilette*, viz., putting on my brown woolen stockings, I paced up and down my chamber *al fresco*, occasionally admiring my person in the glass, and occasionally nature through the window. I combed out, with some difficulty, my long, sandy-red beard, and hair of same color, and would willingly have given one half of it to have had the other half black, but consoled myself by calling it blonde —blonde, the most admired shade in modern France and ancient Rome. So, having made my beard classic, and of the same hue as the hair of one of the most lovely empresses of Europe, I was so led away by my vanity and the good spirits it engendered as to conclude that I was not at all in that sad state in which Seneca recommends suicide or a change of life.

As I looked out upon the smiling landscape, I wondered why all my European brothers hated me so. When young, like Joseph, I had been an outcast into a far country. The probabilities were, I should never be heard of again. My father's house was glad to get rid of me. I settled down in a wilderness among a savage people; the most frightful desolation reigned around me. I struggled through fire, sword, and famine, while my brothers feasted; I overcame all; I grew strong, and, when famine came upon them, I have filled their bags with meal out of my plenty; I have fed their famished, clothed their naked, and reformed their degraded; and still they hate me, because I refuse to bow down to their golden idols.

What a change has come over my lands since I inhabited them! With what fat fertility the once sterile fields now reward the labors of the husbandman! How the mighty rivers, that but lately floated the lazy drift-logs through interminable forests to the sea, now resound with the paddles of gorgeous steamers, laden with the produce of a thousand fields! My possessions, once a barren spot "on a stern and rock-bound coast," now extend from ocean to ocean; my sails whiten every sea; and every land is allied to me by ties of blood. That my mode of government is good, that it is the most natural one for man, and best tending to his happiness, is even proven by the lips of my detractors, since the very criminals, with which they say I am so flooded, cease their crimes and become good citizens; for no people on earth can produce so great an aggregate of happiness and purity of morals as my people. I am ridiculed, it is true, by my brothers because I can not paint, and carve, and chisel, and write poetry, and dance, and fiddle; but, like Themistocles, I can build cities. And history, with its far-seeing, retrospective eyes—history, to whom a century is as a day—history, who overlooks the actions of men as in a battle—history will not ridicule me. She will write that my advancement in arts and sciences has been more rapid than that of Greece, or Rome, or England, or France, or any other nation that ever existed, and *that* while performing Herculean labors on my farm. And, making all allowance for the century in which I live, for the many intelligent persons that come to my shores with all their skill, and for my direct descent from a great nation, yet, the moment that I step ashore in this other world, poor and in a barren land, though I were a Milton, an Angelo, or a Titian, that moment must I exchange my pen, my chisel, or my pallet for the spade and plow—my art is lost. I must relearn it, after having first acquired the *leisure* to reindulge it. And that leisure acquired even, the taste is blunted. Habituated to labor, I feel continually as if I had something *practical* to perform. I can not believe in my leisure; the latent talent is there, but I am too preoccupied to draw it out; and this process will go on until the immigration becomes small compared with the fixed population.

I see some dark spots on the fair surface of my country, and among them, I must confess, that my blacks look at present the *darkest*, as is their right; but this is more on account of meddlers, and misguided as well as misinformed philanthropists, than for any real cause inherent in the object (of course, excepting the color of the skin).

Therefore a grave wrinkle steals over my brow. Unfortunate inheritance, I would you were all on the coasts of Congo! For you, my children quarrel; for you, false philanthropists become martyrs; for you, the press of Europe *studiously* sow the seeds of dissension in my happy family; for you, they dare bandy about the word *Disunion*, that its hateful *sound* may become familiar to the ears of those on our beloved soil who but lately banished the *thought* of it even as high treason; for you, happy as ye are, thousands would see the land reeking with blood and ruin. Abstract principles would snatch the bread from your mouths, as well as from the mouths of myriads more, to carry out an idea—to free you on the spot from bondage, to make you the slaves of misery! But it is my duty to take care of you, and I'll do so. My conscience is not so tender about abstract principles as to be beyond the control of common sense. I had a fever once, and was nearly killed by abstract principles. I ate a hearty dinner of roast beef, because roast beef was healthy and nourishing. It nearly cost me my life, but taught me the lesson that right and wrong are modified by circumstances.

Slavery in the abstract is wrong. I have no right to enslave my fellow-man; but if I have the slave already, and if he have lost his capabilities of self-government, and even of self-protection, by long generations of inherited servitude, or, indeed, which is more nearly the truth, if he never possessed such capacities, then I have a very great responsibility upon me, and commit a *crime* by immediate emancipation under a romantic idea of abolishing one.

My black boys, ye number over 3,000,000 of people; ye compose nearly an eighth of my population; and, believe me, ye are happier than the *lower eighth* of any nation on earth. Could ye go over the world, and see those sad lower eighths, yea, and in some places a few of the higher eighths, ye would thank God for your position.

My black boys, a book is yet to be written about those lower eighths which live in countries whose highest eighths weep over *your* miseries as they weep over plays on the stage, which will make your blood curdle with horror! Ye have to work, it is true; it is our universal curse; but your work is not harder than that of the majority of mankind, and, unlike them, you have no trouble or thought for the morrow. Ye have plenty to eat and drink; ye have a kind doctor and attention when ye are sick; ye have a good bed to lie upon at night, while that sad eighth of which I speak have either none, or lack some of these things.

My black boys, if you had seen, as I have, a cargo of your brethren landed from Africa on the shores of Cuba, you would think there was a great deal more difference between you and them than between them and monkeys; beside them your faces shine with the superior lustre and intelligence that distinguish the white face when placed beside your own. It was a wicked thing to take you away from your own country, but it has raised you infinitely in the scale of being; it has made you *less a slave than you were before*, and it may yet be the means of elevating and redeeming your whole race.

My black boys, the world is full of misery, of which you can have no idea. Your greatest measure of human trouble being the pain of a whipping, which the majority of you never felt even, but may have heard of, and not having known the sweets of liberty, ye do not even long for it any more than ye long to be in Africa, or Boston, or any other land of which ye know nothing and never think. Then I truly think that ye enjoy life as much as at least one half of the human race. To be sure, a few of us look down from our high stations, and, placing *ourselves in your position*, wonder how *ye* can be happy, or, rather, how we could be, under like circumstances. Judging in this way, every man below the king is miserable in the king's eyes, though happy in his own; and perhaps that is a right belonging even to slaves—to judge of their own happiness.

My black boys, do not believe those your best friends who shed most tears in your behalf. There are tears which assuage none, and there are dry eyes which wipe away tears. The luxury of tears is as necessary to man as the luxury of smiles; and those with whom life is a continual sunshine seek this luxury as they do others, driving in carriages to enjoy it in theatres on cushioned seats, and with accompaniments of music, dress, gas, and suppers, whereas they might have had more real cause for tears nearer home. Or they view the stage at a distance of 1500 or 3000 miles, and the actors are black, and they perform their parts so well under the master direction of a Stowe that the amphitheatre of a world weeps—weeps in comfort at a distance, while misery in every shape is pleading for pity and succor at their doors. But tara ra ra la la goes the music, and ten times ten thousand cambric handkerchiefs dry sympathizing eyes, and crack goes the whip, drowning—the crack of that single whip, at a distance of thousands of miles—drowning the groans of myriads of human beings, who can not be heard because they happen to be of an unromantic color—*white*, and at an unromantic distance—*near home*, and because the audience don't go to the play to dispense charities, but to have a *good cry*. . And you might say to this audience, How much untruth may be conveyed by an improper way of representing truth? And you might suggest to them that, as life is not very long, it would be better to cease *crying* and commence *doing;* and that, since the relief of the misery of mankind is the grand object, at present, of all benevolent minds, it would be more systematic as well as charitable to begin with the most miserable first, just as a surgeon attends first to the wants of his most dangerously-wounded patients. But then, my boys, it would be long before your turn would come!

Still, I wish ye were all in Congo, instead of increasing upon my hands at the rate of more than 70,000 annually, or in more rapid ratio than any other race on earth, which at least shows how easy your condition is.

But I assume the responsibility, as my son Jackson said. I will keep ye and take care of ye until some one can give satisfactory evidence of being better able to do so than myself. If the world can not take care of the poor and wretched now at their charge, what will they do when 3,000,000 more are thrown upon their charities?

So, my black boys, as long as you have a good dinner without the trouble of seeking it, a good bed, and plenty of fresh air, believe that your masters are your best friends; and after picking cotton all day in the field, don't go home and pass sleepless nights, making your brains as kinky as your hair in trying to decide if Philip Francis were really Junius, or if the man in iron mask was the son of Louis XIV. and the Duchesse de la Vallière, or if his mask were velvet instead of iron. Leave these questions to me, and go to sleep like good niggers! and, in the mean time, I'll try and solve three other questions which puzzle the world, viz.:

"What becomes of all the pins?"

"What is done with all the newspapers?"

"And what shall be done with the slaves of the United States?"

Jonathan was here seized with a sudden chill, owing to his demi-toilette, the magnitude of the questions, and the hole in the window-pane. So, beginning where he leaves off with that vexing question which few can touch on either side without flying into a passion, I say it is utterly impossible that simultaneous emancipation can ever take place in the United States; or if it does, it will only be with the blood, smoke, and ruin of the whole South—a consummation, I trust, few abolitionists even desire.

As this is the opinion of most persons who have lived for any length of time in the South, I was very anxious to see what opinion a French philosopher and a very impartial observer would give after a short residence of a month or two in Cuba and New Orleans. Professor Ampère is a member of the *Académie Française*, and although a great many of the learned men of France, including Montesquieu and Voltaire, have been unsparing of ridicule on the Academy, still they are always proud to get into it, and the forty chairs are always full, as they would be if there were eighty. Therefore I confess to very great reverence for a member of the Academy, and was anxious to hear the opinion of one of its members, a man of so much education and talent as Professor Ampère. I almost expected to see the whole question resolved at once; but what does he say? Hear.

"After having traveled through the country, after being impressed more deeply with horror of the system, and after having heard the opinions of those statesmen most opposed to this scourge of their country, *I see no more than the first day any practical means of immediate deliverance.*"

So says a philosopher who has the greatest horror of slavery, and who lives in a country where mulattoes go to balls and dance with white girls, and where I have seen jet-black men walk with white women in the streets.

Professor Ampère evidently is in favor of amalgamation. That seems to me contrary to nature. I have always observed, while living in the South a good many years, that mulattoes, while mentally superior to blacks, but inferior to whites, were physically inferior to both, and more vicious than either. Exact information on this point would be useful.

The first thing to be done by *very* conscientious people to assist the abolition of slavery would be, as Professor A—— very properly remarks, to deprive themselves of sugar, tea, coffee, or any thing known to be slave-grown. (Some good ladies in England have already done this.)

For the present I shall take only *two* lumps of sugar in my coffee instead of *three*, which some people take. I shall read carefully both sides of the question, and never get excited on a warm day, as a lady of my acquaintance did when I handed her once a copy of the London Times containing a review of "Uncle Tom" that did not please her. Because that practical sinner did not choose to go into *Uncle Tomitudes* like the rest of the world, she tore my newspaper up and trampled it under foot! Still, she was a good woman, although she uses sugar on her tarts!

However great a crime slavery may be, however sinful it might have been at first to bring these creatures from Africa, still I think that, in the year 2056, the world will say that *the greatest blessing that ever happened to Africa was the slavery of a portion of her people in the United States!*

This is a very queer letter. I have suffered Jonathan somehow or another to get hold of my pen and run away with it, whereas I had intended to apply a salve to the wounds made by my last.

Seriously speaking, why does almost every European who goes to America think it necessary to write a book, turning every thing he has seen into ridicule? We shall look at this matter a little, and see who these persons are, and perhaps the ridicule will turn against them. Without being so personal as to inquire into the private life or character of any them, we may observe that there is hardly a name among the whole list of slanderers that has risen from obscurity, and they are most of them notorious rather than celebrated, for their books of trash on that country. Their names have become by-words, if they are ever mentioned at all; and what they have written to excite the smile of their countrymen has ended in causing disgust. On the other hand, those who have been just, even while they have censured, compose a list of names every one of which is distinguished. Chateaubriand, De Tocqueville, Ampère, Laboulaye, Thackeray (who has merely published some remarks on the country), Chambers, and others, have had mind enough to see things rightly, and comprehend what they see, which is certainly a very difficult thing for a European to do who has not studied the genius and institutions of the country. It is more pleasure to be censured by such men than to be praised by the Trollope-Fontenay class. When they sit down to write a book on the United States, they feel the responsibility and difficulty of the undertaking; they know they are about to speak to hundreds of thousands who have their eyes turned toward that land as their future home; they know they are speaking to statesmen who have diplomatic relations with the government of that country, and to whom it is not only important to have much, but correct information; and, lastly, they feel an interest in watching the progress of freedom and the development of the resources of a country under a form of government so different from Continental forms, and conducted by so heterogeneous a people.

It requires rare qualities in a traveler to be able to judge of any country correctly, even on a lengthy visit. This every one must feel if he will only compare his impressions of a place received while suffering from headache, or under disagreeable circumstances, with those received on favorable occasions. It requires a philosopher to be uninfluenced in his opinions by trifles.

The United States, of all countries, is the one where travelers are most liable to arrive under unfavorable circumstances. To cross the Atlantic is more terrible for Europeans than to venture a voyage in a balloon. To Americans it is more a pleasure-trip; they have an innate aptitude for travel, and an American woman will bear a sea-voyage better than a European man; the latter are always whining and crying like babies before, during, and forever after a little ocean toss. The only American we ever knew to take on so about it was Greely; and whining over trifles is his nature: he can't help it; but Horace would whine on board a steam-ship and smile in a dungeon!

Therefore Europeans generally arrive in America cranky and cross, colorless and attenuated, nervous and susceptible to the slightest noises. In this condition, instead of being carried in close carriages straight to the Hospital, there to remain a few days, they are launched into the most awful rush of rumblings, rattlings, trampings, crashings, bangings, bell-ringings, that ever greeted human ears from the days of the brick-makers of Babel to the comparatively modest music of a modern Chinese concert. The consequences are evident; they rush away into some distant room, bolt and bar out men and noises, and commence their lachrymose complaints of America. One French gentleman, Mons. D'Almbert, commences a chapter on the ocean with "*Funeste Manie des Voyages*," and then has the good taste to say in his preface, "We were in a bad humor on landing at New York, and if we judge America with some prejudices, it must be attributed to our sufferings on the passage, and to the bad impression which is first produced by a country where one must arrive by so abominable a road as the sea."

Another, in going aboard the steam-ship, repeats to himself the words, "The other world! there is something sinister in the thought." "Frightful voyage! the sea is the most awful punishment I know."

Others, again, besides these hinderances to correct judgment, are influenced by personal feelings. One goes with his head full of international copyright projects, and the failure of his darling scheme instantly claps the blue spectacles on his nose. Another very respectable milliner, hearing that the people are all democrats in the United States, and all equal, goes over to have a gossip, and is quite piqued as well as astonished to find that all the doors of Fifth Avenue and Chestnut Street do not immediately fly open to her. "Lor' bless your soul, marm, I was intimate with the Countess De Pettypois!" (in the nursery, while making babies' dresses.) And so she tosses her head, expecting to rule in hell after having served in heaven—her heaven, an aristocracy. Of course, she is much surprised to find that she is still where her talents placed her, not only serving, but in hell besides.

Another comes to spout Shakspeare or Racine, and very strangely imagines that touching the soil of America has changed him in a twinkling into a genius: he is a Gulliver coming among the Liliputians—a Saul, "a head and shoulder higher" than all those about him. He expects every man will feel honored by being allowed to pour golden eagles into his lap! By just so much as he has mistaken his height and importance, by just so much is his mortification deep and bitter.

The Paddy heard the streets were paved with gold, therefore he would not pick up the half dollar he saw on the quay on landing. He, too, went home with heart of gall!

All these people take their revenge, as is their right, and we laugh at them. We wince too, not only because they tell a great many truths, but because they tell so many untruths, which, although they would be of no consequence to us if we were an old, stationary nation like England, with a policy well known and understood by all the nations of the world, in our present position often tend to alienate governments from our friendship with whom we should otherwise be on good terms. Many think they injure us likewise by checking emigration. Of this we should be glad. A thousand people arriving every day at one port alone is too many. We can not wash, dress, and educate them fast enough, and before that their influence is bad.

Different from all these is Professor Ampère. He comes to see, know, and appreciate justly the country. He is a philosopher. The loss of a friend, a toothache, an indigestion, or even a dirty waiter pitching a dirtier napkin over his face while sleeping, and calling out, "Haloa, there, *comrade*, get up," do not at all affect his serenity. If he travels a whole day through a prairie, he does not write, "Your country is flat as a pancake." If he should wander for weeks among the Alleghanies or the interminable Rocky Mountains, he would not say, "You have nothing but mountains in America." If he travel for many days on the upper lakes, he does not think the United States a place fit only for boatmen. He sweeps the whole horizon, and takes in the vast panorama at a glance; he sees mountain, forest, lake, river, plain, on a scale of magnitude such as he had never yet imagined, and admirably adapted for the purposes to which they are being now devoted—the regeneration of mankind. He sees ugly spots too, such as swamps, cane-brakes, etc., but they show only a proper prominency in the picture, and in nowise injure the general effect of the whole; and he knows that even those spots will be certainly effaced in time.

As he sees physically, so he regards morally.

The pigmy beside him can not see beyond the dark spot. He isolates; he has not grasp of mind to combine.

The one is the *man*, who, standing underneath the dome of Saint Peter's, sees in the mosaic work above him a beautiful picture; the other is the *fly*, which, alighting on a bit of that mosaic an inch square, sees only a bit of dirty-colored stone!

Professor Ampère landed at New York, and visited most of the important places in the Union, and his criticisms are generally just.

He points out more faults than perhaps even the caricaturists, but gives them their proper prominency only, instead of making them most conspicuous. If he mentions our bad taste in architecture, he awards more credit to our sculptors. After a page devoted to the ridiculous points and untruths of a tragedy called Savonarola, which is a caricature of the noble and unfortunate enthusiast of Florence, he devotes a dozen pages to the literature of America, noticing many of the principal authors very favorably. He smiles at such attempts in architecture as the Smithsonian Institute and the Medical College at Columbus, but, after criticising the latter, says, "Here is something better than feudal construction in honor of Hippocrates;" he then mentions the fact of a thousand laboring women at Scioto, out of a population of 11,000 souls, *hearing lectures in chemistry while knitting stockings.* He found no greater *questioners* than himself, and always found every one ready to answer all that he was disposed to ask. If the Yankees are going to be laughed out of asking questions, I shall be sorry. "He that asketh much shall learn much," says Bacon (provided it be not of the price of rings and watch-chains). He and De Tocqueville both say that in the United States we have no school of philosophy, and attribute it to the strong religious check upon philosophical speculation, as well as to our practical utilitarian habits. The latter author says that America, of all countries in the world, is the one where they study least, but follow most the precepts of Descartes.

And now, to show you that I make a distinction between just criticism and caricature, I quote some remarks of De Tocqueville, where he very graphically illustrates our national vanity.

"The Americans, in their relationships with strangers, appear impatient of the slightest censure and insatiable of praise. The smallest eulogy pleases them, and the greatest is rarely enough to satisfy them; they harass you continually to obtain your praises, and if you resist their entreaties they glorify themselves. One might say that, doubtful of their own merit, they wish to have the picture of it continually under their eyes. Their vanity is nót only *thirsty*, aride, it is restless and curious. It allows nothing, demanding every thing. It is supplicating and quarrelsome at the same time."

"I say to an American, 'Your country is beautiful.' 'That's true,' he replies; 'there's not a finer country in the world.' I admire the liberty enjoyed by the people, and he answers, 'Liberty is a precious gift, but there are very few nations worthy of enjoying it.' I remark the purity of morals which exists in the United States, and he says, 'I can easily conceive that a stranger, who has been struck with the corruption observable in other nations, should be astonished at such a spectacle.' I finally abandon him to the contemplation of himself, but he returns to me and refuses to be satisfied until I have repeated all I had just said to him. It is impossible to imagine a more annoying and prattling patriotism. It fatigues even those who honor it."

This hits the nail exactly on the head. It is true as if written by a god. And it is so recognized in Europe that this vanity must be fed or war ensue (between individuals), that I hardly ever make a new acquaintance but he begins forthwith to praise America, often in the most ludicrous manner.

Persons who are very vain are generally easy tools. To use a man, find first his weak point. The European press have found out the weak point of America, and I fear they are beginning to turn it to tremendous advantage. I fear more their flattery than their censure. If the mortifying remark made by a gentleman in London lately, that "*the press of Europe hold the key to the American heart*," be true, it is high time that we have another *lock* put on.

I close this letter with the following striking remarks of Legouve, also of the Académie Française. In reviewing Ampère's work, he says:

"America brings good fortune to those of our great writers who speak of her. It seems as if one could not touch that fruitful land without acquiring a greater strength. Chateaubriand brought away a new poesy; De Tocqueville found there a *chef d'œuvre* of political philosophy; Monsieur Ed. Laboulaye has produced from the study of the American Constitution a book which, although still unfinished, counts already as a durable work; and, finally, Monsieur Ampère returns to-day from this new world with that which is most wanting, perhaps, in our old continent, a religious respect for the dignity of human nature."

OVER THE USUAL HIGHWAY OF CITIES TO THE RHINE.

On a fine moonlight night toward the end of April, and not many days since, I saw the familiar domes and spires of Paris rapidly fading in the distance as the express train rapidly hurried away toward Brussels. The flare of the Boulevards, the smooth rumbling of coaches over the level Macadam, the promenading thousands, the merry gardens, the lofty column, the stately Madeleine, the tasteful Louvre—sights and sounds that had become almost a necessary part of life—were in an instant left miles behind, exchanged for the big, round, and solitary moon. A few puffs at cigars (what spot on earth is free from cigar-smoke ?), an arranging of traveling-caps, loosening of cravats, and muffling of throats by the gentlemen, and a general fixing by the only lady in our compartment, occupied my three fellow-travelers for the first half hour of the journey, after which, and a few words of conversation, every body fell asleep or a thinking. When we were awakened after midnight to attend to the passport nuisance, I found the lady reposing her head as quietly on my shoulder as if she had been my wife—a position that startled her quite as much as myself. Observing that she was alone, I invited her to take some refreshments, which invitation she gladly accepted, partly, perhaps, as a pastime, and partly to avoid the chilling effects of the midnight air while we were awaiting the examination of our passports. Another nap, and we awoke in Brussels at 6 A.M., a dull, frowzy hour to arrive any where, particularly after sleeping endwise. To go to sleep a gentleman in a railway carriage is to awake a rowdy. People have such a sour, grizzly, rumpled look after passing a night bolt upright on a stuffed cushion! They look as if they had been tussling with one another during the whole twelve hours for corner-seats or leg-room. Cravats are twisted one way, caps another, heads and beards shaggy, eyes bloodshot and wild, so that I wonder the guards dare open the doors to let loose such a lot of ferocious-looking animals.

Think of arriving at Brussels before breakfast, after having eaten your last dinner in a cabinet of the *Café Anglais* at Paris! Ugh! Oh, that I had just left the fogs of London, the waves of the Channel, any thing but the gay and lively million of Paris! Belgians of Brussels! what a contrast! I have heard Englishmen often call it a gay, delightful city, but then they had just arrived from their *own* country, and things are beautiful or the reverse only by comparison. I have also heard it called a miniature Paris. It looks about as much like that capital as the rough plaster copies of the Venus de Milo look like the original. There is evidently an attempt at imitation of every thing Parisian; the people try to dress in Paris style, to walk Paris, to build Paris, and to have cafés, Boulevards, and gardens à la manière de Paris. But all these things only cause one to heave a huge sigh and long for the original.

Nevertheless, the people are most kind-hearted. A gentleman of whom I asked information concerning a public building was not only so kind as to tell me all I desired, but walked about the centre of the city with me during a whole hour, pointing out its curiosities, and that before breakfast, too, when *civilized* people are always cross and dumpish.

Of three inquiries made in Brussels, every one was answered in a manner exceedingly rare in America—the persons accompanied me to the spots I desired to find.

Brussels is a characterless place—a sort of neutral ground between France and Germany, both lacking the elegance and refinement of the one, and the whole-souled simplicity of the other country. It will end by becoming thoroughly French, that, too, being the language spoken there. Indeed, all Europe is getting very Frenchy at present, and in all that pertains to refinement, luxury, and elegance of manners, Paris may be said to be the heart of the world.

At Antwerp I remained four hours, and saw only one picture. What is the use of rushing through long galleries of paintings till eye and limbs are wearied, and the taste is blunted by abuse? The effect is to create unpleasant reminiscences of the finest things in art. It is like running over all Europe in a month to say you have seen it. You can not see chef-d'œuvres, whether of architecture, sculpture, or painting, in a hurry, any more than you can enjoy a grand dinner at a railway station with the bell sounding in your ears; and whenever I hear a person say, "Oh, I am so tired of looking at pictures, and these long galleries are so wearying!" I infer at once that, in his greediness to see every thing, he has enjoyed nothing. If you have only a day for the Louvre, for instance, and will give yourself to the enjoyment of half a dozen pictures only, you will carry away a treasure to last a lifetime; but if, in one day, you are determined to see every thing in the Louvre, you will not only have no pleasure in looking back upon your visit, but will always experience a secret dread of picture galleries, which you will be ashamed to confess, lest it betray a want of taste.

I would give a great deal to know what the polite guard of the railway station at Cologne said to me as I descended from the carriage; but, whatever it was, I remembered that a safe answer to make a German on all occasions is *so-o*, so I brought out a *so-o-o* with the most virile energy an untrained tongue was capable of infusing into such a little word. The effect was magical; he unstrapped my baggage with great alacrity, submitted it to the inspection of the custom-house officer, who, instead of touching any thing, adjusted his spectacles on his nose, and gave the command to restrap. No more words, only a few silver groschen, passed between the guard and myself, and as I put them into his hands he put me into a drosky, and in ten minutes I was whirled into the awfulest stench I ever smelt in my life—and this they called Cologne!

Every body here is named Farina. Farinas are merely scented Smiths and Joneses. For a long time Jean Marie Farina was a prefix to the name of every new-born babe, as Jean Marie Farina Schwartzberg, Jean Marie Farina Petzkuchen: it was a fortune to the family to be able to sign that name. But, now competition has spoiled the trade, the name is common as the article it represents, and people say, indifferently, a bottle of Farina water or a bottle of Cologne water.

Who ever sat down to his dinner in Cologne without seeing the Cathedral? I did. However, I saw it after dinner. It would be ridiculous to say a word of this beautiful building—as ridiculous as to praise Shakspeare. Nations have grown into grandeur and dwindled to a name since it was commenced, and yet it still remains unfinished, and will always remain so, because time pulls down one end while man rebuilds the other.

Truly, Gothic is the architecture for churches, as

time is their consecration, and the Roman Catholic religion their best preserver!

UP THE RHINE AFOOT.

THE whole valley of the Rhine was asleep.

The landlords had grown fat and lazy after an idle winter, and sat in their doors with drooping pipes and eyelids, awaiting the approach of *the season.* A few solitary travelers, Cologne merchants perhaps, trod the decks of the steamers, heedless of the well-known scenery around, or sat dozing under a genial April sun until awakened by the tap of the bell announcing the approach to Coblentz or some other river port.

But Mein Herr of the Königlicher Hof at Bonn was the stoutest sleeper of them all—the Rip Van Winkle of Rhenish landlords. He sat in his easy-chair at three o'clock in the afternoon (a sleepy hour, it is true, to those who dine heartily at midday, as do these good Germans), and snored and puffed, and puffed and snored, just as if he had not been puffing and snoring in the same position during a whole winter. Shaking and pulling had no effect, except to shake the pipe out of his mouth; but the instant I shook my pockets he started to his feet, and looked smiling and good-natured as but few men can, awakened out of a comfortable sleep at midday. The first thing he did was to take off his hat and describe a half circle with it, a process which I imitated with great success, but a little too rapidly in movement, so that my head was recovered first. Conscious of a serious breach of German etiquette, I endeavored to correct my error by uncovering again just as the good landlord had covered, at which he leisurely removed his hat a second time. In this heat I tried to come to time, but was too quick again, having had a little the start. In the third heat the landlord led off in fine style, his hat moving in the same graceful circle, but with greater speed. I was not far behind him, but I could see that bets among the hotel-boys standing around were largely in his favor. This discouraged me, and I *broke* after the fourth heat, the judges declaring him winner, and showing me to my room over the Rhine.

The next day I awoke just as the morning sun was rising behind the hills.

The Rhine Valley was asleep—all asleep except nature, the peasants, and the birds, which never sleep while the sun shines.

I threw my windows wide open to catch all the early morning air, all the chirpings of the birds, and all the beauties of nature, lavished so bountifully under my eyes in the winding waters, the green meadows, the blooming trees and flowers, and the glorious background of all, the blue hills of the Siebengebirge. A pretty little bridge spans two hilly grass-plots in the grounds back of the hotel, and under this bridge, after bathing an instant in the Rhine, came darting up the sun's rays right into my window, making me envy them their rapid and picturesque bath, and at the same time loth to lose a moment of such a view in dressing. But Drachenfels, eight miles distant, seemed to beckon me away; so breakfast and dressing were soon dispatched, and my trunk forwarded to the city, while for myself, *armed to the teeth*, viz., a cane, comb, and tooth-brush, I started off afoot to see the celebrated mountain of Drachenfels.

It was the end of April, the maidenhood of foliage just budding into beauty ere ravished by the heats of summer. The trees were, perhaps, less green than they would be a month hence, but, from the immediate contrast with the black branches of winter, the eye seemed better to appreciate their loveliness; the grass was blossomed with dew-drops sparkling and fresh in the morning air. Peasant men and women were already going to the fields; the latter stout and strong, with broad backs, broad waists, and broad hips—walking parallelograms in petticoats. They looked as if they had been made by the mile, like Dutch ships, and then cut off in lengths to suit. Like their vessels, too, they are solid and substantial, made rather to *carry* than to *go;* and the two are just exactly the reverse of American women and ships, which are both *clipper*-built, and sacrifice solidity and strength too much to elegance and speed.

Most of the women had heavy baskets on their heads, with which they walk many miles, and which give them a stiff, sturdy carriage, though they are entirely devoid of that grace and ease with which a Southern slave carries her burden: the latter sways her body coquettishly, and even tosses her head without dropping her load like the milkmaid in the spelling-book. Sometimes, too, their basket will be a little cocked to one side, like a dandy's hat, while they go along singing and trying to catch the eyes of their black swains. But the German peasant women bend down to their work like great Norman horses; their heads are all sun-tanned, for they wear no covering over their hair, and their faces are of every hue, from nut-brown to blazing red. When they are young, their faces are good-looking from excess of good nature, but hard out-of-door work in the hot sun or cold air soon dries up their good looks, leaving generally a kind of resigned, quiet expression, as if they accepted their condition, and never hoped for, or even thought of, any other. Those peasant girls who early quit the fields and go into family service have certainly the most innocent, sheep-like, good-natured physiognomies to be found in the human race. It is surprising how human beings can go through the wear and tear of life, and be so little worn and torn as many of these girls are at thirty.

Crossing the Rhine in a small boat, I was soon surrounded by a crowd of men and boys, who addressed me in English, French, and German, to know if I wanted a guide and an ass; but informing them of my ability to act in both capacities, I shook them off, and was soon standing alone on the "castled crag of Drachenfels"—alone, but amid a crowd of images that came grouping around, and peopling the rocks, walls, and crumbling stones of the ruin with the only beings that should accompany one to such a place.

Drachenfels is a worthy commencement of the scenery of the Rhine, and, like the overture to a grand opera, its views comprehend glimpses and foreshadowings of every style of scenery that is to follow: the sloping mountain, the frowning crag, the green islet, the smiling vineyard, and the vast plain dotted with cities and towns, amid whose humble roofs rises the towering church-spire, proud, lofty, and rich, fitting emblem of the mighty power wielded by a few clergy over the superstitious and ignorant masses around them. And amid this lovely landscape rolls the Rhine as far as the eye can reach, seeming like a silver ribbon to bind all these beauties to earth.

But who shall dare description where the Childe Harold's foot has trodden?

It was but a few months previous that I had stood on the top of Monte Diablo at the other side of the globe. The similarity of names is the only resemblance between the two mountains (Dragon's Rock and Devil's Mountain). But the suddenness of transition made comparison irresistible. My grandfather, who lived to the good old age of ninety years without ever having read of a steam-boat explosion, could hardly have imagined so rapid a flight.

God makes mountains, but man maks them revered. A hill consecrated by the foot of a poet or by the hut of a philosopher stands higher in men's minds than the highest peak of the Andes. Association, and not height, is the charm of the mountain. But to the pure worshiper of nature the mountain is dear for itself too, though doubly dear when it can tell its story.

Monte Diablo is three times the height of Drachenfels, and its scenery is as much grander and more masculine as are the bold, manly features of a warrior than the gentle, smiling face of a Grecian girl. Monte Diablo is a giant, born among the grandest works of nature. He looks up to the towering Sierra Nevada on one side, and down to the vast Pacific on the other.

His feet bathe in some of the finest bays in the world, and every where scattered around are dark ravine, forest, river, and plain. He has no story to tell but of wild Indian and bear, and of the silent though grand operations of nature which his hoary head has witnessed for thousands of years. But he now commences a tale for future centuries, which, when consecrated by time, shall far surpass the pretty little stories of Drachenfels. He will tell how he saw a city spring up in a day; how it was repeatedly consumed in a night, and rebuilt in the morning, and how it went on increasing in size and numbers till it became the greatest city the world had ever seen; how its broad bay teemed with the ships and commerce of millions of the human race, that till then were shut up in the walls of their own vast empires; and how the mainspring of all this action was sordid gold—the gold that he had seen streamed forth along the sands and in the river-beds by Dame Nature as tempting prizes to induce men to leave their homes and cultivate the plains of the West. He will then relate how men, having sinned and suffered for gold, their evil passions spent, formed themselves into industrious communities, and not only made their own land smile, but carried civilization and commerce across the ocean. All these things will the venerable old mountain say, and poets will sing of him, and of his wild glens, and of his trout-bearing rivulets.

Long will I remember thee, dear old mountain! and the night I slept on thy bed of leaves, in a dark ravine, beside a purling brook, with a wall 2000 feet high between me and civilization, will never be forgotten. Few but beasts or savages had ever trodden that spot;

it was miles away from any habitation of man; black forests and huge overhanging rocks inclosed it, as if for a banquet-hall for the spirits of the mountain. Long before the sun had set in the distant Pacific, its rays had disappeared from the hall of the spirits, and the morn was visible in the heavens hours before its orb hung on the cliff o'erhead.

Farewell, thou fine old majesty! No polished rocks of storied Rhine or icy Alps shall change my love for thee!

After remaining some hours admiring the sweet views around Drachenfels, and wondering where all its thousands of worshipers were, since none had appeared, I sorrowfully wended my way down the hill, turning up (or rather down) my nose at the steamer a thousand feet below, and thanking God for legs and a cane instead of paddle-wheels and smoke-pipe.

> "Though sluggards deem it but a foolish chase,
> And marvel men should quit their easy-chair,
> Oh! there is sweetness in the mountain air,
> And life that bloated ease can never hope to share."

I recrossed the Rhine at Königswinter, and was soon climbing the hill of Rolandseek.

A buxom, red-faced girl came bounding out of a house half way up the hill side. I asked her if I was in the right road. Without further ceremony, she took my coat from my arm and began to lead the way, talking and laughing as she went. Now I knew it was of no use to wrestle with a Dutch girl; I had measured too many of them with my eye on the road to attempt that; besides, it would have been very ludicrous to tumble down the hill together in the midst of the village of Rolandswerth! So she kept my coat, and I kept the first guide I ever had in my life in the open air. After having been trotted through palaces and towers to the measured pace and mumblings of showmen some years since over half Europe, I resolved never again to take a guide for any thing—they are the iconoclasts of imagination and reverie. Learn all you can beforehand of a place, and then trust to your wits, and your soul shall have a feast. If you have not time for that, let the object go unseen, and you have something left in the world between you and satiety.

But, after all, thought I, it is a fine thing this, a female guide up the mountain of Rolandseek. A petticoat will assist the imagination in calling up the lovely nun of Nonnenwerth; and so I made the best of my position; and my guide chatted and laughed, and I chatted and laughed, and she understood what *she* said, and I understood what *I* said.

However, I quickly dismissed her on the top. The nuns were chanting in the convent on the little island in the midst of the Rhine. Soon a number of them went out into the garden. It was easy to fancy Hildegarde among them, and the hermit-nephew of Charlemagne looking out from his castle opposite, and hopelessly pining for his lost bride. The picture was one of perfect tranquillity and rest. The hill sides covered with vineyards, the mosaic-work plains, the dreamy atmosphere, the sleeping cities in the distance, and the peaceful Rhine, over which the soft melody of the nuns was floating, seemed to invite one away from the world into this paradise. But, alas! experience proves that the world we would escape from is not the noise, toil, and bustle of life among our fellows, but the passions of our own breast. "Earth's troubled waters are that little sea within our own bosoms."

> "What exile from himself can flee
> To zones, though more and more remote?
> Still, still pursues where'er I be,
> The blight of life—the demon Thought."

But, by hickory-sticks and hob-nailed walking-shoes! let us not become sentimental on such a day as this. Many a merry mile is before us between this and Mayence—not French merriness, which must have a band of talking companions continually a-chat—not a merriness, indeed, that *every* one will allow to be very merry, and yet, to him that understands it, it is the very soul of fun. I verily believe that many men are born pedestrians; they can not help it; they have certain little muscles in the feet that are always in a state of unrest; they are like a Frenchman's tongue, which is constructed on different principles from all other tongues; they must go, company or no company. It is pleasant to have lively companions with one, but really a true pedestrian has made so many acquaintances in the woods, and among the mountains, and through the meadows, and along the streams, that I have rarely seen one who could not relish a walk of several days or more entirely alone.

When I run away from a city, the first thing I like to feel is my independence. I throw away my suspenders because they are bonds. I cut my straps because they restrain my liberty. I won't have any luggage, because it is more trouble to take care of one's trunk than of one's self.

Then, what a delight it is to roll in the dirt like a horse assuring himself that his harness is off, and to get up again without having a dozen garçons flying at you with brushes; and *then* what health inflates your lungs! what an appetite! what rollicking spirits! what castle-building! what reviews of life and hopes for the future! Your heart swells and beats with a will to dare and do any thing. Every body seems in a good humor with you. The peasant women show you how to bind the vine-twig to the stake—one can always converse easily with women, though *they* be Samoyedes and *you* a Tongatabootan, and both languages without a dictionary. But with men it is different; yet even the men, from the polite way in which they bow, evidently regret that they are so stupid as not to be able to speak English and have a conversation with you. At the hotels they know just what you want before you ask for it, and your steaks and ale are before you without the blue-eyed maid cutting up any *garçonicalisms* for your entertainment—great walkers these steaks and ale! they almost start off without you, they are so accustomed to it. The poorest walker in the world is your pumpkin-pie. The "*yellow-faced rascal*" that haunted Tom Hood on the Rhine was a pumpkin-pie! It is a sad invention that, and capable of turning a whole nation to saffron. Why, every thing about it is yellow: the eggs are yellow, the butter yellow, the sugar regular *yaller Muscovado*, and the pumpkin itself (or *punkin*, as the élite of Connecticut call it for brevity's sake)—Heaven knows if that is yellow—no doré about that; it is the true color all through, from husk to seed.

But to return to our steak, which was just about walking off (aided slightly by a hungry-looking dog)—there is a relish about that dish, eaten on a board table, that if I could collect and bottle up would make my fortune in Paris in six months. My *fortune!* Ah! there's a walker for you. I have never caught up to it yet, and never shall. But no matter; as my Lord Bacon saith, "riches are the baggage of virtue," and I hate baggage. One can never go through the eye of a needle with baggage on his back. It's hard enough to get through without it.

I spent nearly two weeks in walking leisurely up the Rhine, visiting its robber castles, tarrying in its principal cities, and crossing and recrossing the river as circumstances required. I had many a pleasant adventure, and met many a pleasant companion, and at one of the hotels was glad to become acquainted with a Spanish family, as, not speaking German, I was sometimes doomed to silence in the hotels. However, it is rarely that one will find any difficulty along the Rhine in respect of languages, provided he speak French.

But the Rhine—the Rhine, past whose beauties we steam in a day—it would fill a summer's walk, it and its neighboring valleys! It would even fill another book! But one feels afraid to speak of it any more. It is one of the things society has tacitly agreed to observe silence upon, perhaps for its reverence, perhaps for the majesty of the names which have celebrated it. It would be snobbish to talk of the Rhine. We enjoy it secretly and quietly, as we enjoy love and Paradise Lost.

But let us take a glass of Johannisberg before parting. The day is warm, and there stands the chateau on the top of the hill, not invitingly, but dazzlingly bright. One does not feel at all like climbing up there, and nothing but the presence of the prince himself, or—his cellar, could induce one to take such a journey in so warm a day. I arrive at the gate before having thought even whether there might not be some formalities required preparatory to entering the chateau of a Metternich; but it was too late; "fools rush in where angels fear to tread," which is just what I did on that occasion, and was treated, too, very angelically for my temerity by the good-natured lady who has charge of the house. She conducted me through all the various apartments, showing me a bust of the prince, his dining-hall, sleeping-rooms, and even his bed, which, all covered with halo as it was—in her eyes—I would not have exchanged for my comfortable bed in Paris. But there was one room I could have wished to spend weeks in; not for any thing it contained, nor for its associations, which, after all, are of nothing but pipes and puncheons, but for what it did not contain—its lovely view of the Rhine and the extended landscape through which it passes. It is almost as fine as the view from the Niederwald, some distance below it.

I asked for a bottle of wine, inviting my conductress to sit down with me, which, after some blushing and display of modesty—natural modesty (for the Germans are all modest)—she consented to do. I examined carefully the seals, the labels, the bottle, and the cork, and watched with a midday-fifteen-miles'-walk-in-the-sun eagerness the cool flowing forth of earth's only nectar! The glass touched my lips, when, without tasting the wine, I replaced it quietly on the table, planted my hands on my hips, with elbows akimbo, and asked her *if it was genuine!* You may laugh, but it was the most natural question in the world. I am a connoisseur, and do not like to be cheated in my wines. Besides, did you ever see Monsieur Doré, of Paris, with eye-glass on eye, and resting his elegant form on the cushions of the Café Riche, sip his wines without asking that question?

Have you observed Mr. Snob, of West End, with what supercilious satisfaction he regards his country guests as the white-cravated waiter, with judicial emphasis, pronounces the wine "*genuine Johannisberg*, sir?"

And Mr. Humbug, of New York, with what a dashing air he calls for Delmonico himself, and "A-a-r, I say, Delmonico, my boy, my friends here have just returned from Europe; a-a-r, give us a bottle of that real Johannisberg: no nonsense, you know; for, by the living powers! I can tell from the color of a wine whether it grew on the east or west side of a house!"

Captain Yellowlump, of San Francisco, Nugget, of Sydney, and old Rupee, of Calcutta, all indulge in the same style, all drink Johannisberg, but all are first very careful to ask, *Is it genuine?* and being assured by the smiling landlord, in presence of their friends, that it is, they sip, and sip, and sip with unctuous satisfaction.

From England to India, from Maine to California, from California to Australia, the landlords all over the world will give you just whatever wine you choose to order — Tokay, Rüdesheim, Asti, Lachryma Christi, Lafitte, sparkling Catawba—no matter what. They are all in league with the accomplished gentleman that tapped the tables in Auerbach's cellar. A gimlet, a table, a cellar, and a few casks is all they require. By the genius of Cagliostro and Barnum! but men *do* like to be humbugged. They have a natural tendency toward that, as toward pride, selfishness, vice, luxury, aristocracy, or whatever else tends to make men mean and slavish.

The Johannisberg estate contains only seventy acres. A single prince will sometimes buy a whole year's produce, paying often as high as five dollars a bottle on the spot! and yet the whole world drinks Johannisberg!!!

I emptied the glass at a draft, and another, and another. I felt disgusted with the world, and took another—to think that men *will* be so bamboozled—one more—when they can get the real thing, right on the spot, too—a sip—and no false bottom in the bottle—madame's good health—wonder if she's not the daughter of the prince—sip, sip, sip—amazing large bottles, but the road long—*vita brevis est*—positively no more, *Madame Metternich!* She looks at me with disdain. "What! leave a drop of Johannisberg to dry in the bottle!" It was very pretty to reply, "My dear madame, not that I respect the wine less, but my head more;" but the bottle was too nearly empty for such a speech, and presently the last drops went purling along my palate—and I knew how Bacchus became a god!

As I strutted down the hill, with hat pompously cocked and cane performing the most surprising evolutions, I felt as if the chateau, the vineyards, and the whole estate belonged to me. My peasantry saluted me with uncommon deference and courtesy; they, no doubt, thought I was a scion of the house of Austria; and at that moment I would not have been at all surprised to see a messenger dashing up and placing dispatches in my hands from his majesty the Emperor of Austria! I was already revolving what advice I should give in the affair of Naples, when my toe struck a stone, and I fell in the mud. Astonishing how quickly the Emperor of Austria, the dispatch messenger, my estates and peasantry, all fled! There were only a few grinning boors about me as I got out of the puddle covered with slime—and then I knew how Bacchus became a beast!

I was glad to arrive at Mayence to repair damages. If I committed a sin in entering its big red-sandstone Cathedral *merely* for rest, I consoled myself by the thought that the motive was at least as worthy a one as curiosity, and a better one than that of the French, who converted it only forty years since into a barrack and magazine—the heathen! But I little thought what awaited me at the table d'hôte of the *Rheinischer Hof*. My neighbors were four whole-souled Germans whom I had never seen before. We became travelingly well acquainted during the dinner, so that, after the second bottle of Champagne, they were kind enough to inform me that I had met with *la crême de Mayence*—the very flower of the city. I responded by saying that America always sent her best men to European courts! (What if they had seen one of them issuing from a mud-puddle the day before!) Bows and salaams from both sides.

After dinner they invited me to take a drive with them. We went to two or three of the neighboring villages, in one of which they collected a party of young ladies and a few gentlemen, so that we had music and a dance. In another they asked me if I would take some beer. "Certainly." But imagine my surprise at seeing a whole keg brought up and placed leisurely and in a business-like manner upon the table! At sight of it I felt a sudden contraction of the abdomen, but at the same time chuckled in my coat-sleeves, "All right, silly youths! New Orleans and San Francisco *versus* Mayence!" I rapped the keg every time our glasses were empty, as if to show my readiness for more beer, but really out of anxiety to see what progress we were making. The operation was slower than I supposed; and not desiring to make a Bacchus of myself again in any shape, I struck my colors at the sixth round, and I had reason to see afterward that the defeated do not always finish the battle in the worst condition. *Au reste*, we passed a very delightful evening, returning to Mayence at about 11 P.M. After getting safely into my room, I found it necessary to reconsider my principle of doing in Turkey as the Turks do. After careful examination, I found it perfectly correct, but capable, like treaties, of several different constructions. Certainly, the best way to know people, their manners and customs, and to enjoy as well as benefit by travel, is to mingle with them as one of them, not insisting dogmatically on having your own ways, but indulging an amiable *laisser aller.* On the other hand, however, if one is continually changing places, he is apt to be continually entertained, and the consequence is, he is not doing as his entertainers do among themselves ordinarily, so that he may let his *laisser aller* go too far.

Truly, it seems as if all the hearts, vats, bottles, and cellars of Germany had lost their keys. I resolve to retreat forthwith to Wiesbaden to provide for this unforeseen difficulty!

To Wiesbaden is but a step. I have scarcely time to read one side of a newspaper before the gilded mausoleum of the Grand Duke's wife appears in view, and I am in the green basin of hills that contains the town, with its smoking springs—a delightful place in June, although that is not the fashionable month. To discover what is most comfortable, most agreeable, prettiest, or most convenient, find first what is most fashionable, and then select the reverse. Fortunately, I met here a very pleasant family from America. It was delightful to enjoy a little family life again after so many months of cosmopolitanism; it was delightful to trot to the springs every morning with Julie and Lulie, and drink hot *chicken-broth* instead of Johannisberg and Bock beer. No necessity for asking if it was genuine, because we saw it dipped right out of the cellars of the earth—deep, deep, no one knows how deep those cellars are. And then what a puffing and blowing to cool the hot beverage as we walked about under the colonnade in the cool morning air! and what long and serious consultations upon our various complaints, and the quantity requisite to cure each! Our faces would grow so serious on this point that we might have been taken for a school of peripatetic philosophers, the old baronet very well representing Plato. Mr. R—— was too fat; he wanted reducing. The baronet was too thin, and wanted to be fattened; the children were too lively, and wanted sobering; Mrs. R——, heaven only knows what she wanted; it was certainly not more color in her cheeks, nor more brilliancy of eye, nor more youthfulness, for the gentlemen always used to inquire of R—— how his *three* children were—he only had two (besides his wife)—but that she required mending in some way was evident, or else she would not be at the springs. The fat, the thin, the feeble, the strong, the delicate, the healthy, the rosy, and the pale, all feel as if something wanted repairing the moment they arrive at the springs. There was no ailment that chicken-broth would not reach; there was nothing it could not accomplish. If I were going to study Sanscrit even, I would go to Wiesbaden and drink chicken-broth!

Many were the surmises as to how far down were the kitchens where the soup was made. Did the chickens feed on pecan nuts, that aristocratic dish used only by Southern capons and Christmas Turkeys, or did they eat simply corn-meal mush? Did the cooks use Soyer's or Mrs. Leslie's cookery-books? Where did they get pepper and salt? What sort of a machine did they use to raise their soup to the surface? and why did they not send it up in the midst of Saint Giles' or Five Points, where the poor could help themselves, and thus save large cities the expense of soup societies? The wisest men of Wiesbaden could not answer these questions.

So much philosophy and salt never failed to produce an appetite by eight o'clock, and the little table at "The Rose," which was just big enough for four, was *very* snug for five; but the old rule that a breakfast for four is a breakfast for five proved fallacious in this case at least, and I should think it would always depend a good deal on who the fifth person is. What delicious little simplicities those Wiesbaden breakfasts, with the windows thrown wide open, and the fragrant June air filling the room! June air, and June roses, and the roses on children's cheeks, with their innocent flow of spirits, and country scenery—who can be subjected to such influences and not feel happy? *Ennui* was never known in such society; it is found just exactly in the spots where men expect it least, and where they go to avoid it—in the midst of noisy gayety and pleasure. It was born in the very city where there are most facilities for exciting and highly-seasoned enjoyments. The world can not produce so fine a specimen of an *ennuyé* as your true Parisian.

Satin and jewelryism have not yet made their appearance at Wiesbaden. The London season is hardly over, and imperial baptisms are occupying the Parisians, but Wiesbaden looks lovely nevertheless. A single tree is prettier than a whole tiara of diamonds; or, if you will have those beautiful gems, the fountain back of the Kursaal jets them up by millions, sparkling in the bright afternoon sun, and all of the *purest water!* What satins can compare with the fine sloping lawns! what society with the forests and rustic solitudes of the Taunus Hills!

The walk to the old Schloss is two miles. The

path runs along beside the noisiest brook that ever disturbed a meadow's quiet. Now it babbles, now it roars, now it makes a hollow, sonorous sound; it is just like a wild schoolboy trying his voice to see how many different noises he can make. I took that path so often that it seemed more like a stroll around a flower-bed than a four-mile walk. At other times *our* family would be seated under a tree by the pond, listening to the band of the Kursaal mingling its notes with the falling waters of the fountain. Our favorite spot was a bench right over the water, hidden from the main walk by a thicket on one side, but open toward the pond. Here we could see without being seen, like an Italian lady behind her jalousie. We were as much surrounded by natural scenery as if miles away by a lake in a forest; and at such a moment, to hear suddenly a piece from the last opera, or a polka played by a fine band, produced a confusion of sensations as singular as agreeable, the gayeties of Paris flitting about like fairies amid the pretty scenery of Wiesbaden.

FRANKFORT AND FIRST IMPRESSIONS.

"EVERY thing depends on first impressions," as the Irishman said when he broke loose from an experimental shower-bath where he had been standing a quarter of an hour, *cooling himself* before pulling the string. "Every thing depends on first impressions," as Lord Chesterfield observed to his son, who was starting forth on his career in the world. "Every thing depends on first impressions," as all travelers must have observed a thousand times over, whether in respect of men or cities. The only exception I am aware of is the impressions received during a "honey-moon," which are woefully deceiving, as I am informed by a French lady.

Rousseau entered the dark side of Paris, and said that, in spite of all the splendors of that city with which he afterward became acquainted, he never could entirely eradicate his first disagreeable impressions.

There are few travelers who are sufficiently self-commanding to see things at all times in any thing like their true light. A bilious stomach makes a jaundiced eye; a man with a tooth-ache will be sure to find every man he meets irritable, and tight boots and corns will destroy the finest architecture in the world. London, on a sunny day, would be nearly as handsome a city as Paris on a wet day.

I confess to considerable weakness on all these points. Good health, a blue sky, and a generally balmy state of self-satisfaction are to me very important ingredients in a fine landscape. Without them I had rather suspend an opinion.

There is no city of Europe with which I was more anxious to be pleased than with Frankfort; there is none where I less expected it. It is true, *Free City* said for my republican ears a great deal; even though it were merely a name, it recalls pleasant association; but I heard so much of its Jews and sausages, of its retail details and parsimony, of its lack of public spirit and dullness, that I was prepared for the *würst!* Even its praises, instead of being an inviting picture of what there was, rather suggested what there was not. What is to be seen in Frankfort was always answered by "The Ariadne," and "Rothschilds" when at home; when not at home, his house and gardens. Even Goëthe has been stolen by Germany, like Homer by Greece; and the Frankforters, to revenge themselves, at last erected a colossal bronze statue of him. Shakspeare undoubtedly belongs to England; but little Stratford-on-Avon is so proud of him, and cherishes him so much, that its name can not be mentioned without instantly recalling, before any thing else, that of this poet. Great cities should early take care of their great.

"And is *that* all there is in Frankfort?" said I to an Englishman at the springs. "Not another thing." "Then I have need of the sunniest day, my best spirits, and loosest boots; for, by the loves of a host of German cousins, if I don't like Frankfort, I'm a ruined man!"

So I picked out one very fine morning in the month of June, and left Wiesbaden in an early train, so as to arrive there at about eleven o'clock. There are not many days in the month of June (*certainly not thirty*), nor in any other month, more beautiful than that particular morning. A recent shower had not only laid the dust in the roads, but washed it off the trees, the flowers, and the grass, at the same time giving the atmosphere that peculiar freshness that man and nature both feel after a shower-bath.

Nowadays one's first impression of a city is generally received at the railway dépôt, and there is nothing on earth more practical looking than a rail-road dépôt. The heaps of iron and useless wheels, the piles of boxes, barrels, hogsheads, bags, bundles, packages, etc., together with long rows of empty luggage-cars, or heaps of coal, all smell of just what a traveler for recreation wants to get away from, viz., the every-day realities of life. Moreover, the city dépôt is generally placed so that one has to thread the very worst and dirtiest part of the town to get to and from it. I was prepared for all this too; so my surprise was great, on emerging from a clean and well-arranged dépôt, to find myself in a flower-garden where I expected to see only filthy lanes. There is hardly a city of its size in Europe that meets you on a fine summer day with such a cordial, welcome smile as the garden-belted city of Frankfort! So much for the inanimate greeting.

After washing off a little of the traveling dust at my hotel, I repaired to the house of my friends *who were to be*, although I had never seen them, rather curious to get a first insight into German family life, but a little dubious as to how things would move on the score of languages, I speaking no German, and ignorant whether they could speak French or English.

There is certainly nothing more ludicrous for a *third* person than to stand by and watch two parties who wish to be very kind and polite to one another, but yet who are incapable of making themselves understood. They use their tongues quite freely at first, which not being followed by the expected results, they gradually resort to signs and gesticulations, then to grimaces, and finally settle down into fixed grins, which, being an uncomfortable position for the features, soon grow into a very grim and savage expression, and the chances are that they will end with a fight!

My fears were speedily dissipated on passing through the Zeil, and entering the house occupied by the gentleman I wished to see. He welcomed me in excellent English, and immediately called his wife, who did the same in French, and it was not long before the whole family, nearly every one of whom, including the children, could speak French, and often French and English, were around me. I have never in my life, on entering a strange city, felt so completely at home on the first day as in the city of Frankfort. How many questions they put me about their friends in America, and with what eagerness they pressed up to me to hear my answers! They were all to dine with some relatives of theirs that day, and as the dinner-hour was half past twelve, of which it only lacked half an hour, I was taken without any ceremony to their friends' house, and made one of the party. There were parts of three families represented, and, including the children, there were at least twenty persons at the table. I was at first perfectly bewildered with the number of children, and could hardly tell which was which; but beginning with the Fritzes, of which there were two little ones and one big one—the three comprising all the roguery of the party—I gradually sorted them all out. If you see a Fritz in Germany, you may be sure he is *tant soit peu fripon*, just a little bit of a rogue, sometimes a pretty big bit. They are like the English Jacks, always cunning and mischievous. Wilhelms are generally sober and quiet, with a good many solid qualities—slow, but sure, just like our Williams. I was amused at the suppressed fun that, while kept in at the mouth, would leak out at the eyes of the eager faces around me; and, as I anticipated, it only needed a few spoonfuls of soup and a few mouthfuls of white wine to warm up the whole party of little ones, and melt the ice which restrained them. They were of all ages from six to nineteen, and all brothers and sisters or cousins, and on that day were met together to celebrate the confirmation of one of their number. They were therefore allowed to let out their mirth almost unrestrained; and though it never reached too high a pitch—at any rate, never so as to be boisterous, yet they were occasionally checked a little, perhaps in anticipation of their getting the bit in their teeth and going off at a break-neck, or, rather, break-plate-and-glasses pace that would be difficult to stop.

A German dinner is a serious business, as every one knows, and performed at a serious hour of the day, particularly when the thermometer stands at 90° Fahrenheit. I therefore prayed for strength to be enabled to go through the performance creditably to myself and the polite hostess, as well as to show the children that a *free American citizen* was not such a savage but that he could dine on a dozen courses as well as on fruits and acorns; for I did not yet know what might be the character borne by my countrymen in Frankfort, having only a little while before been asked by a Prussian gentleman what color the Americans were, and what language they spoke. I turned a little pale as I thought of the big dishes of *saur kraut*, and *leberwursts*, and other German *delicacies* which I expected to see momentarily enter; and I must confess that, after doing justice to a great many good things, as asparagus, delicious chickens, etc., I was surprised and somewhat disappointed to see neither the one nor the other of the looked-for dishes appear. In short, my first dinner in Frankfort, and the cordial spontaneity with which I was invited to it, will long be remembered by me with pleasure. The hospitality that will admit a stranger suddenly to a family holiday-party is very rare, and the perfect cordiality on all sides that will make him feel a welcome guest on such occasions is perhaps rarer still.

After the coffee, my friend Herr F—— took me around to his brother's house, where we spent an agreeable evening with the family, consisting of five persons. Here there was the same genuine welcome as before, accompanied by that hearty earnestness and simplicity which so distinguishes the German character. The afternoon being pleasant, a walk was proposed by Herr W——, to which I willingly acceded, although it cost me a new Paris hat. Nearly every citizen we met took off his hat, struck his right knee with it, and then replaced it. I thought at first all these bows were intended for myself, supposing that, perhaps, it was a polite compliment paid strangers, but afterward I learned that I had been walking with a senator and late burgomaster of the city. However, sticking to my rule to observe the customs of the country, I took off my hat every time any body else took off his, performing the operation fifty-three times by count (to say nothing of touches to *unimportant people* and boys), and completely breaking down the rim of the right-hand side of it; but I did not regret this at all, for who knows but that this very habit of airing the head so often may keep away the cholera from Frankfort (which, it appears, never visits that city), and so may be conducive to general health?

We walked around the beautiful gardens which girt the city, and which are laid out in shady paths and secluded walks, along which numerous seats are placed. Here the Frankforters resort during the warm summer afternoons to enjoy the fresh air unheated by bricks and mortar. These grounds were formerly the ramparts of the city, and Frankfort is not the only city that has discovered that trees and shrubs are a better protection for towns than stone walls and twenty-four-pounders. Mannheim and a good many other European cities bear testimony of what a sad misfortune it is to be a fortified town. Fortifications place them in the position of those individuals who carry revolvers to protect themselves, but which generally invite their destruction. Is this the beginning of that great change which is prophesied, in which all the swords are to be turned into plowshares? The present state of Europe does not look like it. Austria is showing her teeth to England because John Bull is peeping through the gratings of certain dungeons; Naples is snarling; Spain is melting up all the roofs of the houses, the leaden spoons, gas-pipes, and gutters, to make bullets to decrease her own population; Sardinia is polishing her bayonets and throwing up breastworks, the dust from which, in a west wind, blows right into the Emperor Francis Joseph's eyes, who is afraid to stop Victor Emanuel's sport lest John Bull step in and substitute his big fist for Piedmont dirt. The Russian bear feels uncommonly strong. He never knew his strength until lately; he is now sharpening his claws and teeth; he will be the most terrible animal in Europe! Brother Jonathan looks on quietly, and is thankful that 3000 miles of ocean roll between him and this quarrelsome, distrustful family of nations. The Millennium is not come yet.

We continued our walk to the new cemetery, where Herr W—— pointed out to me the fine bas-reliefs by Thorwaldsen on the tomb of the Bethman family, as well as the Reichenbach monument, etc. This cemetery is well worth visiting, too, on account of the views it commands. There is no spot near the city affording so fine a view of the Taunus and of the city itself. A supper at eight or nine o'clock at the house of Herr T—— closed the day and my first happy impressions of Frankfort.

My intention had been to remain there only two or three days, but, hardly suspecting it, I soon found that I had staid nine, and was among a circle of warm-hearted friends, in which I could very willingly have remained nine months. Every day there was some excursion to be made, or some long walk to take to a neighboring wood or about the town itself. But, with the exception of the old Cathedral and the Römer, I did not go into a single public building of Frankfort in nine days, having absolutely not a moment to spare from the living curiosities. So the Städel and Senkenberg museums, and even Dannecker's statue, not visible at the time of my visit, together with the public library, must form part of the amusements of a future visit.

On Whit-Monday it has been the custom from time immemorial for the whole city, man, woman, and child, to move out en masse to the Frankfort wood to spend the day, or a portion of it, in such rural amusements as may suit the various tastes of the parties concerned. I must acknowledge that, after all the picture-galleries, and libraries, and statues I had seen in different parts of Europe, such an opportunity for seeing the people, and their habits and customs, presented more charms to me than all the best paintings of the town, particularly since the collection of the latter is not very large nor celebrated when compared with those of more favored cities.

"The proper study of mankind is man,"

and it is not often that a whole city is so obliging as to spread itself out for your inspection under the shady trees of a forest.

At two o'clock in the afternoon we started in a large party for the wood, going down to the banks of the Main, and intending to take one of the boats which were continually moving down, laden with passengers, to the appointed spot; but they were all so overcrowded and looked so top-heavy that, though the ladies were not afraid, the gentlemen were afraid for them, and we therefore all started afoot down the river banks, which were lined on both sides by thousands of pedestrians.

I have always observed that in Germany a party of ladies and gentlemen going on a pleasure excursion will generally separate, and you may mix them up together as often as you choose, but you will soon find the ladies by themselves again, while the men will be at a little distance off, as if entirely unconscious of their presence. Whether they are afraid of one another, like the Methodists in their churches, or whether the Germans are *built* on different principles from the rest of mankind, and prefer, each and all, their own sex to the company of the other, I can not say, but the consequence of the fact is that the German ladies have learned very well to take care of themselves. They can leap any gutter you can leap, walk as far as you can walk, and, in short, I think, if all the men were to emigrate, Germany would march on straight forward, or, rather, stand stock still, in spite of all innovation, just as she has done for centuries.

Long before we arrived at the wood we could hear the hum of many mingled voices, occasionally drowned by the music of a circus band or other instrumentation of that genus. As we approached, the crowd with which we were borne along grew more dense, as its flow was momentarily checked by that which was circulating among the trees. Now the tables spread in the vicinity gave notice that we had arrived at our destination, and, in fact, we had to go but little farther to find ourselves in the very midst of the *new* Frankfort.

The whole appeared like a huge picnic party, or as the children of Israel may be supposed to have looked during one of their forty years in the wilderness; and, indeed, there were a good many of the children of Israel there on the present occasion, only, instead of *manna*, they were feeding on *sausages and bock beer*, which I have no doubt they preferred to the delicate diet over which their ancestors grumbled so much.

Eating and drinking seemed to be the principal part of the ceremony, and beer the principal part of the drinking. The beer flowed in rivers, and yet the people were always thirsty (the consummation most devoutly wished), or, if not thirsty, huge slices of *leberwurst* soon made them so. I looked on with fear; for, being a lover of beer myself, I was afraid that the city would be entirely deprived of that beverage for a week afterward. In some places long rows of tables were placed, surrounded by broad, good-natured faces, more fleshly than spiritual, and groaning (not the faces) under jugs, mugs, bottles, bowls, and any thing else that would hold the national beverage; while the interstices were filled with bread, rolls, *petzkuchen* (a pet cake in Frankfort), *boobies' shanks* (I spell it phonographically; there may be an error of a letter or two), *brödchen mit umständen*, saur kraut, cold puddings, and the ubiquitous *würst*. In other places a large party would be seated on the ground—I do not say because they *could not get up*, though one of the Fritzes slyly insinuated something of the kind, but because they could not get a big barrel around which they were seated up with them; they therefore preferred to be near the faucet; and it made one thirsty on that warm day to see how eagerly they held the long glasses under the steady flow of the golden-colored liquid, and how, with sparkling eyes, they put it to their lips, as if Paradise lay in the bottom of the mug. Your true German likes to drink his beer out of a glass a foot long, and, if they were not so tenacious of old customs, they would soon have the glasses a yard deep instead of a foot. He likes to regale his eyes with the long sea of beer between his lips and the bottom of the glass; and as he turns it slowly but surely down, he watches the foam breaking against the sides, and delights his eyes with the little beads rising to the surface and bursting into tiny spray! As he approaches the end of the draft, he sighs, and puffs, and sighs again, to think how fleeting are all earthly enjoyments; and when the last drop disappears, he closes his eyes and smacks his lips in an ecstasy of delight, meanwhile bringing his glass down *whack* upon the table, which, if there is a waiter near, is merely a signal to have it filled again forthwith and without further notice. It is a singular fact, but history never mentions the case of a German who has had as much beer as he wanted! Capacity always fails before appetite.

Scattered among the merry crowds were booths and stands where refreshments of all kinds were sold, including even wines, of which the white wines of the country were most prominent. There were also many women who were occupied in making coffee in big kettles, and over big fires, and there seemed to be a pretty good demand for that too. I was disappointed in not hearing more music; in fact, I did not hear a single good chorus, and but little singing of any kind.

After walking about for an hour and viewing every thing that was to be seen, we were fortunate enough to find two vacant tables in one of the prettiest parts of the wood, where the ladies took their seats, while Carl, Fritz, Wilhelm, and Adolf were dispatched for refreshments; and, gauging our thirst by their own, they were not long in returning well laden with bottles, nearly one a piece, I think, for the whole company, not counting what they had drunk on the way. A plentiful supply of substantials accompanied the bottles, and we all satisfied our thirst and appetite, leaving enough behind for our successors to set up a small shop.

Not being yet well acquainted with German customs, I committed a great mistake in the forest; and though I did it quite innocently, I can not say I look back upon it with any feelings of regret, although I am sorry to learn that it caused for a while great excitement among the young beaux of that city, who thought they were about to have a young lady removed from their midst and carried away to America. When the crowd grew pretty thick in the woods, some were in danger of getting separated. I offered my arm to the Fraulein H—x on the one side, and the Fraulein G—tle on the other, never suspecting that I was committing one of the gravest errors known to the German code of manners; and I never discovered till a month afterward, in Heidelberg, that such an act between unmarried persons indicates an engagement. Coming from America, too, I have no doubt many thought I must be a Mormon and had made two converts! I do not know what the young ladies themselves thought, but must commend their good sense and absence of squeamishness, and, I might add, *good taste*, in quietly accepting the proffered arms, and not fainting away on the spot, as a French lady would under like circumstances.

We arrived at home at eight or nine o'clock, still leaving thousands upon the grounds.

On our return we found the usual nine o'clock supper prepared, which in Germany is rather a heavy meal. It generally consists of eggs or sausages, and salad, with white wine. There are marvelous stories in circulation about German eating, which are not without foundation, but which, at the same time, are by no means of universal truth. They are best retold by repeating what a nephew of mine said of his school in Frankfort. Adolf, like all schoolboys, after raking his brain for grievances, eagerly seized upon my question as to whether he had enough to eat as a very proper outlet for a growl. He couldn't exactly say he didn't have enough, but there were times when he couldn't eat at the regular hours, and then he was sometimes hungry before the next turn came. "Well," I inquired, "how often do the turns come?" "Oh," he said, "in the morning we have our bread and milk; after that the *ten o'clock*, and then comes dinner at twelve; then we have the *four o'clock*, with tea at six, and supper at nine!" "Very well, my boy; I don't wonder that you lose your appetite sometimes when the *regular turn* comes."

I found that this routine of meals (excepting the tea) was very common in some parts of Germany; but there are many families who take no morning luncheon, though sometimes a light sweet bread with their coffee at two or three o'clock in the afternoon. Thus the German style of eating is very simple. They eat when they are hungry, and a man who takes rolls and coffee only at seven or eight in the morning is sure to have a pretty good appetite at twelve or one. The style of the New Englanders is just the same, only that they take no wine, but little meat in summer, and tea at six o'clock instead of a wine supper at nine. That is still nearer nature. The savages approach nearer yet; they eat whenever they can get any thing to eat, provided their wants and opportunities coincide. I do not think it so great a virtue, this approaching to nature, as many suppose. Our heads were given us to improve on nature. It is a very easy thing to approach nature a little too closely, as in dress, for instance, but this is only tolerated among Feejee Islanders. I am not particular about what I dine on, nor when I get it, provided I am *sure* to get it. I have made a very fine dinner at eleven o'clock in the morning among naked Indians who had never seen a fork or a table. We were squatted around a fire on the banks of the Coquille River, and the dinner consisted of two courses: first, some large fat mussels, just picked off the rocks in the Pacific Ocean; second, hazel-nuts that grew in the woods behind us. In New Orleans, a plump Pompano always found me ready at three. In New York, a "plain roast" and potatoes, with "*circumstances*," as the Germans say, was always welcome at five. In New England, at twelve I invariably sent up my plate three times for *succotash*. I never gave an extra snore at night for having indulged too heavily in black plum-pudding and XX at six in Old England; and I have performed a day's routine at a German table without the first sign of a nightmare. But, for all this, I have my preferences, which are, to get my feet under the mahogany at six, and to let them rest there until half past seven, while the top of the table is served *à la Française*.

I do not at all believe with Buillat Savarin, who

says, "Tell me what you eat and I'll tell you what you are," that because a man eats pork he must certainly be a pig. (He certainly tends that way, however.) But I do believe that the French have studied the art of eating for centuries to some purpose, and come nearer obeying one of Solomon's wise hints than any other nation. For when that great man says, "Woe unto thee, O people, when thy princes eat and drink in the morning," he evidently intended that they should eat and drink in the evening, when the business of the day was over, and when they had leisure to be sociable. As every man who will go to America may be a prince, therefore the "woe" applied to the whole world; and therefore, as the Germans have commenced innovations in the matter of railways, they might as well go a step farther, and make Savarin a classic, and pay Soyer a pension to live in their country.

Frankfort is one of the pleasantest cities in Germany for a residence, and the new town is conspicuous for the splendor of many of its buildings, as are also the suburbs for that, and for the beautiful large gardens which are attached to them. The people are hospitable and intelligent, and if the place is not distinguished for its curiosities and public buildings, like many other cities, still the stranger who may be already tired of such things will not lack for amusements, particularly during the summer. He will find himself in the very centre of watering-places, excursions, and fine scenery. At the Casino he will find more newspapers and periodicals than at almost any club-room in Europe—a great many more than at Galignani's at Paris, while Jugel will give him a book on any subject in any language. The advantages for education, too, in Frankfort are great, particularly for young ladies; therefore the people are generally very intelligent. It is very common there, as elsewhere in Germany, for people to have their *specialités*. One will be a thorough botanist, another a geologist, a third a chemist, and a fourth an amateur painter, and all this while attending to their mercantile or ordinary business.

I was quite astonished, in taking a party of the children to Wiesbaden, to see these little people, while walking through the grounds, suddenly stop their play. One would pick up a flower, examine it, class it, tell all about it, and stow it away in her tin case. Adolf startled me by suddenly diving, like a duck upon a June-bug, upon an insect upon which I was about to tread, and the animal was forthwith stowed away in his bottle, to take its place beside some two or three hundred he had collected and classified. This induced me to examine the party on arriving home, the result of which was that Carl played on the piano some fine music of Beethoven; Fritz showed me hundreds of seals he had collected of all the different states of Europe, coats of arms, etc.; he also makes fancy boxes, toys, and little useful articles with a skill quite surprising for his age, which is about twelve or thirteen; another had a large botanical collection, and nearly all excelled in some one department.

But the whistle sounds—the train is off! Farewell thou fine old city! Thy nine days' hospitality has made my last impressions as agreeable as my first.

A DAY IN THE ODENWALD.

Having been well drenched by rain at the ruins of Rheinfels, and had my coat whitened by a mid-May snowstorm among the Taunus Hills, I felt prepared for any thing that might happen on the top of Melibocus, even for fine weather. All the landlords of Germany as well as myself had been praying for this during the last three weeks; but as the peasants and farmers had, perhaps, been making counter-prayers with better reason and more faith, the rain continued harder than ever, and with a good west wind, which promises, in this country, plenty more of it.

I left the train at Bickenbach, walking along the Bergstrasse as far as Zwingenberg, and there commenced the ascent of the mountain. A slight shower was falling, but as the sun had appeared at intervals during the morning, I hoped to be favored at the top with a good view. Taking one of the short cuts through the woods, I soon discovered that I had taken a very muddy as well as a very slippery one; and where it was not muddy and slippery, the long grass, dripping with rain, wet me thoroughly up to my knees.

How delightful are the beauties of Nature! thought I, as the mingled rain and perspiration dropped from my face. The next moment I slipped and fell on my knees in the mud, and, though it was neither the first nor the last time, I toiled on, reaching the top of the mountain in about an hour and a half. The boy at the tower seemed to look "What fool's this?" but bustled about in search of his spy-glass, which had a winter's cobwebs over the glasses, and also gave me his register and a last year's pen to inscribe my name. I dislike putting my name to any thing, even to a bill payable, but most of all upon tower walls and registers; it's quite enough to fill a line in the hotel book, while the curious landlord rubs his hands and watches for the profession you may insert—and, by-the-by, it's always better to fill up that space with something—traveler, merchant, misanthrope, etc., or you will find that mine host has made a *rentier* of you next morning—on paper, of which, unfortunately, you are on too much already.

At the top of the tower I and my ill humor had reached our climax; neither could get any higher. I looked at the boy diabolically; he was screwing the glass to the stand. Evidently he was mocking me; a thick haze shut in the foot of the mountain even; what the de'il to do with a glass when my eyes were of no service! My fingers itched to pitch boy and glass over the tower wall, instead of which I gave him a dozen kreuzers and descended, ashamed that a little mist between me and the sun could have such an effect upon my spirits; but I am not philosopher enough to enjoy a thing without possessing it.

Descending on the side toward the pretty village of Auerbach, the sun came out brightly as I reached that lovely valley between it and the mountain. A good many peasants were scattered along the road, returning from a funeral. They were dressed in their best last-century fashions—that is, the men having long-tailed coats, such as the dandies of to-day in

New York are pleased to consider handsome, and the women short-waisted gowns. Other peasants were mowing in the field, and the half-wilted grass sent up a fresher and more agreeable odor than that which comes from rose-bushes. The road, winding around the foot of the mountain, and in a narrow valley, seemed walled on all sides with green. Every step brought a new view. How quiet, peaceful, and contented was the face of both man and nature in this happy spot, lighted by the warm sun! My equanimity of spirits returned amid such soothing influences, and I was rejoiced at not having pitched the boy and glass from the tower, but could not help thinking that the world at the top and the world at the foot of Melibocus were two very different worlds.

Auerbach, if not examined in detail, a scrutiny no German town can bear, is one of the prettiest little villages on the Bergstrasse, and with its castle, and Melibocus, and lovely valley, and the shady walks leading to them, may well tempt the passing traveler to linger a day and visit the neighborhood. The houses, though rustic and common, have a picturesque look, owing to a cornice of vine-leaves over the entrance and first-story windows; and as this vine, which extends in a horizontal line along the whole front of each house, is nourished by only one stem, and that so small as to be often unnoticed, the village has the appearance of being decorated artificially for some holiday, rather than of wearing its every-day dress of green.

Mine host of the Krone Inn will give you as good a beefsteak as you ever ate in your life to fortify you for a day's fatigue, but, like all steaks in Germany ordered by an Englishman, it will be only half cooked. The poor cooks over the whole Continent have been so berated for a number of years by John Bull for cooking all the juices out of their meat, as is the custom throughout Germany, that now they go to the other extreme, and serve up beef to an Englishman literally raw. They imagine that for the Bull as for the Lion, a little shaking in the sun is all that is necessary to render a steak palatable.

The English deserve the thanks of the traveling world for what they have done to improve the hotels on the Continent, even though they have neglected their own at home. They have drilled the landlords of the Rhine until one can fare better at most of the inns near that river than he can in England, and this in respect of the very comforts on which the English pride themselves most, viz., beds, room-furniture, and cooking. Comforts! indeed, the word is obsolete in English hotels, but cost remains. It was once comfort by comparison, but the pupils have surpassed their teachers, and one may now have a better dinner better cooked, a better room, and better bed, and better service in the larger cities of Germany than in England; besides which, he will not have to pay a shilling every time he turns around or a sixpence a bow to a white-cravated, sexton-like waiter. 'Tis true, the roast beef of England is still unapproached; it occupies a proud pre-eminence; but for the pudding I must declare in favor of Germany, particularly after a hearty dinner. The English are very fond of what is old, and point with pride to that venerable *old bed*, which has been pressed by eleven thousand three hundred and twenty-five travelers of every age and condition—of cleanliness; and to that revered old carpet, laid down in the time of the Georges; and to those dingy worsted bed and window curtains, that have filtered so much breath, fog, and smoke. A feather bed is, fortunately, never to be met with on the Continent. It is a bad enough thing to have one at home that none but yourself has used; but in a hotel, to give feather beds to travelers, as in England, is really a barbarity.

But leaving beds and inns, and particularly the krone of Auerbach, where I had made a very good dinner, I walked along the Bergstrasse, hoping for a finer afternoon than the morning had been, in which I was disappointed, for it soon began to rain, and it rained at every place where there was any thing to be seen: it rained at Benshiem, and it rained at the Abbey of Lorsch, and it rained at Heppenheim, and at Starkenburg Castle, and I began to think the Bergstrasse but a very sorry road, after all the praise it has received. To be in harmony with the elements, I gave up sight-seeing, and entered an inn to drink some beer. Two Germans were talking politics and smoking pipes over a bottle of white wine—that is, one talked all the time, and the other said *ja*, or *ja, ja—a!* A gray cat sat on the rough board table, of which there were several, and these and the landlord were the only occupants of the large, smoke-impregnated room. The latter came up, bowing low, and inquired what I would choose, as if his cellar contained all the vintages of the known world. Upon my replying *beer*, he raised himself up with surprise and majesty, and said that in *first class hotels* they did not drink beer. Glancing around at the board tables, dirty Germans, gray cat, and smoked walls, I felt like begging to be shown a *second class hotel*—a glance, however, that the worthy Herr no doubt mistook for one of admiration, as he smilingly went after a bottle of *Tischwein* which I ordered. This is a very queer thing in Germany. Beer is every where; every body drinks it; every body likes it: beer may be said to flow through the streets even—in *bodies and bottles*, and yet there are in the villages certain dirty fourth class inns, assuming to themselves, however, the title of first class, where you will really give offense by being so vulgar as to call for beer, in place of which, if you drink at all, you must drink some sour wine—the poorest made in the neighborhood. As a beverage, I had much rather have their good beer (which I like better even than English ale or porter) than most of the ordinary Rhine wines; and the German enthusiast is not wrong who says that Bavarian beer will soon be drunk the world over. He may see it already drunk in immense quantities on the Pacific coast of America. Another strange thing about this beer-drinking is, that although high and low pour down beer at all hours of the day and night, they never drink it at dinner.

The rain had now ceased, but neither returning serenity of weather nor of spirits could induce me again to try the road and the sights, or, indeed, any thing else but the quick and sure railway train, which would pass in an hour. I followed a lane leading to the station, which, like most stations in Germany, had a large and pretty garden around it, while the walls of the building itself were covered with ivy-vines, the whole having as rural a look as the most confirmed lover of country life and country things could desire. No poet, whose dreams beside a purling brook have been destroyed by the shrill whistle of the train; no conservative old gentleman, who sighs for the olden time, and the crack of the driver's whip, and the bustle of the post-inn, but would, in this country, become a convert to railway systems, particularly if, for want of one, toward the close of a wet day, fatigued and muddy, he found himself compelled to walk fifteen miles to the next city, or lodge in a dirty room in some small village. To see the finest scenery now, it is not necessary to count hours and days of jolting in a stage-coach before arrival at the spot to be visited; the train is ready—it starts at the minute—it whirls you over uninteresting ground, and drops you where the view is fine, and, instead of getting out and walking through scattered car-wheels and bars of iron to enter a severe, business-like station-house, you walk between rose-bushes and shade-trees, and into a pretty ornamental building clad with ivy, which rather arrests your attention than makes you turn away with disgust.

It was five o'clock in the afternoon, and the weather had become warm and lovely; the sun was shining brightly, and the grass was nearly dried. To while away an hour, I threw myself down on the green lawn by the road side, near two peasant-girls who were resting themselves, with their large baskets of grass beside them. The air was fresh and pure, as ever after a shower, and richly perfumed with the blossoms of the cherry and apple orchards which grew on all sides.

Along the road were passing carts drawn by *cows*, yoked up and doing the work of oxen; and in the fields were women hoeing, and planting, and doing the work of men. It is painful—it is a shame to see women at work in the field—to see our mothers, who are weaker than we are, do double the work that we do; for they must not only do their household work, and suffer all those pains and trials peculiar to their sex, but they must undergo this after having toiled in the midday sun. It is wrong, contrary to nature, and adverse to the interests of a nation. Keep your women and your Sabbaths properly, and your nation will *never* grow old and die. Every thing else will take care of itself. The two peasant-girls and myself were soon good friends; they were both young—that is, from sixteen to twenty years of age, and both had faces not very pretty, but full of good-nature and modesty, the chief characteristics of all German faces. After some ludicrous attempts at understanding and being understood, I managed to discover they had carried their baskets (zwei stunde) two hours. Now all the way from Bonn to Heppenheim I had been wondering what might be the weight of those baskets carried by the women, and a better chance to try could not be found than the present. So, very much to the surprise of the maidens, I took the basket of the larger, and was trying to lift it upon my head, when, very much to *my* surprise and their astonishment, it tumbled over t'other side, like vaulting ambition. They both turned very red, which I supposed was an evidence of putting themselves on a war footing, a contest I was certainly anxious to avoid with Amazons who carried such weights, not to mention their personal solidity; but when they could hold in no longer, they both burst out laughing, in which, though at my expense, I was too happy to join, and we laughed and picked up the grass together, and I helped them to raise their baskets on their heads, and saw them move chattingly away with their *guten abends* and burdens just as the shrill whistle announced the arrival of the Frankfort train.

In five minutes I was dashing past the pleasing beauties of the Bergstrasse—which I had intended to view at a pace of *three* miles an hour—at the rate of *thirty* miles an hour. Thirty miles of mountain, forest, vineyard, vale, and brook in an hour, and by the glowing light of the setting sun! It was a sin, but a lovely, delicious sin, and I leaned back to enjoy it leisurely and consciously, after taking a survey of my fellow-travelers in a third class carriage. I must tell you that a third class carriage does not make a third class man, as you are apt to suppose in America, for in that country you are beginning to out-aristocrat all aristocracy. On the Continent, and in Germany particularly, people of third class *means* know how to behave themselves; and though I have traveled but few times in that conveyance, I have always found exactly as much decorum and decency as in the first and second class carriages, and of course more simplicity. The words rowdy and rough have no synonym in Germany: no such character exists. I am sorry I can not say as much for my own country and for England. The rough and the rowdy have their homes among the Anglo-Saxon. The former has no idea of the qualities belonging to a gentleman; and the latter, who dresses like and pretends to be a gentleman, never is one. The latter is the worse character, and belongs to America; the former is English.

My fellow-travelers were composed of bourgeois principally (with some few peasants), who were taking a pleasure excursion to various places on the road. Opposite me were a gentleman and his daughter, who was a very pretty and modest girl of some eighteen years of age. They were from the neighborhood, as I inferred, because the father was reading aloud from some German poet, which seemed much to interest both; but no poet could steal the attention of a stranger to such beautiful scenery from the very works which inspire poesy. What a poet could not do, however, the young maiden did for me very frequently, for I could not help watching her changing and artless expression as she gave vent to her feelings in her face. So I was leaning back to enjoy these double charms of nature without and within, happy with either, but doubly happy with both, when suddenly, ere ten minutes of enjoyment had passed away, a large cinder flew in my eye, and gave me such keen pain that I could not open it again during the remainder of the day, nor did I get even another glimpse of scenery all the way to Heidelberg; but I thought I saw through my falling tears some evidence of sympathy on the part of the fair girl who sat opposite, which was gratifying, and yet, perhaps, her sympathy was for some fictitious character of the poet. There is nothing certain in life but death—a fact confirmed by my experience of a day's anticipated pleasure in the Odenwald—a day I had dreamed of for half a lifetime—a day of repeated allurements, followed by repeated disappointments—a day emblematic of all the days of man's journey through life—man ever pursuing and never attaining.

The Odenwald shall not be revisited, but it shall remain mapped in memory as it is, the most useful chart of all my voyages, to serve as a guide for a longer voyage than any I have yet made.

The cinder baffled all efforts to extract it, but was felt till long past midnight, when kind Nature did for me, with my eyes shut, what I and others could not do with them open.

HEIDELBERG AND THE BARBER'S SON.

Heidelberg is a jewel because of its rich setting; strip it of that, and view it in the midst of a large plain, and it would remain as unnoticed among other German cities as a Scotch pebble among diamonds and pearls. Whatever pertains to the town is unremarkable; whatever pertains to the environs, even to the very borders of the town, is full of beauty. Its churches are not particularly interesting, and its buildings, save one, are unattractive. That one, *Zum Ritter*, shows what Heidelberg must have been as a *town* before it became the constant butt of thunder-bolts and bomb-shells, a plaything for French armies.

But if Heidelberg, with its long Haupstrasse and short side-streets, considered merely as a collection of buildings, be a dull place, there is certainly no city in Germany that has more attractions in other respects to render a residence agreeable. The castle, situated above the town, is an unfailing source of pleasure from its historical interest, from the views it commands, from its winding, shady walks, and from the varied society from all parts of the world which selects its grounds during the summer for an afternoon promenade. In fine weather a band of music enhances the beauties of this charming spot. The neighborhood abounds in delightful excursions to suit every taste. The climbing enthusiast may mount the Kaiserstühl; the lover of a quiet, secluded nook may seek the Wolfsbrunnen, and regale himself on delicious mountain trout caught under his own eye, while his mind is regaling on the ever-changing foliage of the mountains, slopes, and valleys around; the invalid may make a most agreeable excursion, either by carriage or steamer, up the valley of the Neckar to Neckarsteinach, or even to Heilbronn; in short, whichever way the traveler turns, he finds something to invite his attention. All roads lead to Rome, but from Heidelberg all roads lead to beauty.

Like many another traveler who comes here to remain a day, I find myself engaged for a month. With a quiet room overlooking the Neckar, and said to have been last occupied by a prince, which, although not saying much for princely life, is most likely, as they form the majority of the population in Germany, I am now prepared to scour the whole country, like the robbers of the Rhine, but in search of treasures which can not be handled, but which may be carried away, nevertheless, in the brain.

It is hard to get away from Heidelberg. To the

traveler who has come from Brussels over the usual highway of cities, it presents features entirely different from any that precede it. It is to the glories of Switzerland what Drachenfels is to the Rhine—a new overture to another opera. The scenery has suddenly become as majestic and grand as is compatible with perfect elegance and grace. A little more boldness of the mountain, a little more view of naked rock, a little more precipitousness of the sides of the valley, and you would pronounce it wildly grand. It is just at that point at which we have seen some rare men, who, though the very type of all that is bold and masculine, display a refinement and delicacy of expression and manner that would ornament the finest gentleman of Paris. A little addition of weight, or size, or strength, or of fire in the eye—in short, a particle more of virility, and they would be too coarse. From descriptions we have read of him, we fancy Kit North (Professor Wilson) to have been such a style of man.

My corner window sweeps the landscape far and wide, including in its view the castle, the Kaiserstühl, the city, the Neckar, and its charming valley, so modest, like all German people and valleys, that, after running but a short distance from me, it hides behind a jutting hill and is seen no more, unless I chase it, when it will play hide-and-go-seek with me all the way to Heilbronn! At night, when the moon is high in the heavens, and its rays come reflected up from the water, the valley looks especially lovely, and then it is musical. All night long I hear the rippling of the river over its rocky bed, and now the whispering voices of the leaves under my window, and now both are blended together. Sometimes, in the earlier part of the night, their music is interrupted by the patriotic chorus of a party of students returning from their mountain ramble; sometimes it is the more unpracticed song of the peasants, and again it will be the guitar and violin of a young couple seated by a fountain in a neighboring garden, who often delight me with their music.

But when morning returns again the valley is quiet, or, rather, its music is drowned by the noises of day.

Now, as the sun rises, the market-women begin to pass my window and cross the bridge over to the city, for my room is opposite the town, in a space between mountain and river so narrow that if the former were to take a freak of crowding a few feet, it would topple the house and contents into the water. Boats which have floated down the rapid current to Mannheim without wind or steam, like the flats on the Mississippi River, unlike them, are now being drawn up again by horses, empty or laden with coal, etc. The English are starting out for their morning walks, and companies of students are to be seen strolling around in all directions, for these boys are omnipresent. Go to the top of the mountain, and there is a student; sit down to any table d'hôte in the city, and there is a student; plunge into the highest or lowest beer-shop in the city, and there is a student. They consider themselves a part of the scenery of the place, and therefore depute one or several of their number to every visitable spot in the vicinity, where they may be found at all hours of the day and night. It is foolishly supposed that these young men come here to study, but I am happy to correct such an error; they are too sensible to lose the heydey time of life over musty books. Life is to them a masquerade, and, to keep up the illusion, they wear travesty; they deck themselves with yellow, scarlet, white, and gold-banded caps, and wear shawls for *style* in hottest weather—a set

"Of merry fellows, free and gay,
Regular rioters are they,
And their whole life is holiday.
The requisites for happiness
Are few, are—what these men possess:
With lively spirits—self-conceit—
And little, very little wit—
'Tis the same life the whole year round,
The self-same set together found;
Each night their songs—their drink—their game—
Their mirth—their very jests the same;
And as its tail diverts a kitten,
So they with their own jokes are smitten.
They ask no more than thus to sup—
Without a headache to get up—
And while the host will credit give
Are satisfied—and thus they live."

In the morning they fight duels in swaddling-clothes; in the afternoon they sit in the confectionery shops and eat sugar-plums; and in the evening they drink beer and smoke, and smoke and drink beer, and sing songs.

In any other part of the world, when you see a man with a scar in his face, you suppose he has won it in battle. The scar in the face is the soldier's proudest medal; it is a grand cross which the united kings of Europe even could not confer, and the soldier is proud of it—ay, jealous of it, and he likes to meet it on others, for he says, "There goes a hero; there is a brave man." He inquires who is the wearer of that scar, and in what action it was won. He is informed, "Oh, my dear sir, that young man received his scar at Heidelberg, in what is there called a duel; that is, the combatants are carefully swaddled by their nurses, so that they can't hurt one another: their legs are swaddled, their breast is swaddled, their right arm is swaddled, and their head and eyes are covered, so that they can only be pricked a little in the face; and for fear the police should interrupt these terrible duels, a picket guard of *women with knitting-needles* is thrown out on the side near the town, who will give notice if there is any sign of interruption." And it is said that some of these fierce duelists, in their thirst for blood, get the maids of the picket guard to prick their faces with their knitting-needles when they have failed to gain a scar in combat! But I suspect this is a slander. After the duels, these Heidelberg chicken-cocks, with their twopenny chivalry, march to the town with their handkerchiefs to their faces, in great apparent agony, and then sit down to a good dinner and talk over the *hot work* of the day.

If you meet any of these Quixotes in the afternoon, always allow five feet distance in passing between you and them—that is, three feet for their canes and two for their arms—or you may lose an eye, for they are always making passes when walking, now at a beetle, now at a butterfly, and now at some imaginary adversary. Many of the students here are very wealthy; but, as they generally have only a certain allowance per week to spend, they do as all students do the world over—"go on *tick*." There are therefore certain Jews about town, at whose stores they buy, and promise to pay double when they get money; when in funds they buy at other places where they can not get credit. They often get in debt for many thousands of florins, but generally pay up after finishing their course. There are now 730 students in the University from all parts of the world, including several from the United States and Cuba.

I was walking the other evening with a French lady, when several students passed us with their gay caps and shawls. "*Fi donc!*" said she; "see these babies, with their colifichets; that's not *chique*. One of our students at Paris would have his mistress, and his ball, and his pipe, and no money left for dress." The remark was very Frenchy. But I must confess I think the Heidelberg students superior in all that makes a man to the students of the Quartier Latin. With all their little foibles (which children in swaddling-clothes will have every where), they have free spirits, a manly bearing, and more good sense than some of their customs would lead one to suppose.

Shortly after my arrival here I had another instance of the *folly* of not knowing German. I went into an out-of-the-way gasthof a short distance from Heidelberg to get something to eat—the first want of nature. Now this is a feat that I have never found difficult in any country or in any tongue. Beefsteak and love are the same in all languages, and there is no polyglot like a Napoleon. This trinity is a synonym of the universal thought, and perhaps will be the foundation of a universal language, which, let us hope, will never again be confused. But one can not live forever on beefsteak and love, nor can he always have his polyglot interpreter beside him. Having eat, walked, and dreamed beefsteaks from Bonn to Mayence, I began ardently to long for a change of diet—a little lamb with mint sauce, a *chapon au riz*, or even a plain leg of mutton with turnips; but all these dishes, though simple enough in English or French, were very complex in German; so I resolved to take the very easy word *chicken*, fondly hoping, as bread was *brod*, and butter *booter*, that chicken would be *shicken*. I accordingly called the girl who attended, and demanded fearlessly *shicken*. She immediately began to titter, and ran out of the room to bring another girl, with whose assistance she tittered harder than before, and these two joined to them a third devil—for as such I began to view them—and stood peeping and laughing at the door. To end the trouble, I resigned myself to the old dish once more, and called out beefsteak; but they had come to the foregone conclusion that every thing I was to say they were not to understand, and now they wouldn't understand even that. Finally, enter the landlord bowingly, with the air of a man who knew a thing or two, who, on my repeating the mysterious word, promptly replied ja, ja, *shincken*, and brought me a great slice of very *salt ham!* Though burning with thirst from a long and dry walk, I swallowed that and my disgust together, and rushed off to Heidelberg, determined immediately to begin the study of German.

On my way to the house of a professor who had been recommended to me, I stopped at a barber's shop to have my hair cut, and, while seated in the chair, observed the barber's son, a youth of about 20 years of age, earnestly engaged in study during the intervals he could get from the sale of pomatums and Cologne water. I addressed him both in French and English, and found that he spoke both of those languages with grammatical correctness, and hence inferred he would know his own tongue at least equally well. I immediately thought of Johnson and Goldsmith toiling in garrets; of Hugh Miller to-day standing side by side with Sir Robert Murchison as a geologist, while yesterday delving in a quarry or laying stone walls with the most ignorant laborers in wet ditches; of Rousseau waiting on a table in Italy as a laquais; of Franklin's drudging in a printing-office; and I thought—as I have always thought—that where a man is found toiling in poverty, yet ambitious and studious, there is surely something in him, and he ought to be assisted by every passer who has it in his power, for such men are not only aided by the pecuniary gratification received, but also by the stimulus afforded.

I made the barber's son my German teacher, and that night was deep in the twistings of the first letter of the alphabet. I have no doubt that the morning after crossing the Rubicon Cæsar cried like a babe. One feels so very cool on first awaking in the morning (provided the thermometer is not above 90°)—one is so flat and passionless—so unexcitable! A nun who has sinned away thirty years of her life and all her passions could not be more repentant than every body is inclined to be in the first waking moments of the morning, after having performed some doubtful, daring deed the day before.

The first thing I thought of in the morning after

awaking was my sudden resolve, *in hot blood*, the day before, to learn German! The first thing I saw was a long sheet of foolscap covered with this deformed character, in various degrees of ill-shapedness—𝔄 𝔄 𝔄 𝔄!! Positively, I never saw any thing look so ugly. It recalled the ghosts of Latin, Greek, Spanish, and Italian dictionaries and grammars, rapped knuckles and dry bread-and-water dinners, cranky, old, snuff-taking French masters, and roots, dialects, and declensions—words, words, words! And, in German, what a list of them between Alpha and Omega! I put the sheet over my head (not the *sheet* of paper, which I dashed into the stove), turned over in bed, and went to sleep again, during which I had the most awful morning-mare imaginable. A sea-turtle on a London alderman's chest is a trifling thing; he remains quiet, merely gazing curiously down the snorer's throat. But the gender and the article danced quadrilles on my head; the verb sat on my breast and played trombone; my legs got tangled up in the letters as in a Mexican chapparal; next, my jaw-bone snapped in trying to pronounce a long word! Fortunately, at this moment I was released from fancied miseries to encounter real ones (often the lightest) by the entry of the barber's son, who awakened me as the clock struck nine. *Ce n'est que le premier pas qui coute*, as Santa Anna said when his leg was taken off by a round shot as he made his first step toward the enemy. And I will lead you no farther into my conflict with the barber's son.

DOES YOUR TRUE GERMAN HATE A FRENCH-MAN?

MOUNTAINS and rivers are the noblest engineers on earth. All others are essentially practical; these are æsthetical. Stephenson is a pigmy beside them. What a pretty looking earth we should have without them! The degrees of latitude and longitude, instead of being so many imaginary lines, would be marked by turnpikes and railways straight as a carpenter's rule. The earth would look like the top of a balloon covered with meshes, or be a fac simile of an engineer's brain, a net-work of rectilinear feet and inches!

The theodolites had about as much to do with the making of the pretty road from Heidelberg to Heilbronn as Queen Victoria has to do with the government of the British empire, or the golden-chained Seogun of Japan with the management of his island kingdom! They were there, it is true, but only to endorse every thing willed by the mountain and river. The mountain would have a lovely sloping bank here, and a cliff-clinging forest there, and the river is always peeping into every valley that lies near its course, thus constantly thwarting the straight lines of the engineers, till they finally yielded, and made their road to run where the river and mountains allowed it to run, and thus we have one of the prettiest roads in Germany. Doubtless many picks and plans were broken in the contest.

It was in following the windings of this quiet road

that I spent most of my afternoons and evenings, after having passed the whole day in studying German: it was a delightful recreation, after the noise and bustle of cities, and it is surprising that there are not more families selecting Heidelberg as a Continental residence. Economy, education, beauty of scenery, and quiet may all be combined here, and more intelligent society can hardly be met with in any city of its size in Germany.

Here, as in most parts of Germany, one forms attachments—in France, acquaintances. The German character is just the reverse of the French. They are modest, sincere, affectionate, simple, yet earnest. In Germany there is nothing *doré* either in the character of the people or in their manner of living. Their furniture is as plain as their manners. There is not the slightest disposition toward *humbug* among them. I doubt if there is a people on earth with whom the act is more an index of the thought than with the Germans. They think more of the matter than the manner of things, hence they are often rather rough. The French think more of the manner than the matter, hence they are often over-polite. The German fondness of home is carried to a surprising extent. It is almost inconceivable to Americans to see persons who are able to travel, and who are well educated, living in the neighborhood (say at two or three hours' distance) of remarkable places without ever having visited them. You find many in Heidelberg who have never been to Frankfort, and in Frankfort who have never been to Heidelberg and Mayence—places that they might visit even between a breakfast and supper at their own houses. Railways are breaking through this custom, however.

"Your true German hates a Frenchman," says Goëthe; perhaps he ought to, as the French have so often desolated their country and burned their fortresses. But if that be true, then there are very few *true Germans* in this day. In fact, it is impossible for any one to *hate* the French; they are too chivalrous, and lively, and gallant, and polite ever to be hated. But the Germans evidently admire, and are beginning to copy after them; and I have seen Germans, I am sorry to say, who wished they had been born in France—who would exchange all their true, hearty, solid qualities of the heart for gay colifichets. None can help *admiring* France, but I should think few would wish to be French. We imitate insensibly what we admire, and as all Europe is admiring la grande, la belle nation, the prediction of Napoleon would have been truer if he had said, In fifty years Europe will be *French* or Cossack!

French ideas, French habits, French manners may be observed forcing themselves every where, even in antagonistic England. In Germany the new element often appears in rather a ludicrous way. French dinners, for example, at *midday* are an absurdity. And French manners do not always ingraft well upon the style of German barons. Can Bruin dance a minuet? Fine Paris furniture ill assorts with an uncarpeted or unpolished floor.

However, we all want mixing up; we want to extend our moral as well as our physical commerce. To-day there is no Sparta that would wall out the world, and no Canaanites, excepting the Japanese, who are afraid of their neighbors coming to spy out the poverty of the land. The world is full of traveling Anacharses. We shall all modify one another's habits and manners till we grow very much alike. England will be less foggy and fogy, America will be slower, Germany faster, Russia more civilized, and with fewer tendencies toward *Mohammedanism;* Turkey will be more *French and English;* but as for France, no one can tell what she will be—the coquette. She is the *lady nation* (though Amazonian in war) whom we all court, and bow, and smile to. Let us hope that, at least, she will not become less lady-like in her manners.

Verily, if there is not a musquito on my boot! What a bungler! He can't get his bill through; he has been a whole minute poking about without getting the first suck. In the same length of time a New Orleans musquito would have made his meal through a double-soled shoe, and have been singing about your ears for his digestion, preparatory to taking a more delicate bite out of your cheek.

Stupid as was this musquito, I thought he might learn something, and then invite his friends to dinner. So I packed up my German books after a long and agreeable stay, and went to Baden-Baden. I should have liked much, however, to have caught that musquito to send to Staten Island, the summer residence of the New York moneystockracy, where they never saw a musquito! Think of a people passing a whole summer without a single musquito-bite! It seems incredible.

ON THE ROAD AGAIN.

Baden-Baden is a beautiful spot; it is very beautiful, but the summer abode of *dorédom* and gamblers. It is therefore a good place in July and August to see the *world* without traveling all over it. It is a good place to see the *country* in May, June, and October. It is a good place to get damp and the dumps in winter, being one of the dampest and dumpiest places in Europe at that season. A little of the "West-End" of London, a bit of the Boulevards of Paris, a section of the Schottenviertel of Vienna, a portion of Fifth Avenue, New York, with a vast admixture of adventurers and deputations from the "hells" of those various cities, and you have Baden-Baden.

Let us away to Switzerland.

We refresh ourselves a day at the Rhine Falls near Schaffhausen. We are not disappointed with them because we have seen Niagara. We are never disappointed with any thing when we have once seen the limits of which it is capable, but until that limit is known the imagination can easily outstrip all realities. One who has seen the World's Fair of '51 will not be disappointed in his expectations of an ordinary fair; and when we have seen the ocean, we can very easily imagine the proper proportions of a lake; but many have been at first disappointed both at the World's Fair and the ocean, as well as at Niagara.

We get up three times in the night to see the water foaming, and boiling, and seething right in front of our window, and to have the pleasure of being put to sleep again by its roar. We watch it by the hour in the morning, and, *en passant*, would like to throw that machine-shop to which it is harnessed on one side into the very deepest part of the pool. Why, in America they would hardly put a waterfall to such base uses. We should like to make the place a good deal wilder than it is. But what do you think? A railway bridge now passes nearly over the fall itself, and in another year the train will rush by, drowning the noise of the waters, and the passengers will look out of the windows and say, "Ah! the Rhine Falls!" while in another instant, with a chut! chut! from the locomotive, as if to reprove idle curiosity, they are swept past, and on toward Zurich, where *we* arrive, however, per diligence.

The environs of Zurich are beautiful. Clean white cottages, and houses with green blinds, all freshly painted; large gardens, blooming with flowers; isolated and scattered groups of trees in their deepest green, line both sides of the lake to the water's edge, as far as the eye can reach. If you climb an eminence, you will see dwellings scattered all over the plain, instead of blocked down in solid masses, as in Germany. This gives the country a very pleasant look, and reminds an American of the United States. Indeed, while thinking of this similarity myself, I met two graduates of Harvard College, who remarked to me, "How much that looks like New England."

We take the steamer to Horgen, and thence our legs to Zug, twelve miles, over the Albis ridge, which separates Lake Zug from Lake Zurich, and arrive half an hour before our fellow-passengers in the diligence. Many of us had intended going to Arth to commence the ascent of the Rigi on that afternoon, but the cloudy state of the weather prevented, so that nearly all of the passengers continued on to Immensee, and thence to Lucerne.

A Londoner, who was traveling with his bride, offered me a seat in his coupé at Immensee, whence the diligence goes as far as Küssnacht. They were a very agreeable couple, and I was congratulating myself on such a pleasant rencounter, when a young lady whose nationality I had been puzzling over, for she was brunette, delicate, and spoke three languages nearly equally well—none of them English characteristics—came near the door and looked inquiringly into the coupé. I could do no less than offer her my place, although I would have given any thing if that seat had been long enough for four. I afterward learned that this young lady was from Crewe (I thought there was nothing at Crewe but machine-shops; as great a mistake as those ignorant people make who think that we all wear skins in America).

On that same evening, this young lady and her father entered the reading-room of the Schweitzer Hof at Lucerne, where I was sitting, and took the only two chairs vacant, one on each side of me; but, had they not commenced conversation, I should have sat a thousand years beside her without opening my lips, merely from my very anxiety to open them. She belonged to that minority of English ladies who do not look as if they could go down to their husbands' office and carry on the business during his absence, or lead a troop of cavalry to battle. It may be an error, but it always appears to me as if the English ladies managed and directed their husbands, great stout fellows as they are too; but a very little rudder will guide a very big ship, and a very little woman will manage a very big man; in fact, my observations in all parts of the world have convinced me that all women govern their husbands, and the man that boasts most of his independence is generally the most skillfully managed; he is merely allowed to *appear* to rule. At all events, the morning after that fatal knot is tied, I shall say to my wife, "There, dear, take the reins, only don't drive to the devil!" Depend upon it, it is the shortest way, and saves a life-long contest for the mastery.

All the agreeable people of the world are certainly traveling this summer. At Lucerne I became acquainted, also, with a very pleasant French family, who were full of animation and life, amused at any thing and every thing, ready to go any where or do any thing by which they might see, be seen, and be sociable. Then there was an Irish bride, a sweet woman, with that rare combination of boldness (perhaps frankness would be a better word) with modesty and simplicity that one never sees out of Ireland. Her husband was an entertaining companion, as all Irishmen are. They proposed my joining them in the small boat which they had taken to go to Alpnach, and thence to the Bernese Oberland, but having formed a party with the Londoners to go to Bern, I bid them a reluctant good-by as their boat glided away on a fine sunny morning under the stroke of two stout rowers.

I had a fine midday view from the top of the Rigi;

but the sunset, toward which hour some forty persons —English, French, Dutch, Americans, etc.—arrived, was clouded, and the landscape, too, was mostly shrouded in mist. It was a cold evening, and a more melancholy, disappointed company could hardly be found than that which stood shivering on the peak, trying to force out the sun. One old Irish gentleman amused me. He and his son, an officer of the British army in India, had gone up with me early in the day, and we were almost the only persons that had a fine day-view; but the old gentleman was determined to see the sun set, and stood resolutely by the flag-staff watching a black mass of fog in the west where the sun ought to be. The crowd thinned off gradually; one by one the most ardent slipped quietly away, until at last the most enthusiastic had gone, and we three were left alone in the twilight. The rattling of knives and forks, and glasses, and the lighting of the dining saloon, showed unmistakably that even the landlord was convinced that there would be no performance that evening. Still the old man said, "I don't give it up yet." The shades of night deepened; the breeze blew colder; savory odors issued from the hotel, whetting our appetites, already sharpened by the breeze; but the old man stood firm; indeed, he said "he thought he saw a streak." We left him, hoping he would follow us in; but, after waiting ten minutes, we went out again, and there he stood, buttoned to the chin, while it had now become quite dark. His first words were, "Oh, I don't give it up yet!" And it was fully a quarter of an hour more before we could get him away from his flag-staff, and the thick banks of fog which rolled by not ten feet from his nose. As he entered the now lively dining-room, he said, "I think, if we had remained only a few moments more, we should have had a view!"

In the morning it *rained*, and I left the Rigi-Culm before any one was up, descending on the side toward Goldau. Fortunately, I met a French gentleman at the lower hotel, and we waded down together through mud and rain. It was a fitting day to see such a picture of desolation as was presented by the ruins of Goldau, and the gloomy, sterile-looking Rossberg opposite.

I left my companion, and in the pattering rain walked over the spot where four hundred and fifty persons were suddenly buried alive; and I felt indescribably sad as I looked at their tombstones, larger than the mausoleums of kings—huge masses of granite, bigger than the "Invalides," the mausoleum of Napoleon. These—the instruments of their death—were their only fitting monuments. But nature, that provided them tombs, was not unmindful of their decoration, and they were mostly covered with ivy, or with green bushes and small trees. The valley on both sides of this ruin was lovely.

From Goldau I skirted along the borders of Lake Lowertz to the farther end, and then crossed over to Brunnen on Lake Lucerne. The rain still poured in torents, and the beautiful Bay of Uri looked grandly dismal. Fortunately, at the Golden Adler hotel of Brunnen one can find other enjoyments besides those required as necessaries. The daughters of the landlord were good musicians, and their parlor resembled somewhat a concert-room, being filled with music-books and musical instruments—at least a harp, guitar, piano, and violin. During the afternoon, a priest whom I had seen before near Lake Lowertz came in, and, being an excellent pianist, played while one of the ladies sang. Thus I passed the time agreeably till the steamer from Flüelen hove in sight, and I embarked in her for Lucerne. She was crowded, but with a dripping set of tourists, and we were all glad enough to get into the comfortable quarters of the Schweitzer Hof.

One might sit forever and enjoy the magnificent view of Lake Lucerne, the Rigi, Mount Pilatus, and a dozen snow-capped peaks visible from the front windows of the Schweitzer Hof. The wild and rugged mountain scenery which surrounds the lake gives its waters, on a day in which there is no wind, an appearance of the very deepest quiet and seclusion, such as the smoothest sheet of water surrounded by level, or merely hilly ground, can never show. On such a day Lake Lucerne is the very emblem of silence and repose—a quiet, philosophical soul in a stormy world.

It was hard to leave; but, after a three days' rest, we settled our bills, and were soon seated in a carriage en route for Bern. Our party consisted of four—the London gentleman and his bride, a young Frenchman, and myself, and we had the whole carriage to ourselves. A merry day's ride we had of it too, so that when we arrived toward evening in the city of bears, we all felt sorry. It was the first time I ever wanted to remain a moment longer in a diligence after having driven nine hours. Where the nine hours went to it is impossible to say; but, what with our walks up hill, our halt for dinner, our gay spirits, the fine day, and pleasing though not picturesque scenery, the hours flew by so that the lady even was not at all fatigued. At Bern our party still kept together in promenades, tea-table talks, etc., and it was with real sorrow we parted two days afterward to spread in three directions. What a pleasure if we could keep all our traveling acquaintances, and carry them home with us, and with them all our fine views! That would be living *en prince*. I think I would select first Lake Lucerne and the young lady from Crewe, and plant them down near the Hudson, to break the heart of Lake George and of the Belle of the Highlands!

At Bern I shouldered my knapsack again and started afoot for Fribourg, not for any particular beauty of the scenery, but for delight of air and motion. I dreamed away the whole day over this twelve or fifteen miles walk, now bathing my feet in a cool brook, now lying on my back under a tree on some green slope, with a book in my hand, alternately reading and watching the fleeting clouds, and now accompanying some Swiss peasant-girl for a mile or two to the hay-field, and there watching them make hay. In the afternoon I found a delightful little nook, secluded away in the bushes beside a deep brook, where it had enlarged into a sort of natural basin: the peasants had here constructed a bench for bathing. A full porte monnaie lying in the road could not have afforded me so much pleasure as this discovery. I undressed as leisurely and comfortably as if in my own chamber, being completely shaded from the sun by the overhanging trees, amid whose branches the birds were singing, almost as happy as myself. Two or three carriages, containing parties of English tourists, passed within twenty feet of me, and I could see distinctly their gay, rosy faces, and hear their conversation, without being seen.

Since the world is so large, and country air, and country houses, and trees, and brooks are all so much cheaper and better than city air, city houses, paved streets, and leaden pipes filled with water, how surprising it is that such numbers of the human race find their difficult way to dirty back garrets, where they starve for want of food!

Ca-chug! like a bull-frog, I plunged head first into the water at the thought, seeming to wash off city cobwebs and back-garret odors as I entered the limpid stream! After a refreshing bath, not finding any towels hanging on the trees, I was compelled to dry myself as Adam did, by walking up and down in the sunshine, for which I felt nothing loth.

I walked into Fribourg at 6 o'clock that afternoon with all the delight of rollicking health, and thinking, as I passed over its aerial, bridge-spanned chasms, what a simple thing is true happiness. It can not be described, and will not be directly sought, like pleasure, but is often found when unexpected, and oftenest by those who seek it least, and who live with most simplicity, as Nature intended those to live who would be well and happy. A walk over both those wonderful suspension bridges which the Fribourgians use as a promenade in the evening, passing in mid-air, like spirits from world to world, and an hour spent in hearing the organ of Moser, one of the finest in Europe, played by an amateur, closed one of those few days which occur in life where there was not a single thought even (except the garret and cobwebs) to remind me that this world was any thing different from a promised paradise! and yet there was not an incident, or a view, or a circumstance, other than the possession of a single book, but what is within reach and capacity of the majority of the human race. But if I had owned ten thousand shares of railway stock, and suddenly found a newspaper announcing a decline of an eighth, I should probably have been very unhappy.

My next day was passed in the banquette on top of a diligence. The conductor and myself were in full and sole possession, and we had not been there half an hour before he told me that he could tell at a glance whom he could talk and laugh with; which, interpreted, meant "a glass of beer at the next change of horses, if you please, sir." He was a very fine fellow for all that, and much better and cheaper than an edition of Murray.

We arrived at Vevay at about five o'clock in the afternoon, the loveliest hour of the day to arrive at a lovely place.

I shall never forget the sensations experienced as that placid lake, reposing in the warm sunshine of a summer afternoon, first stole upon my view. We descended slowly, amid vineyards and country houses, the winding road that leads from the hill-top to the borders of the lake, now lying like a mirror before us. Opposite were the Savoy Alps, whose green bases, bathed in the waters beneath, raised their lofty, snow-covered summits with glittering and defiant brilliancy toward a July sun. In many places their green slopes were suddenly changed into black, craggy peaks, plumed with clouds, or presenting an irregular, many-hued outline against the blue sky behind. Immediately under us lay Vevay, nestled among trees, and in the midst of a most charming landscape. I was afraid to look farther either to the right or to the left, lest I should enjoy too much at once.

Who does not feel a reverence in approaching this lake, consecrated perhaps more than any other spot on earth by the aristocracy of all nations—the true aristocracy of earth—that which is generally farthest from the throne—which dwells in the garret oftener than in the palace!—an aristocracy to which succeeding generations render more homage than to the kings who ignored their names while living?

To-day an apprentice is locked outside the gates of Geneva, and runs away from his native place for fear of punishment. To-morrow the same person, a vagabond escaping from service as a common waiter in Turin, again seeks the shores of his beloved lake and settles at Lausanne, duping the people by giving lessons in music, of which he knew nothing. The next day, but late in life, and after innumerable hardships and sufferings in other lands, this erratic genius is yet again back to the shores of the lake he worshiped, locked in a room at Vevay, peopling his mind from nature; and the result of this last visit is "La Nouvelle Héloise," and to-day the marble statue of Jean Jacques Rousseau stands beside those of Pascal, Malherbe, Voltaire, and other noble names of France in the palace of the Louvre, while his memory is more lastingly enshrined in the hearts of all who revere genius, whatever its faults.

In a garden of acacias at Lausanne, and with this same Alpine view and placid lake before him, another descendant of obscurity made himself and the spot where he wrote famous by penning the last words of "The Decline and Fall of the Roman Empire."

At Ouchy, right over the water, is the room where Byron wrote "The Prisoner of Chillon. Madame de Staël, Voltaire, Sismondi, and a thousand other names of the aristocracy made by heaven, and who wear their "orders" on their brows instead of on their breasts, have worshiped nature beside this lake. Therefore it is holy.

But our driver is beginning to crack his whip furiously, a sure sign he is getting where he will be seen. We are entering the streets of Vevay. The doors and windows are full of maids and urchins, who dodge ludicrously as our important man with the reins flourishes his long lash right and left, to the great danger of all eyes within whipping distance. The heavy diligence rolls on with a lumbering, lazy motion, and a banging noise, which fills the windows of the upper stories with curious young ladies, just in time to convince me that the animate beauties of Vevay are far behind the inanimate!

And now what a bustle at the "Hotel of the Trois Couronnes!" It is as if a section of Broadway were suddenly planted in Vaud. Travelers arriving and travelers departing; garçons strapping and unstrapping, and running against one another; disappointed families grumbling because they can't get front windows; supercilious gents, elegantly dressed, smoking their cigars coolly as they gaze at the becapped, dusty, tumbled, red-faced, and excited-looking new arrivals; and then such a clatter of tongues of all nations—English, French, Russian, and German—all talking together, and all pouring in with Alpine sticks, which are covered, some with the trophies of their excursions, marked in branded letters, Rigi-Culm, Montanvert, St. Bernard, etc., and others of virgin white, betokening the novice just starting on his tour. The English noises prevail; in fact, a Swiss hotel in midsummer is either English or—Bedlam!

I was very glad to climb past all this noise, and went even up to the roof for the sake of having a window over the lake. And then my first movement was to take a towel, and go off a quarter of a mile from the hotel to as secluded a spot as I could find, and there plunge into the cool waters, right under the snows of the Alps!

The weather that evening was delightful—delightful to sit still in, which was just what every body seemed inclined to do. The bustle at the hotel had died away, and in the cleanly-shaven, well-dressed gentlemen who sat conversing, or leisurely promenading in the pretty garden over the lake, which adjoins the hotel, you would scarcely recognize the rough-looking people who had arrived two hours since. With the ladies the change was still more magical. Brown traveling dresses were exchanged for fresh, cool-looking muslins (I believe they were muslins, for to this day I do not know the difference between a muslin and a calico or alpaca); their awkward hats were thrown aside, and heads, that before would have answered to a description of Meg Merrilies, were now as smooth and shining as brushes and pomatum could make them; but, what was more astonishing, every one of the ladies had grown two or three feet in circumference—a very surprising metamorphosis, considering the time occupied! The sun had set; a bright pink tinge fringed the tops of the opposite mountains, which appeared the more brilliant for the contrast of the deep shades below; the stars were hardly peeping forth: it was the moment of their struggle with the last rays of day; the lake lay without a ripple, except when the quiet oar of some romantic young lady, alone in a small boat, disturbed for a moment its peacefulness. Now and then a boat would pass with a musical party, whose songs were particularly beautiful as they grew more distant, and the sounds came faintly over the water. And there by the railing, looking down into the water, stood a man who for twenty years had not been away from the midst of a million of people with their din of trade. His forehead was coruscated with wrinkles, and his face marked with cent per cents. For twenty years the money article and the market article had been his only literature; for twenty years he had worn his soul and body threadbare in the pursuit of some imaginary prize, of which he supposed gold the representative. He has got the gold, but searches in vain for the prize; he is rich, but unhappy. In the midst of this lovely scene, he is estimating the profits of his last investment. He suddenly starts, and pulls out his watch in a hurry, as if he had some engagement; he will return to London to-morrow. What a varied company parade over the graveled walks of that beautiful terrace! What extremes are brought together! the happy and the miserable, the rich and the poor, the author and the student, the miser and the spendthrift, and every one sees a different scene in the quiet view spread out before him.

The next morning, at daylight, I started for a leisurely walk as far as Villeneuve, at the end of the lake. I stopped at Clarens, some four or five miles, to take a cup of coffee. I entered an inn by the road side which has committed the crime of terming itself the "Bosquet of Julie," and of hanging a most frightful daub over the road, so that every traveler is forced to see it, representing that heroine in any thing but an agreeable light. It was not much after sunrise; and as I entered the *Bosquet of Julie*, I was saluted by a cloud of dust and cigar-stumps, brushed out by a dirty porter. I passed that and went into the coffee-room, where the chairs were all standing upon the tables as they had been placed while the room was being swept. A mixed smell of beer and stale smoke filled the room, which was carefully closed, as if to keep out the fresh air.

"Clarens! sweet Clarens! birth-place of deep love!
Thine air is (*not*) the young breath of passionate thought:"

at least so much of it as was allotted to me at that moment. In fact, nothing could have been more unfortunate than the necessity that compelled me to have something to eat and drink at Clarens, and I was delighted to escape from the *Bosquet.*

But, apart from the hotel, nearly every one is disappointed in the village itself; and the reason is, we all look *at* it instead of *from* it. Certainly, there is nothing *in* Clarens that ever inspired Rousseau's pen, but it is the ravishing view afforded by this spot in looking away from it.

I walked on, and could now see distinctly that sulky monument of tyranny, Chillon—a foul blot on the loveliest spot of Leman. The deep blue of the waters that washed its base, the green foliage of the trees that waved against its walls, the huge mountains overhead that shaded its dingy turrets, seemed to ask, Why art thou here with thy foul presence? Every steamer that passes sends its wave of compassion to burst in a shower of tears against the dungeon of Bonnivard, and the tomb of—Heaven only knows how many innocent men!

I soon reached the castle, and descended into the seven-pillared dungeon, celebrated as much for its Byron, who spent half an hour there in carving his name on a stone pillar, as for its Bonnivard, who passed six years wearing, in wearying windings, a hollow circuit in the stone floor—an eternal protest against "man's inhumanity to man." And civilization comes to Chillon, and reads this protest, and weeps, just as it will weep three hundred years hence when visiting the dungeons of Italy, where hundreds of Bonnivards lie at this moment, in their own lands too, pining for liberty, or for the death to which they will soon be led. The great, the noble, the brave—the victims of Austrian tyranny—at this moment pace their weary rounds in damp cells, and stop and hark at every sound, as if in this nineteenth century they expected foreign deliverance momentarily to unbar their doors. Here is a chance for interference; and if the nation that is so fond of *protection* (the doré name for fillibustering) had sent her troops to Italy instead of to Constantinople, she would not be complaining of want of sympathy from America. She would not have what is called an active sympathy, it is true, because the most active and efficient sympathy America can render is "masterly inactivity," and it is more powerful in its influence on the world than the action of combined European forces; it is the working of a principle which is changing and will revolutionize the whole world.

I spent several days in wandering about the shore and visiting the cities of this beautiful lake; now crossing by boats, and now walking along the margin of its waters; but if I made you travel with me as slowly as I travel myself, you would be long in arriving at your journey's end.

So here we are in a steamer leaving Geneva for Villeneuve. It is two o'clock in the afternoon. The sun is clear and bright, but a cool wind tempers its heat, rippling the waters into a freshness which reacts upon the atmosphere, because it destroys the mirror-like reflection of the sun's rays, and also brings more water in contact with the air. I do not know a single person on board. There are at least forty travelers on deck, and as the passage is a short one of four hours, I do not intend to speak to any one. I take a book and a quiet corner, and pass the minutes, now in reading a paragraph, and now in gazing at the varied scenery we are passing, and now in a glance of observation at my fellow-passengers. I had not been occupied in this pleasant manner more than twenty minutes, when an English lady, who was standing near with her husband, asked me in French if Mont Blanc could be seen from our present position. I was about to reply in English, but checked myself, and answered in French, which she interpreted to her husband, for it is very rarely that English husbands speak French. She then commenced an agreeable conversation, for which I was very willing to lay aside my book; and as I saw she wished to *practice* on me, I would not be so cruel as to betray what, if she had known French but little better, she would have easily discovered, viz., that I was not a Frenchman. The moments passed delightfully; the ladies never appeared so amiable, for on my right were two young ladies with black hair and eyes, whom I mistook for French until they spoke, when I discovered by their accent that they were not. However, seeing one of them trying to cut open the leaves of her book with her fingers, I lent her my knife, with a thousand apologies for my kindness *à la manière Française*, and this, of course, led to an acquaintance with them. They were Americans, and had been residing for some time in Europe; they were now going with their mother to Vevay to spend a few days with some friends.

I do not know how long I might have played the Frenchman with these pleasant ladies had I not heard the husband reading a glorification article from the London Times, in which that journal was comparing England to the lion resting in his strength after his recent Herculean labors, and occasionally uttering growls of defiance at his enemies. I burst out laughing, and said, in good broad English, that the roaring of the lion sounded to me a good deal like the noise made by the animals that carried some ladies to the top of the Rigi the other day!

A real lion's growl would not have created more astonishment; the gentleman laughed, while his wife turned crimson, to think she had spoken first to an American; however, better that than to one of her own countrymen, for an English*man* will hardly speak to an Englishman, much less would an English *woman* think of doing so. She was piqued, and looked prettily piqued, but suddenly seemed to reason, "Well, I know him now, and he will not bite, I am sure;" and so she continued her amiability, while her husband continued the article in the "Times," which went on to say that the "lion had taken a kick from the jackass over the water," when I begged to inform him that it was quite a mistake; the jackass might have switched his tail in the lion's eyes, and the noble animal, being a little nervous after two recent visits to Cronstadt, had mistaken that for a kick!

At this juncture, one of the long style of real down-East Yankees, who had been quietly listening, stepped up, and, addressing the Englishman, said, "Look here, neighbor!" We all looked, and I must confess I felt a little uneasy, for fear he was going to "pitch in" to Mr. Bull, so serious was his manner. He continued: "I say, if that 'ere jackass does kick, the lion will have a headache all the rest of his life, sure as you're born!"

The whole party burst into a roar, during which the steamer touched at Ouchy. The gentleman inquired if I did not dislike the "Times" newspaper. I told him I liked it better than any sheet published in the world, and would rather see any half dozen newspapers that might be selected destroyed than that; that I liked an able enemy, and thought the Times generally said the best that could be said on the side which it might choose to take.

From lions, jackasses, and newspapers, the conversation turned to travel talk, comparisons of routes, plans for the future, and so forth. My countryman was going to Moscow to see the coronation of the Emperor; the Englishman and his wife to Chamouni, where I had the pleasure of meeting them afterward; and the American ladies were already domiciled for the summer on the shores of the beautiful lake over which we were passing. Altogether, it was a lovely afternoon, and one long to be remembered; and when I saw the whole party get off at Vevay, I could hardly resist following them into the boat that was to take them ashore.

If I had shut myself up in supercilious selfishness, as intended, what a pleasant episode would have been lost. I resolved, more than ever, to let the key of my heart always hang outside while traveling. With a good deal of experience, I have never yet found any one to abuse this frankness, and I think I should be able to protect myself if they did. 'Tis true, I met once a gentleman on a Mediterranean steamer who wanted to borrow the price of his passage home, and I loaned it to him, and received it again a year afterward. I had never seen him before, and if I had had any doubts about the payment, I would have told him frankly that I could not lend the money.

After passing Vevay I was left nearly alone. At Villeneuve I took the top of the omnibus at about 7 o'clock in the evening, and arrived at Bex, in the valley of the Upper Rhine, at half past ten. It was a beautiful night, and a chamois hunter, who sat next to me, entertained me with interesting descriptions of the various mountains and localities passed.

After a light supper, I retired to a tolerably comfortable country chamber, eager for the morning light and the walk which would follow.

CATHOLIC OR PROTESTANT?

THERE is not a more delightful sensation than that experienced by the pedestrian who starts with the sun, on a fine summer morning, for his Alpine excursion. By a pedestrian I do not mean the man whose joints are stiffened by his daily cramped rides, and who walks only when are to be seen the fine views. No one has a right to assume the name of pedestrian who can not get up in the morning, after a thirty miles' walk the day previous, without blister, pain, or ache. There are two classes of advisers on the subject of pedestrianism. The first, who are heel-and-toe rabid, recommend you to walk all the time, from the beginning to the end of your journey; the second, to walk only through the finest scenery. The truth lies, where it generally does, "*au juste milieu.*" If you walk all the time, you will certainly lose more time than most people can spare, besides stultifying yourself by long, flat, and uninteresting miles. If, on the other hand, you select only the finest scenery and the mountains for your walks, be assured you will enjoy your selections but little. The sudden fatigue and violent perspirations attendant on climbing high mountains by persons unaccustomed to it will not only mar your pleasures, but leave painful reminiscences as well as aches behind. I climbed the Rigi with a lieutenant of artillery from Bengal and his father. The Rigi is not much of a climb, certainly, but the old gentleman, fresh from the easy, quiet life of London, broke down before half way up, and we should have been compelled to return with him but for the fortunate discovery of a neighboring châlet, where we procured him some milk mixed with kirchwasser, which so restored the hearty old gentleman that he said he could climb Rigis on Rigis! He went to the top in fine style.

The true way to enjoy pedestrianism is to make it a point to do at least your ten or twelve miles *every* day, even where the road is flat as a pancake; this keeps one in practice. But in countries like Switzerland or the Tyrol, the less one has to do with the diligence the better, and the more one walks the more he enjoys it.

Such were my sensations as I left Bex, a little village of Vaud, situated at the foot of the Dent du Midi. It was only 4 o'clock in the morning, and, with limbs hardened by some hundreds of miles' walking, I started forth as light as a feather, or, rather, as 140 lbs. avoirdupois, exclusive of knapsack. But weight is only a comparative thing after all, and the 140 lbs. and knapsack, when weighed in the medium of youth, health, strength, and Alpine air, might still be said to be light as a feather—so light as to go bounding along through the crisp and bracing atmosphere, with feet scarce touching earth.

My course was toward Martigny, about twelve miles distant only, and lay through the valley of the Rhine, here commanded by the snowy peaks of the Dent du Moreles on one side, and the Dent du Midi on the other. At but a little distance from Bex the bridge of St. Maurice is passed, which links the cantons of Vaud and Vallais, spanning the Rhone, here a torrent, and otherwise an almost impassable gulf, and separating two religions as well as two cantons.

But there are boundaries more marked than mountain torrents that separate the Protestant Vaudois from the Catholic Vallais. The cleanliness, healthfulness, industry, and intelligence of the one people were changed for the filth, wretchedness, poverty, and degradation of the other. No place in Switzerland, perhaps, offers such a marked contrast, in this respect, as the unfortunate village of St. Maurice. I was truly pained to see the miserable beings of this town, so picturesquely situated, living positively in greater filth than New England swine, which sometimes live quite genteelly. Sickening smells issued from the dirty doorways of the houses, and poor humanity was to be seen on all sides afflicted with goître, cretinism, and other diseases.

It would be unjust to suppose that St. Maurice is so wretched merely because it is Roman Catholic. St. Maurice is an extreme case; but in voyaging about the world I have had so often to bring in immediate contrast Protestant and Roman Catholic communities, and always unfavorably for the latter, that if there were no other reasons for the opinion even, I should feel certain that the Roman Catholic religion is unfavorable for the progress, happiness, and general welfare of mankind, while Protestantism is connected with whatever tends to the advancement, elevation, and prosperity of the masses. I would not attack any one's conscience or religion. I do not. I have often wished I could serve my God with the same devotion I have seen a poor ignorant peasant do in a Catholic church. He does the best he knows how to do, and I have no doubt he will be rewarded for it. But it is for that poor peasant I speak. I speak of the system which, with his religion, has ingrafted so many superstitions. I speak of the system which saps, like a vampyre, the juices of the many to nourish the few. Talk with this Catholic peasant, and then go yonder and talk with that Protestant, who is in the same position in life, and note the difference in intelligence. Go to the little canton of Appenzell, and here you see again this marked contrast. This small district of Switzerland is divided into two parts, called Inner and Outer Rhoden. Outer Rhoden is Protestant, and distinguished for the neatness of its dwellings, the cleanliness of its inhabitants, and its general appearance of prosperity. Inner Rhoden is Roman Catholic, and remarkable for its dirt, filth, and poverty. Show me the churches of a town, and I'll tell you what its people are. I do not speak so much of large cities, where the *gilding* and splendor of the few, wrung from the mites of the many, hide the poverty and distress behind; but even here, if you will but rub off a little of the gold with which every thing is *doré*, you will get a glimpse of the truth.

Oh, these glorious-looking, gigantic, Gothic cathedrals, how they have drained the fat of the land! How they have impoverished the people! Not a fertile field which their large roots have not traversed, sucking its strength and its sweets, while withering the fruits of the land! Not a handful of earth on the most barren rocks but its thirsty tendrils are there, seeking nourishment! The most lofty prince contributes to their support, and the meanest peasant shares his scanty pittance—twice shared, because he, after all, first pays the prince. The tendency of Roman Catholicism is to keep the masses down to a certain point of ignorance, for that is the only way in which they can be kept down to a certain point of subjection. The tendency of Protestantism is to educate the people, to throw the Bible and all knowledge widely and freely open to them, to permit and to teach mankind to think for themselves. The two greatest representatives of freedom on earth, England and America, are Protestant, and the very arch friend of the Pope in Europe is the very archest enemy of liberty among civilized nations. The sword in one claw and the cross in the other of the double eagle of Austria is an alliance that speaks volumes! In England and America all religions are free as air. Where the Protestant himself is free and truth is free, he has no fear of Catholicism, Judaism, or any other ism. He relies on education instead of the sword, on truth instead of force. Depend upon it, that's a poor religion that must be bolstered by the bayonet, or by the state, or by any other coercion, and it is very different from the pure and simple religion of the open air, and of the mountain, and of the sea-sides of our Savior. How the poor and weary soul, disgusted with forms, and ceremonies, and tinsel, and gilding, and filigree, and outlandish images, rejoices to get away from such distracting trammels, and, while worshiping God in the mountains, feels that it was there, above all places, that his Savior, the simplest of men, delighted to retire for prayer. The sea-side and the mountain were his churches—his Gothic cathedrals, and his worship and all connected with it was perfect simplicity. O man! how darest thou to make that so complicated which the Almighty made so plain?

But knowledge is power, and power is tyranny. The truth is universal, and universal knowledge will be the only check to the tyranny of the Church!

In passing on through the town of St. Maurice, I thought how much I would like to see one of those little white wooden churches, such as one sees in New England, planted right down in the *dirtiest spot in town*, and beside it a little white wooden school-house, with its green blinds. How amazed the people would be at first, and how they would turn away their unaccustomed eyes from the brilliant glare of the light, and run into their dark houses! And then they would look at it through the window, and, gradually becoming accustomed to it, would go to see it, and finally go into it. Afterward you would see the man who lived next door to it getting up a little bit earlier, just to wash his door-steps, which, he really didn't know why, had never appeared so dirty; his neighbor, ashamed to be outdone, follows his example, and in a few days all the scrubbing-brushes in the vicinity are at work, and the little white spot spreads all over the town. If they don't begin to bathe after that, I'm mistaken; and when people begin to bathe, their salvation is nigh at hand. From the bath-tub to Paradise is but a step.

Leaving St. Maurice, and passing the fine waterfall of the Sallenche, where I stopped half an hour, I arrived at Martigny at about nine o'clock; and after resting a little, took a good breakfast or dinner (as you may choose to call it, according to your habits and the country in which you live) between eleven and twelve. At two o'clock I started again for Chamouny, of which trip I defer the account till my next.

SOPHIE AND THE TÊTE NOIRE.

From Martigny to Chamouny there are two rival roads, which have had as many partisans as the houses of York and Lancaster: the one is by the Col de Balm, and the other by the Tête Noire. The first has its one glorious view, grander than any thing on earth, as Europeans say (probably meaning by earth that quarter of the globe inhabited by themselves); the second is the more picturesque and savage of the two routes, but has no single view equal to the first.

After reading and hearing all the arguments in favor of both sides, and being very near witnessing a fight between a Col de Balm man and a Tête Noire man, I found myself exactly in the position whence I started —the conclusions of the day unconcluded by the night, like Penelope's task. In this melancholy state I left Geneva for Villeneuve, and fortunately met a young lady in the steamer who belonged to the Col de Balm party, and who decided my course by saying, "If you are going to Mont Blanc, take the Col de Balm; if you are coming from it, take the Tête Noire." As there was nobody to say any thing on the other side, I thought her advice very sensible, and resolved to follow it.

It is a great satisfaction to come to a decision about any thing, but one is often so puzzled to arrive at that decision as often to prefer not having a choice in order to save the trouble of selection. This was exactly my feeling with regard to the two passages, and a dozen times I wished that either the Col had never been made, or that the Tête were stopped up with an avalanche. So, when the matter was decided so promptly for me, I felt as if a load had been removed from my shoulders, and started on my way with the confident air of a man who not only knows *what* he is about to do, but is sure that it is just the *right thing* to do. But man proposes, and *woman* disposes, as I have often before had occasion to observe, and as you shall see presently.

It was a fête-day at Martigny. The patron saint of the place was holding a grand jubilee, in consequence of which all the villagers, and all the neighbors for miles around, were thronging the lanes and roads in the vicinity, and enjoying themselves under a bright July sun with that heartiness which freedom from habitual labor only can confer. They were all decked in holiday attire, the women particularly having a most picturesque appearance, owing to their fanciful Vallais bonnets, or rather hats. (Peasant men never do look picturesque, at least when you can see their faces.) As I wound along the rocky path, between green fields and under cherry-trees laden with ruby fruit, I heard the frequent *gut'n tag*, but the more frequent *bon jour* (for in this district the German begins to give way to the French) from many a smiling face. The sight of so many joyous couples and so much sociability made me desire a companion, and I was almost sorry that I had not taken a guide, merely for company. The wish had hardly expressed itself in thought when, just as I was commencing the ascent of the Forclaz, I saw a large pair of hazel eyes under one of the most fanciful of those gold-embroidered Vallaisan hats staring full upon me. The gaze was so fixed, and came from a girl so fair in comparison with the other girls, that I involuntarily stopped under the shade of the same tree, and with a bon jour commenced some ordinary conversation about the weather. She stated that she, too, was going up the Forclaz, and, without any verbal agreement in the matter, we both started together, followed by her uncle and one of her female companions.

No sensible persons, in traveling, excepting the English, will ever wait to go through all the ordinary routine of forms before making an acquaintance. Traveling friends are like traveling dinners—they must be seized quick or not at all. A carpet-bag should always serve as a letter of introduction to another carpet-bag. This is the principle upon which every people under the sun act, always excepting the English;

and with them it is better, as a rule, not to speak till you are spoken to—a demeanor not to be observed from any ill feeling, but simply for your own protection and to avoid being "snubbed." I must confess I have never followed my own advice, and have never met with any thing but cordial politeness from all classes of Englishmen in traveling, but they have often acknowledged to me that it is a custom of theirs to snub their own countrymen particularly very frequently. "Why, sir," said one of them to me, "I am afraid to be sociable with my countrymen, lest some one might wish to borrow a five-pound note!"

Well, to return to my companion, it needed neither carpet-bag nor any other letter of introduction to make us acquainted. The hilly miles of the Forclaz, while retarding our pace, advanced rapidly our friendship. I yielded myself up willingly to her guidance, indeed without ever bestowing a thought as to where she might lead me, while leaving the main path and crossing wheat-fields, or wandering through thick woods. The afternoon was a most lovely one, and the scenery around was of that mixed character which, by contrast, renders the mountain and its savage pass more wild, and the quiet, peaceful valley more pleasing. At our left was the pass leading to the great Saint Bernard, in front the Forclaz mountain, and behind us one of the most beautiful and extended views of the valley of the Upper Rhine, with the white Simplon road running along its side, to be had any where in the Alps.

My fair Vallaisanne looked like a queen. She was one of the only two pretty Swiss girls I ever saw, for female beauty does not flourish in Switzerland. She was about nineteen years of age, and her name was Sophie—a name I detested till made beautiful by a Swiss Sophie. She was full of talk, but modest, and innocent to a degree that astonished me. How a person could live on this earth nineteen years, be so intelligent, and yet possess so much simplicity of style and thought, was certainly wonderful, but more charming than wonderful. What a contrast with the young Parisian lady! How different this child of a secluded Alpine valley from the sophisticated society I had just left even! She had never seen a railway carriage or a steam-boat, and *had never tasted beer!* Good Heavens! a person living in the year 1856, in which there was beer enough made to float the whole Baltic fleet, who had not even tasted beer! By the vats of Bavaria, the world is not yet civilized!

But, though she had seen neither locomotives, nor steamer, nor beer-mugs, she could tell all the remarkable or pretty spots of her neighborhood; she could tell me how she and her friends lived, and what they did to pass the time—the short and simple annals of the poor; but she related it all with so much modesty, that, though I was more sincerely interested in her than in any person I had met for some time, her manner seemed to say, like Goëthe's Margaret,

"You do but play with my simplicity,
And put me to the blush. A traveler
Learns such good nature—is so pleased with all things
And every body—my poor talk, I know,
Has no attractions that could for a moment
Engage the attention of a man who has
Seen so much of the world."

At the summit of the Forclaz, the two paths leading

to Mont Blanc diverge; the one—*mine*—ascended the Col de Balm; the other—*hers*—descended into the black and savage valley of the Tête Noir. I stood and paused before the two roads, as many a youth pauses in early life, puzzled to choose between the arduous path, which, with much toil and labor, will lead him to the bright summit where stands the temple of Fame, and the easy descent, amid present pleasures, to obscurity. In nine cases out of ten, a woman decides such matters, and what is lacking in her influence is more than made up by a glass of wine.

The bluff but good-natured old soldier at the top of the mountain, who gives return travelers permission to enter Vallais, after complimenting me on my selection of a guide, had his heart and mouth so widely opened by a cigar and a *petite verre* from my flask, that he sat down with us at the rustic board table placed in the open air, and grew very communicative, while his wife provided us with refreshments from her larder, rustic as the table, but expensive as the delicacies of Paris!

The scene at this focus of Mont Blanc pilgrims was very animated. Every few minutes some *puffing* party from below, with blazing red faces, came dragging up their weary footsteps, and reached their hands forward, with inclined bodies, toward the nearest seat, as if their feet alone could hardly perform the little distance left. The men always looked more fatigued than the women, for women can accomplish any thing on great or novel occasions, but sink afterward; and the climbing of a mountain to a city belle is as important an event as for a man to go out to battle.

She therefore summons all her spirit and energies for the momentous undertaking; and, for that reason, I have never known a woman to *break down* in a country ramble, although I have seen them ill for a whole week after it. In marked contrast with these sweltering climbers were the arrivals from the other side. How coolly they came in; with what dry skins, pale faces, standing collars, untumbled ruffles, and unruffled dresses! And their manner, too, how knowing! almost supercilious, I might say. With what pity they regarded the lobster faces of the other party; and truly, they did look more aristocratic! They looked as if they had seen Mont Blanc! They looked as every body in life looks after he has attained the object of his ambition—disappointed! Disappointed, yet elevated—the bliss of ignorance lost in learning that lesson which it is good for us all to learn, that no attainment on earth will ever satisfy our desires. So looks with pity the pale philosopher as he sees the ardent student following the upward path which he himself had so enthusiastically trodden; so looks the disappointed statesman upon the young aspirant for his country's honors; and so looks the wealthy merchant upon the toiler for golden joys.

Mingled with these two parties were numbers of peasants, in holiday attire, returning to their homes after having indulged in the festivities of Martigny; and thus the whole company represented all quarters of the globe: the fastidious Parisian, disguised in *feutre* and hob-nailed shoes, might easily have been mistaken for an invalid Englishman; the tall and ubiquitous American was there, appearing as much at home as if in his own parlor: "*he warn't a talking much, but he was quietly looking into things;*" and you may be sure that, whether he be merchant, scholar, or farmer, when he goes home he will *invent* some way of doing a something better than he saw it done in Europe. John Bull, of course, was *largely* represented, rubicund and rosy, solid and well planted, and equally ready for a smile or a growl. The honest German, too, the truest republican on earth, with his singular admixture of energy of character with modesty (traits that so often run counter to one another), was talking earnestly with his companion, and least occupied of any, I thought, with the immediate concerns of travel. I was going to add Turks and Chinese to complete the picture, but truth compels me to say there were none there.

During the half hour devoted to rest we were joined by a number of other peasants living in the same valley. Some of them had large baskets of cherries, which they were carrying all the way from Martigny to Chamouny, to regale the fat-pursed visiters there. We lightened their baskets a little, though not without increasing the weight of their pockets, and they, in turn, were grateful for a glass of beer or lemonade—delicacies they had rarely tasted. Of course, under such circumstances, the whole history of their valley and its beauties, and the advantages of that road, were poured copiously forth. My charming guide thought it would certainly rain in the morning (I had just noticed a cloud about as big as a fisherman's jacket, but it now seemed to occupy a quarter of the heavens). "Besides," she said, "you are going to see Mont

Blanc any how, and what is the use of climbing the weary Col de Balm in order to see it half a day sooner?" The old soldier saw immediately how the wind blew, and as the finest view on earth to an old soldier is a pretty woman, I need not tell his advice on wind and weather. In ten minutes *we* (*not* the old soldier and I) were wending our way amid flowers and fertile fields, or through the long grass and under the pleasant shade of wide-branching trees, down into the valley of the Trient. And so, for a woman, has many a man descended lower than the valley of the Tête Noire, when he should have ascended higher than the Col de Balm!

The scenery, which for some distance is comparatively tame, though it would be grand in any country but Switzerland, gradually changes, growing wilder at every step, till it assumes a fearful grandeur. The path first trims the edge of a mountain torrent, and then ascending, skirts the edge of a precipice, where, hung in mid-air, the traveler sees above him on one side huge overhanging rocks clasped in the rooty embraces of the hardy pine, which, despising the nourishment of more effeminate trees, seems to grow out of the solid granite; and on the other side, the white, glittering peaks of the satellites of Mont Blanc towering against the blue arch of heaven with indescribable brilliancy, while far below is the black valley, where resounds forever the deafening roar of the Eau Noire.

In the most savage part of this scenery, and nearly under the tunnel through which the road passes, and which any one who has ever traveled in that direction may well remember, there lies, a thousand feet below the path, a beautiful green spot, dotted with fruit-trees and luxuriant in fertility, which, amid the sterile grandeur around, looks like an oasis in the desert. Here, in the lap of Nature, were nestled half a dozen picturesque-looking chalets; and here, completely mountain-locked in one of these chalets, lived my Alpine Sophie —she and her father, all alone; and that spot she had rarely left, even to go as far as Martigny, and hence her childish simplicity.

I have never seen an inhabited place that presented so perfect an idea of seclusion from all that is human, viz., wars, robbers, pickpockets, passions, and misery. There was nothing to fear there but thunderbolts, avalanches, and the sudden descent of large sections of the mountain, which, in the shape of huge rocks, every where overhung with threatening jealousy the devoted beauty which had so long resisted the ravages of time, and it seemed as if a breath were only wanting to detach these rocks and overwhelm in common ruin the last bright spot of this dark gorge.

Nearly over this spot there is a small, solitary inn, where I felt almost afraid to trust myself for one night, on account of the appearance of the rocks above. One of the smaller bits of this mountain (a huge stone, higher than the roof of the house) had fallen at some period within the memory of man, and was lodged warningly close to the building.

The peasants of the valley here rejoined us, for we had walked rather faster than they, and their encomiums and recommendations to the landlady to treat me well, "he was such a *brave garçon*," quite amused, but at the same time convinced me of the benefit as well as pleasure of a little frank civility on the part of the traveler toward the inhabitants of the countries he passes through. I am sure those simple people would have fought for me, and yet I had not given them a single cent of money. I bade them good-night one by one, excepting the *last one*, with whom I could not resist walking a quarter of a mile farther to the path where she descended to her home. I watched her till she disappeared under the trees that shaded her door, and almost envied that peace that I was sure she must possess, and the happiness that she and her father would experience when she related the extraordinary adventures of the day—the fête at Martigny, the firing of cannons, and the splendid service in the Cathedral! And how he would enjoy the little basket of cherries she had carried so far, and how the neighbors would drop in (for in Switzerland, as elsewhere, they "*just drop in*"), and how all the gossip of the village would be rehearsed!

A sudden clap of thunder and a drop of rain dispersed these thoughts and started me at a quick pace for the inn, and I had barely reached my solitary chamber when the rain poured down in torrents, accompanied by frequent peals of thunder and lightning. The view from my window, right over the valley, was very grand, and comprised every description of scenery. Besides the foaming torrent below, I counted seven waterfalls tumbling with snowy whiteness down the opposite mountain; but I was too fatigued to enjoy the view long, and, as night had already set in, I was soon sound asleep.

At midnight, however, I was awakened by the most awful clatter I ever heard. I had forgotten where I was, but thought it surely must be Pandemonium. I leaped from my bed amid a blaze of light, and rushed to the window. Never have I viewed a scene so terrifically sublime. The live Alpine thunder leaped from crag to crag, or plunged into the depths below, shaking the very earth with its noisy boundings. The vivid lightning played from peak to peak, dancing round the mountain summits like fiery imps, and lighting up the black forests and gloomy heights, till the glacier streams opposite looked like torrents of molten silver, that tumbled whistling and seething into the turbulent waters of the *Eau Noire!* Just at this moment a big stone fell on the roof, and I thought of Goldau with its unfortunate population buried by a land-slide, and I remembered that such occurrences are generally preceded a few seconds by a shower of stones! Down they came, till I thought the roof would break through with the weight; nor was my anxiety much allayed upon discovering, by a flash of lightning, that they were enormous hail-stones, for in a country playing such pranks there was no knowing what to expect next.

All the pleasing, sunny events of the day now recurred rapidly to memory: the lovely walk, the odors of the newly-mown hay, the beauty of the flowers, the pleasing landscape of the Valley of the Rhone, the dark and musically-waving foliage of the trees, the blue atmosphere of heaven, and the hazel eyes of the fair tempter that led me down into this, all seemed like a dream—an enchanting dream—and the pleasant odors, and the rainbow hues of the flowers, and the choice beauties of the landscape, and the heavenly blue above, all seemed to blend in one harmonious whole—a woman—a Venus—a goddess. But the bat-like wing of the devil swept away the illusion, and left me in this real Pandemonium. And so, my boy, the path of pleasure does not always lead to happiness.

At the same time, I did not feel much fear, partly because my attention was too much absorbed by curiosity, and partly because, like the newly-arrived Dutch minister at Washington, who sat quietly eating his breakfast during a pistol-fight, I thought these were only the customs of the country; therefore I was not a little surprised the next morning when the landlady told me she was frightened out of her wits, and had never before known so terrific a storm among the Alps!

At half past three the next morning I took coffee and rolls. It was a drizzly, wet day, with a heavy atmosphere. I felt frowsy and heavy, just like the weather, for we both had passed through emotions too violent to allow us to get up the day after very bright. It was hardly light as I started forth, with knapsack rebuckled, amid the pattering rain and sloppy mud. But the cup of coffee, the fresh air, and sight of the mountains soon relieved my spirits, and I felt perfectly unconscious of being in a position in which I *ought* to have been unhappy, or, rather, which, from a comfortable *salon* in Paris three months before, I would have regarded as unhappy. I had walked but a short distance, when, to my surprise, I saw my pleasant-looking country queen standing exactly where Eve stood seven days after leaving Paradise—*at the wash-*

tub! or, more truly as well as poetically in both cases, by the fountain washing her linen, or rather cotton, for neither of them ever saw linen. I was neither shocked nor shower-bath-ed, but went boldly up and tied my white handkerchief (*a clean one*) about her neck; and if, in tying the knot, my lips accidentally brushed hers, it's not the first knot that's been tied by a kiss! In another moment a jutting rock separated us forever.

And that night, in a cloudless heaven, I saw a diadem of stars resting on the snowy summit of Mont Blanc.

A book describing Mont Blanc is sadly needed, and it should have for its title "the 99th and positively last description of Mont Blanc." The hoary old mountain is so tired of seeing himself described, that he exclaims, like John Bull, when his witty neighbor perpetrates a new book on him, "Will they *ever* understand me?"

As I stood the next day by that enormous glacier, the *Mer de Glace*, I experienced a burning thirst—such a thirst as may be supposed to consume a citizen of New Orleans who has had nothing to drink for half a day—and I thought what a waste of good things was here. If that glacier only *grew* in the vicinity of New Orleans, what a blessing it would be! a very temporary one, it is true, for, unless it continued growing, the inhabitants of that bibulous city would pound it all up into brandy smashes, cocktails, and *eye-openers* in the first ten days of July!

A REMARKABLE SPOT.

CITIES and towns, like men generally, have their *specialités*, or, in other words, each has some excellence or superiority which distinguishes it from all other cities and towns.

London is celebrated for its pure, clear atmosphere; Paris, for the sincerity and truthfulness of its inhabitants; New York, for its *cocktails*, abolitionists, and tobacco-spitters; San Francisco, for its temperance; New Orleans, for its healthiness (in its own daily papers); St. Peter's and Rome are synonymes; ditto Bern and bears—you enter the gates between two stone bears, within hearing of the growl of live bears, and, before reaching your hotel, stumble over half a dozen monuments to bears and somebody's stupidity. The odors of Cologne are world-renowned, and always *sweeter at a distance.* Frankfort has an enviable renommée for its *leberwürsts.* The Frankforter, in a foreign land, sighs as he remembers the matchless dish of his fathers; indeed, one fine summer night, after making a hearty supper on leberwürsts and *bock beer*, I sighed myself from midnight till noon! I would have added among the notabilities of Frankfort the Ariadne; but I know that this is a sensitive point with the people—just as if they had nothing to see but the Ariadne! Birmingham is noted as being the only city in the world that never produced a gentleman! At least I read once, in Birmingham, a history of Birmingham, which stated that no gentleman was ever known to come out of that city. I merely mention this to nail it as a vile slander, for I saw a gentleman there with my own eyes. I might go on, and enumerate the comfort and moderation of Liverpool hotels, the quiet of Marseilles, the noise and bustle of Venice, &c., but that I wish to devote more space to one of the most peculiar of all peculiar spots—Leukerbad.

In the first place, you can't find it; but in journeying through Switzerland you may suddenly tumble down upon it unawares, over the German *wall*—called in Switzerland a *pass*. After you have tumbled down this frightful preci*pass* (excuse the pun, if people will call such a declivity as that a pass), and have descended to the bottom of as deep and gloomy a gorge as you ever saw in your life, you are astonished at being told by some Swiss savant that you are still higher than the peak of the highest mountain in Great Britain! On either side of you are perpendicular walls of black rock; behind, the eternal snows and ice of a glacier; and in front—never mind; let us hope that the front is a place to get out by. In such a spot, one is prepared for a *lusus naturæ* of any sort; therefore I was not at all surprised at being told that on the top of yonder cliff was a village, and that the only direct passage for the inhabitants of that village to the baths was by ladders down the rocky wall. Thither my curiosity led me, through a woody slope, and along a rocky path, overhung by steep and jagged precipices, to the very foot of the famous *Leiter*.

And here let me say that the boys of Monumental No. 6, or any other *fire*-boys of San Francisco, would never dream of climbing a six-story building on such ladders, and what San Franciscan firemen won't do *can't* be done. However, six-story precipices are more easily ascended when there are no burning timbers to fall on one's head than six-story houses during a raging fire. Besides, the peasant women here climb these ladders fearlessly, and from their dress you would suppose them to be a branch of the celebrated Bloomer societies of America. From stern necessity, they have banished hoop petticoats, skirts, and whatever else can hinder their upward progress, and have donned—what all women secretly desire to don—the outward badge of masculine authority. Seizing the first round, I commenced the ascent. The ladders are rudely made, and often very loosely fastened to the rocks, so that they shake and tremble at every footstep; and the rounds, instead of being nicely-cut lengths of strong wood, are generally bits of crooked branches, with the bark stripped off, thrust through the holes made to receive them, and protruding frequently several inches beyond the edges of the side-pieces. Sometimes the ladders are discontinued, and steps cut into the solid rock succeed, and these places are more dangerous than the ladders themselves, because there is nothing to take hold of, unless one stoops and grasps the smoothly-worn stones. A single slip here would drop you swiftly down to Hades, with a very slight halt, indeed, on the earthly crust below. But on the ladders, unless you become giddy or nervous, or the rounds break, or a rock from above falls on your head, or the ladders become loosened, *you are comparatively safe!*

When about half way up, hanging midway between heaven and earth, I looked above me, and, to my horror, saw a woman descending. However, she looked like a little thing, and I thought I could easily squirm around her, or over her, or under her even, if she were a better squirmer than I. Still, prudence induced me to stop and await the approach of the enemy, in order that, in case of catastrophe, the fall might be from as low a height as possible, for I have no doubt that in such a tumble every foot of descent contains a lifetime of agony. Down she came, rear foremost, foot by foot, with square and solid tread, cracking the ladders at every step, and shaking the whole framework from top to bottom. As she approached nearer, I could see there was nothing short of two hundred pounds' weight backing down leisurely but certainly upon me. She was now only thirty feet above me. What if she should slip or fall! I shuddered at the thought, and instinctively arched my back, hoping that, the two convex surfaces meeting, she might bound over like the avalanches over the Simplon road. Crack, crack, creak, creak, went the ladders, with the regularity of a pendulum, as the ponderous mass descended, in shape like an inverted balloon, in weight like a meal-bag. I tried to cry out, but my voice was absolutely thick from fright, and I could only pray that she might have another pair of eyes granted her behind, or at least that she might use her natural eyes by giving a glance downward in time to avert serious consequences. But no; she rolled on in all the pride of solidity and security, like the boy in the dirt-cart who goes to sleep on top of his load, sure that every thing on the road will turn out for him. I saw it was necessary that something should be done promptly, and happily cast my eyes on a good big bush growing out of a little scanty earth on the rock's side. To seize a stout twig and strip it was the work of an instant; to grasp the ladder firmly with my left hand and the switch with the right was the work of another, and by this time the enemy was broadside on. I immediately administered a succession of blows, as smartly and as rapidly as I could, on the roundest and most prominent part of her back; and, gentle reader, if you ever saw a cat chased to a tree by a dog, you can imagine how that mass of flesh shot up the side of the cliff! She never stopped, and never looked back till clear out of sight, but hand over hand and foot over foot she paddled away with an ascensive power far beyond her weight, as if all the imps and monkeys of the lower regions were after her. Such is the effect of fire in the rear!

I must confess, I descended as rapidly the other way.

Here I had an illustration of the difference of character between the Americans and English. In descending, I met a number of American boys from a school at Geneva. The first one, a bright-looking youth, who was climbing away rapidly, cried out, in passing, "Pshaw! is this all there is about these famous ladders?" "No, it's not the half," I replied, referring to my own painful experience. He did not stop to ask about the other half, but shot ahead, followed by his companions. At the foot of the ladder was a fine-looking English boy. He was hesitating about mounting, and asked, as I approached, "Is it dangerous, sir?" "No, not if you have a cool head," I answered. "But, after all, what is there to see when you get to the top?" he inquired. "A fat woman!" said I, still stinging from my recent lesson, though probably not so much as somebody else. Now this boy was probably just as brave as the others, but he wanted to be first sure, like his nation, that all was right. The Americans, like all their race, without pause, gave the word "Go ahead."

As all of Mr. Macaulay's schoolboys know, Leukerbad is not so much celebrated for its baths as for the peculiar manner of taking them. The bathing-house is a large room, with four square reservoirs in the floor, resembling beer-vats. Around these vats runs a railing to prevent outsiders from tumbling in, serving also as a sort of rest for visitors who wish to converse with their aquatic friends. During the season there will generally be found ten or fifteen persons (ladies and gentlemen) in each compartment; and as they remain three or four hours at a time, a bench is provided for them to sit on in the bottom of the bath, in which position the water reaches up to their chins. Floating tables, laden with coffee-cups, newspapers, baskets, etc., may be seen sailing about or moored against somebody's nose, and offering the various pastimes of reading, chess-playing, drinking, etc.

As I entered the room, there might have been thirty of these amphibious animals squatted around the edges of the reservoir, engaged variously in reading, chatting, drinking, and laughing. The hot steam rising from the water, which is continually renewed, made the room most comfortably warm compared with the cold, gloomy air outside; and I thought that, after the exciting adventures of the morning, one of those baths would exactly suit my symptoms. I read the laws, and took all needful precautions to get properly equipped for the novel undertaking. I found that a long woolen gown was the only article of apparel required, and having speedily procured that, had it carefully measured, in order that the length might be that required by rule, for it is a fine of *two francs* to wear too short a gown! It was a very simple matter to get the gown on, and it was very easy to stand fifteen minutes afterward, and brush my hair and mustaches before a looking-glass; but all the brushing and arranging of the gown that I could bestow did not at all bring me up to the standard of elegance to which I thought myself entitled: do my best, I looked like a Capuchin friar! and to make my *debut* without collar or cravat, before such an assemblage of ladies, now seated directly opposite, and only separated by a door, was awful. What a contrast to the full-dress dinner-table! With finger on the latch, I counted slowly one, two, three, *and staid where I was.* I counted three three times, and said *Go* every time, but not a budge. At last, beginning to shiver in the cold, I shut my lips firmly, and, without counting at all, opened the door and commenced my descent into the water.

It is my plan, in traveling, to extract information from every body and every thing; and though the lessons are often painful, the fruit of them is always pleasant. In the present instance I established firmly a principle in natural philosophy, about which, it is true, I never had many doubts, viz., that heavy bodies will sink more rapidly than light ones. As the result of this undeviating principle, I found, to my mortification, that, while *I* was descending step by step, my gown had opened like a parachute, and was floating on top of the water! I was already more than knee-deep, and each advance made matters worse. The position of a young lady exposed to a violent gale of wind would be far better than mine, but her efforts to arrange things could not be more earnest. I glanced at the group opposite; a general titter burst from all sides, but particularly from my young lady vis-à-vis at the dinner-table. I resolved to be avenged, and to put my gown where it ought to be all at the same time; so, with a sudden spring upward, I fell on my side, sending a huge hot wave over the laughing maiden.

French, German, and Italian were the only languages to be heard in the baths, and I doubt much if a female Saxon voice has ever issued from those precincts, unless from the lips of a spectator. Still, the greatest decorum was preserved, and I did not see an act or sign that would have been unbecoming in a parlor or any where else. The ladies generally kept very quietly in their seats, while the gentlemen would paddle about, paying visits first to one lady and then to another, or take seats by particular ones and pass an hour in conversation. After soaking four hours, every one naturally had a very keen appetite, and a dinner was prepared at six o'clock, to which a hundred persons, at least, sat down. After dinner the company generally saunter out for a walk, though the weather is cold and gloomy. The evening is spent in dancing, card-playing, reading, etc., etc., pretty much as at all watering-places, though with a good deal less humbug and false show than at many. There are several large hotels in the place (which is but a very small village), and during the season they are pretty well filled; but, for the life o' me, I can't tell what can induce people to remain in Leukerbad one day longer than the time required to see the Leiter, the Gemmi Pass, the Glacier, and to take one bath. These are the very notable notabilities of this strange spot. In scenery there are fifty places near at hand that surpass it; for climate, a worse could not be found: the village has no attractions; there are no fine bands there; and as to soaking in water a little saline, one can do that any where, and have it hot enough to take the skin off into the bargain. Who can tell why people frequent the Leukerbad? In winter the hotels are all closed, and the place is consigned over to avalanches, by which it has been two or three times destroyed.

A TILT AT HOTELS, CUSTOM-HOUSES, AND PASSPORTS.

It is a long road, the Simplon road, and under a July sun a dazzlingly white road, and I should hesitate about advising any one to walk at least the first half of it, unless traveling by short stages, and visiting the numerous picturesque valleys whose ends rest upon it. It commences in the swamps at the eastern end of Lake Geneva, and pursues its course through marshes, over rivers, under and over waterfalls, and beneath the paths of avalanches, skirting precipices, climbing cliffs, and burrowing through mountains, and always moving with a *pertinacity* toward its end unequaled in the history of roads, equaled only by the determined spirit to surmount all difficulties which characterized its great builder. From Villeneuve to Brieg the engineering of the road was accomplished easy enough by the River Rhone, whose course it follows; but at Brieg, where it commences the ascent of the Simplon, the genius of a Napoleon was required to conduct it. It winds up slowly but surely, and grasps that giant mountain in its huge folds, as the boa constrictor grasps the ox. No work of Napoleon showed better the wonderful power of his will than this road in its conception and execution, but particularly in that part of it crossing the top of the mountain—the playground of the high Alps, where the sports are the rolling of avalanches, the roar of waterfalls, and the freaks of lightning. These playful gambols, owing to the ingenuity of the engineer, are not in the least interfered with. The avalanche rolls on its course unobstructed, as it ever has done from the foundation of the world, and as it ever will do to the end of time, sliding harmlessly over a path provided for it, and under which the road passes as through a tunnel. The mountain torrent in some places passes over the road in the same way, in others it goes under it. There are a number of "refuges" on both sides of the mountain to shelter the poor traveler overtaken by storms, and on the top is a hospice, occupied by monks belonging to the same fraternity as those of St. Bernard, and to whose hospitality, kindness, and *good wines* I can bear ample testimony.

It was three o'clock in the afternoon when I left Leuk, and as the day was warm I did not enjoy the walk much until six o'clock in the evening, when the sun dropped behind the high mountains, and a coolness of the atmosphere succeeded which was delightfully refreshing. It was quite late when I reached Visp, after having walked during the day thirty-six miles, which is too much. But after a long walk there is nothing so delightful as to arrive at a good, clean country inn. There are not half a dozen *country inns* on the Continent of Europe, though there are ten thousand inns in the *country;* and at these ten thousand inns, wherever they are upon the line of foreign travelers, you may generally be sure of finding hordes of vulgar white-cravated fellows thrusting upon you their officious civilities and other *garçonisms*, and while making a great flourish about you, really doing nothing to serve you. One seizes your coat, another your bag, and another your umbrella, and all fly off to opposite points of the compass, while *you* are led in a fourth direction by the host. After great difficulty, ringing, and running, you finally manage to collect your little stock of traveling articles together, your umbrella being found in No. 4, your bag in No. 30, and your coat in No. 275. If you descend to take a short walk, one of these polite gentlemen offers to carry your *cane* for you to the door, you meanwhile itching to lay it on his back instead of in his hand. When you are prepared to leave, and have every thing strapped and buckled about you in pedestrian order, these fellows would have you strip again, that they may each carry *as far as the door* some one of all the articles you expect to carry thirty miles. You pay your bill, made out *à la mode de Paris*, with a franc for bougie and a franc for service (although you have been in the house but twelve hours), and then fight your way out through the white-cravated *canaille*, who are all grinning, as a mode of expressing their politeness and the gratitude they would feel at being rewarded for it. Every thing about the majority of these little village inns is a miserable aping of the first-class hotels of cities, but the only result of the effort is a similarity of charges without similarity of comforts.

The whole hotel system of Europe wants overhauling. Indeed, the art of conducting hotels any where is yet in its infancy; but immense improvements have been made within a few years, particularly in America, and, thanks to steam and railways, as travel increases, so will the competition in hotels, and hence additional comforts and conveniences. Travelers are shareholders in a grand joint-stock company, and the landlords of hotels and their waiters are the presidents and directors of that company; and what privileges and profits may be enjoyed by joint-stock companies, the world is just beginning to learn from *credit mobiliers* and banks. The traveling shareholder knows that, by a very small investment of funds in the stocks of the company, he should, in Paris or Rome, at the foot of Mont Blanc, or on the top of the Simplon, have a certain quantity of roast beef; "arf and arf," or Bavarian brewed; clean sheets and silver spoons; decent attendance, cold water, and hair mattresses; the London

Times, Punch, hot and pictorial, or both hot and pictorial, as the London gentleman always is; the New York Herald and New Orleans Picayune, together with a few of the *blanket* sheets, and something from San Francisco in the bargain: all this (and this is not half the traveler wants in the first twenty-four hours even) he knows may be procured for a mere trifle by belonging to the joint-stock society of travelers, which he joined the moment he seized his carpet-bag for a voyage. But to procure an iota of this by himself alone would cost a fortune. For fifteen or twenty francs a day, one may now live at the Grand Hotel du Louvre like a prince. But heretofore princes have known very little about living beyond surrounding themselves with gold and high-ceilinged rooms, and I shall be very much mistaken if, in ten or fifteen years hence, the traveler in America and France (I haven't much hope of England) may not live for a very small sum in a style and luxury never dreamed of by princes—*by German princes*, I mean.

But to return to country inns: what we want to see in them is simplicity, and the very best of country comforts, with some deference to city tastes; as, for instance, we would not like the country inn to be so simple as to have nothing but its village newspaper on the table, and nothing on its walls but the plan of the town, consisting of one long street and two cross ones running at right angles; we would not restrict it to bare board tables and a common washing-room, but we would pitch their attempts at Paris dishes out of the window, and call for fat roast chickens and fresh eggs instead. All the farmers round should bring in their finest fruits, vegetables, and butter; clean sheets, on clean beds, in clean rooms, with water in abundance, should be a sine qua non; we would not at all object to being served by nice, sensible girls, which are to be found in every country, and who would be glad of such a chance of earning one half what is paid many a stupid waiter. We have already seen girls tried in many hotels with great success. Or, pitching head waiters and head cooks *gently* out of the window, we would have a set of plain waiters, who, when told to do a thing, would go straight and do it, and not submit your patience to the ordeal of seeing Mr. Bill or Monsieur Jean, the head serving gentleman, go to tell Thomas to tell the porter that No. 6 wants a foot-bath; the porter appearing half an hour afterward, not with the bath, but to inquire if *monsieur* wishes it hot or cold! Thus every thing would savor of the country, and substantial comforts could be afforded for one half the extravagant prices now generally charged.

At Visp, in the Hotel de Soleil, I found the nearest approach to some of these requisites I have met with in Europe. On my arrival, a cleanly-looking German girl conducted me to my room, threw open the windows, and turned down the white sheets of the bed, brought me a foot-bath, and plenty of water for drinking and washing, and all with so much quietness and celerity, that, after the artistic bungling of the white cravats, I was astonished at how simple and easy a matter service is, if done in the right way. After that, on descending, I found a plentiful supper of eggs, toast, and tea, with strawberries and delicious cream, all spread on a snowy-white table-cloth in a manner that would have even tempted a bishop after a Mardi Gras dinner. Every thing was conducted in the same agreeable way, although there were a good many travelers in the house; and, to crown all, the bill was positively less than one half what I had frequently paid for the same accommodation elsewhere. There are a good many fortunes to be made in good country hotels on the highways of Europe—who will try?

Leaving Visp in the morning, I accepted the first invitation to ride that offered, and which I did not long have to wait for, and soon found myself jogging along in a brewer's wagon as far as Brieg. This little assistance enabled me to get beyond the summit of the Simplon before night, and to sleep in the little village of the same name, where I arrived at nightfall, after having walked the last two hours in the rain. A most gloomy, tragedy-adapted-looking hotel is that large stone building, called *La Poste*, at Simplon. One's first impression on looking at its small, prison-like windows is, that it is a solitary spot, removed far away from society for the purpose of keeping criminals; but, on finding his error, he concludes that if it's not the place to keep them, it's just the place to make them. "Woe unto you," I said to my coat-sleeve (referring to the household); "if I find any bad physiognomies here, I'll take to the road again." An old traveler (no matter how young he may be) becomes necessarily a physiognomist, and, if a man of any observation at all, need never be deceived as to the character of those he meets. (Every bad action is a paint-brush, and surely makes its sign on the features. These brushes are of all sizes, from the broad, full-feathered brush that marked the face of Cain to the delicate pencil that makes a slight tracery only on the face of him who merely harbors a wicked thought.) On the other hand, the good angels paint in pleasing colors our good deeds; and if they be more numerous or habitual, they efface often the black marks made by our evil deeds; and thus it is we often see persons whose features are not well shaped, yet who are handsome by expression; and others, who, though positively plain-looking by nature, have faces we love to look upon, owing to the *goodness* marked in them. For the poor traveler, who is often compelled to choose where he will stay without other knowledge of persons than what he may read in the lines of their countenances, this is a most wise arrangement, and a better protection than half a dozen secreted revolvers. At the same time, inexperienced persons may easily make mistakes, not knowing how to distinguish between the sorrow and care worn faces of some and the pale, student faces of others, which often suffer in comparison with a ruddy-faced fat rascal. But the marks here are as plain as elsewhere; it only requires a little more practice and skill to read them.

The appearance of the *bonne* soon dissipated all doubts, and made me wonder even how such a genial-looking individual could live in such a house, or why, living there, she did not partake of the pervading gloom.

I had hardly finished my tea when a German family drove up with their four horses and traveling atmosphere, and made things more agreeable, though I little thought I was to ride with them most of the next day. I started in the morning long before them, and had nearly reached Domo Dossola before they overtook me. As they had not taken the coupé of their carriage (by the driver's account), I got in there, but had hardly seated myself when it occurred to me that, being now in Italy, and with an Italian driver, the *probability* was that the fellow was a liar. On reaching Domo, therefore, my first act was to apologize to the German gentleman, and ask him whether he had taken the whole carriage. He replied, "Yes." I informed him of the mistake I had made, but he very politely invited me to continue to Bavéno with them, which I did, paying, however, the driver the price of a coupé seat in the diligence.

In traveling in Italy, I always take it for granted that nearly all the low Italians are precious scoundrels, and I am always on my guard with them. Lying and deceit are in that country Machiavelian virtues, which, I am sorry to say, often flourish among a class something higher than the lowest. During the first three days after my descent into that beautiful land, I can not remember a single man who told me the truth where it was his interest to do otherwise. I was not in the least deceived, because I remembered them of old, and was prepared for them, and so always checked their stories by inquiring about the same thing of several persons, taking the *minority report* for truth where all were interested in lying.

From Bavéno I rowed over to the Isola Bella, which greatly disappointed me. One quarter of the money spent on this bizarre folly would have made a little paradise of it. The rare trees growing there in open air, and which have been brought from all parts of the globe, are, of course, both curious and beautiful. And with the grotto, too, I was singularly pleased: it was so cool, and looked so very much like a home for mermaids and Tritons, that I could almost imagine them coming up out of the water and holding levees there. The light of the place had even a marine tint about it, for at that hour the sun's rays could not enter, neither were they reflected up directly from the water, but they came through a watery medium instead of through the atmosphere. No doubt a trout or a perch dropping in that moment would have exclaimed, in ecstasies, "By Neptune! the very light we have at the bottom of the lake!"

I arrived at Milan at midnight, and the diligence was detained half an hour at the gates to examine passports, which I think was the fifth time I had shown the Austrian police my passport on that day. It is an intolerable nuisance, and shows to what a disgraceful position mankind may be reduced by effeminacy and vice on the one hand, and by tyranny and suspicion on the other. As for the Italians, they had better die at once like lions, than live like dogs. The whole passport and custom-house system is an insult to mankind—a disgrace to the age. The traveler for business, the traveler for pleasure, the traveler for health, and the traveler from whatever cause it may be, from the moment he leaves his home, rests under the imputation of being a rogue and a villain! and hence, at every step he takes, he must show his papers at the point of the bayonet, to prove that he is an honest man. At every town in the road a pair of dirty hands are thrust into his trunk. All this is an outrage upon the dignity of man, and the very best excuse (not the real one by any means) that can be offered for it is, that it serves to catch rogues. But rogues can forge passports as well as they can forge bank-bills and drafts, and they are the class least affected by them. No, it is only a portion of that system of tyranny that has so long folded Europe in its grasp, and by which the masses are watched, and their every movement *dogged* and controlled. It is first cousin to the confession-box, and both together tend to degrade man, to take away his spirit, and to make him a mere tool in the hands of a few. I do not believe that the mass of men are either rogues or inclined to be rogues, when left to themselves and to healthy influences. I do not believe they require such a tremendous machinery of government, all *doré* and glittering with splendor, as is exercised to keep them under. All these *dorés* kings, *dorés* courts, *dorés* diplomatists, *dorés* churches, *dorés* palaces, decorations, and grand crosses, form a tremendous and complicated lie, which has grown up gradually, and so dazzles mankind with a brilliancy wrung from the sweat of his own brow, that, until lately, he has not been able to see the *truth* in regard to his melancholy position. But the representatives of the *doré* system have gone too far; they have abused their advantages; the gilding is being rubbed off, and hideous realities begin to appear. And yet things have got to such a position that it is almost impossible for Europe to abandon her lie suddenly. She must keep up the deceit; her diplomatists must still cheat one another; they must semble friendships where they do not feel them. To-day they must ally themselves with the enemy of yesterday, and to-morrow they must declare the nation an enemy and tyrant with which they were but too anxious to be allied to-day. To-day they go to war with one nation, *ostensibly* to protect a worthless people, while at the same moment they see the heroes of the earth and the worthy, who ought to be protected, trampled under the feet of tyrants. Oh, Europe, thou art a doré lie! a vast, an intricate lie—a lie of manifold ramifications!

But the gold is laid on heavily, and hides the deformity in a measure; a *sudden* return to truth would be fatal, for then the lie would show in all its hideousness. Thy position is that of the arsenic-eaters of Peru, who, after having chewed arsenic in gradually increasing doses for many years, in order to render themselves plump and handsome, are compelled to continue the vicious habit, or cease *very* gradually, because, by stopping suddenly, they die with all the horrible symptoms of poison. Such is thy sad state, oh Europe! thou hast taken poison in order to make thyself look splendid with thy dorés trappings, and now thou sufferest for thy unnatural vices and artificial modes of living, and a sudden abandonment of them would be thy ruin.

As for custom-houses, they inculcate dishonesty by tempting men to cheat if they can do it without being detected. There are very few men who will acknowledge openly that to cheat the custom-house is stealing, and yet there are very few men who have a proper development of the moral sense, as most men have, whose consciences do not secretly tell them that to cheat the custom-house is really to steal. But, nevertheless, how numerous are the respectable people, merchants, ladies, gentlemen, and all classes, who continuously steal from the custom-house, and laugh at it as a cunning and clever feat; and how many untruths must they have told to accomplish this! With others, having a natural tendency to vice, the thing goes farther: it is often their first theft, and, thus resting under the imputation of theft, one of the strongest barriers against crime is broken down, viz., the consciousness, shame, and degradation of the first step. It is of no consequence whether a man may really have committed a crime, or only believed himself to have committed it; the effect on his character will be the same. If we perform the most virtuous action, believing, at the time of its performance, that we were committing a crime, the consequences will be as pernicious to our character as if we had actually perpetrated the crime we believed ourselves to be guilty of.

Custom-houses are a great annoyance and waste of time to merchants; they are a nuisance to travelers as well as an insult; they consume the time of a large body of men who might be far better employed; they cost the people an immense addition to their taxes for the collection of revenue, including the pay of officers, spies, clerks, the expense of large buildings, etc.; and they put a large bribe in the hands of government. It is a disgrace to the United States, the great representative of reform, progress, and liberty on earth, that she still keeps her custom-houses open. Away with them, and let us back to simplicity and nature in all things! As for protection, England has taken the glorious lead in exploding that fallacy; all honor to her for it, and for whatever else she may shame us by doing, which we ought first to have done.

After getting through with the passport business, in about the same time as I have devoted to writing about it, we were permitted to enter the city of Milan, and I reached my hotel at about 1 A.M. The streets were quiet and deserted, the cafés were mostly closed, and there was scarcely a person or cab to be seen any where. A gentleman I met, upon my inquiring the way to the hotel, insisted on accompanying me thither, which was a great kindness at that late hour of the night. This is a civility I have so often met with in different cities of Europe, that I am pleased to bear testimony to it, and hold it up to my countrymen as an example well worthy of imitation. I have rarely inquired the location of a place in any city of Europe, as Geneva, Vienna, Leipsic, Frankfort, etc., that the person inquired of has not dropped his own affair, and gone to show me, lest I should be mistaken. At Leipsic I went into a jewelry store, during a hard shower of rain, to make one of these inquiries, and the proprietor immediately put on his hat, and went out in the rain with me to the spot sought, which was some distance. The same thing happened at Dresden. These displays of kindness are most delightful to strangers.

To arise the first morning after having entered a foreign city at midnight, when every thing was hushed and quiet, is like sitting in the theatre and seeing the curtain rise upon a play where some distant capital is represented, with its quaint houses and picturesquely dressed inhabitants. As you sit at your window in the fresh morning air, new and unaccustomed sounds greet your ear—strange-looking buildings, and long, curious streets burst on your vision. Below, you see some people, with their fanciful dresses, promenading as if in travesty or masquerade, while others are attending to their various concerns just exactly as they have prosily done all their lives; but to your imagination the fruit-man is merely an actor, and his musical *Oh! ch'é bella! ch'é bella!* is merely an effort of his to keep up the illusion before you; the long-robed priests, with their shovel hats, are added to give variety; that signora, with a long black veil floating from her head, is only an every-day person dressed up for the occasion; ah! and that splendid Cathedral, with its delicate tracery thrown against the deep blue sky, and its thousands of statues, and its turrets, and its mouldings, and its *alti relievi*, is surely only the painting of the background, in which you think the artist has somewhat exceeded nature: he has made the sky too blue, and the marble so delicate and thread-like, that, if real, the first blast would blow it over. Just at this moment an Austrian band gushes forth its elastic notes, and your heart bounds with exultation, and *you could almost imagine you were in Milan*, which is a strange vagary, in which your imagination confesses how puzzled it is, and that it does not know whether it is occupied with a play or a reality. Descend to the streets, walk about an hour or two, visit the Cathedral, the cafés, the Brera—dine, and after dinner, while smoking your cigar on the Corso Francesco, you will feel as if you had lived in Milan half a lifetime.

Como is but an hour's ride from Milan by rail. It is a delightful little pleasure excursion, and is resorted to by the Milanese as the Parisians resort to St. Cloud and Versailles, the Viennese to Schönbrunn, the Berlinois to Potsdam, etc. Thither I determined to go and spend an hour or two, my time being too limited for more. In compliance with the police regulations, on entering Milan I had given up my passport and received the customary receipt. The following day I had sent the receipt (which must be done within twenty-four hours after arrival) back to recover my passport. This was the day I was going to Como. I therefore had neither passport nor receipt. On arriving at the gates of Milan in the omnibus, my passport was demanded. I replied that it was at the police-office. The officer might have sent me back, but allowed me to pass. In the railway carriages, another officer, followed by a soldier with sword, examines again all the passports. Upon his demanding mine, I answered as before that it was at the police-office. "Well, sir, but do you know you can not enter Como without your passport?" I answered that I had complied with the regulations of Milan, and as I wished to make a pleasure trip to Como, the only way was to come without my passport or not at all. "Who are you, sir?" God forgive me if I replied a little too pompously, "An American citizen!" I could not help it. The freedom and blessings enjoyed in our beloved country came before me in such forcible contrast, that my eyes, my speech, my manner, my whole body must have shown how exultingly I felt the proud distinction. The officer was a gentleman, and in the kindest manner said he would endeavor to get me in, although all he had to do was to tell me to return to Milan. He then went to his office and wrote me a permit on his own responsibility, and returning, said that if I would go to the police-office with a *gendarme* and present that, I would be allowed to enter. I thanked him very much for his kindness, but said that I could not submit to be followed through the streets by a gendarme, and that I should prefer returning to Milan rather than purchase pleasure at such an expense. Turning to the soldier, he whispered *Tempo perduto*, to which I said loudly, so that both could hear, *Non é culpa mia.* I also apologized to him for causing him to write a permit which I refused to avail myself of. Had I known he was writing it I would not have allowed it. We both bowed with perfect civility and separated. I waited an hour and a half for the return train, and went back to Milan without seeing Como or its beautiful lake, though the fresh breezes from its surface had fanned my burning cheek! I shall yet see Como, I have no doubt, but before that day that lovely sheet of water will be freed from the tyrant's rule!

The passports were again demanded in the return train, and again at the gates of Milan, and so the poor Italian, the scholar, and the gentleman, living in his own land, on his own soil, when he makes a pleasure excursion to his own poetic, historic lake, must ask permission of an Austrian, and must, in this short hour's trip, show his passport *six times!* that is, counting departure and return. Can such things last?

I have heard much of the rudeness of the Austrian

police, but I take pleasure in stating that I have invariably found them the most civil officers in Europe, excepting, perhaps, the Prussians. I should say that they performed an unpleasant duty in the most agreeable manner in which it was capable of being performed; and, touching the examination of luggage, I had rather pass my trunk through an Austrian than through an English or American custom-house. Neither at Milan, Venice, Trieste, Vienna, nor at any other place in Austria, have I ever had even the surface of my things disturbed. I have unlocked my trunk, and been requested to lock it again without the weight of a finger being laid upon it. At Trieste, the officer who viséd my passport for Vienna came out and called for Mr. ——, the American gentleman, passed some few complimentary speeches, and absolutely shook hands with me, wishing me a good voyage. It was very pleasing to be attended to first of all the crowd, but I was astonished, at first, at such kindness of manner, accepting it, however, frankly as it was given, and viewing it merely as any similar politeness from a traveling acquaintance. At Vienna a long printed paper is placed before the traveler by the hotel-keeper, with a number of impertinent questions left in blank for answers, and signed by the chief of police. I quietly doubled the paper up and put it in my pocket as a curiosity, at the same time putting merely my name and residence on the hotel-books as usual. One of the questions on this paper asks, Of what religion are you? I immediately went around to the police-office, and in five minutes got my passport, without being asked my religion, or any other question but such as a fellow-traveler will sometimes ask. Yet, notwithstanding this extreme civility on the part of officials, the annoyance about passports is none the less; and if one does not comply with the regulations of the government, he may get into very serious difficulty, as there is no country in Europe more strict in enforcing her laws, in this respect, than Austria. Tyrants see the avenger in every shadow; they tremble at every breath; they flee when no man pursueth. An irregular passport is evidence at once of high treason; it belongs to a plotter, an instigator, a disturber of the public peace. Therefore, if one would avoid all suspicion, and travel through Austria comfortably, let his passport be always *en règle.*

APPLES, TEA, GEESE, GRAPE-SEEDS, TRUNKS, VENICE.

THE last chapters of a book are like the last nights of a session of Congress or Parliament: a great many things must be rushed through at once. I have seized all the most important things I could think of, to "get them in" before the printer substitutes *finis* for "*imprimatur.*" Of all the things at the head of this chapter, Venice is of least importance. Venice is merely a dream, casting its dreamy shadow over the waters. The rest may be trifles, but each calls that a trifle which does not interest himself. The world is made up of trifles. An apple gave us the Bible and a Newton; a small tea-party (at which there were no old maids) revolutionized the world; a goose saved

Rome; a grape-seed destroyed the father of Bacchanalian poetry, if he were not already nearly destroyed by the grape itself; a feast cost Belshazzar an empire; to-day a single bullet, well aimed, would convulse a continent. A cambric needle can kill an elephant, and the elephant's trunk, after striking down an ox, can pick up the needle to commit suicide with—*if he chooses.* And this brings me to *my* trunk (not proboscis), and how I nearly lost it, which let no man call a trifle, because it contained these manuscripts.

In my walking expeditions I had formed the habit of sending my trunk ahead by short stages, and had probably done so twenty times in different parts of Europe, sometimes even without taking a receipt, and never, in any case, had an accident or delay occurred, even where I had intrusted some one to send it after me, though, in such cases, I was very particular about the man trusted.

Having practiced this custom so long and so successfully, I became rather careless and presuming, as most people, *as well as nations*, do, who are too highly prospered; and I thought it was only necessary, wherever I went, to whistle to my trunk to have it follow me like a dog.

From Martigny to Isella, where is situated the Sardinian custom-house, I had forwarded it by diligence; thence, after having had it examined, I was compelled either to wait and travel with it, or to trust the hotel keeper, a very obliging man, to forward it without a receipt (because there was no stage-office there) to Domo Dossola. I adopted the latter course, and at Domo went so far as to give up the key at the stage-office, and direct the agents there to forward it again to Milan; of course, in this case no receipt was given, since they could not be responsible for what they had not yet received. It was the very rashest experiment of travel, and so complicated a movement for my poor trunk that I was sure it would go astray, and began lamenting, repeating, almost from the moment of starting, "It is lost, it is lost, and I deserve it for doing such a thing in any country, but above all others in Italy." These were my pleasant thoughts all the way to Milan. Arrived there, I was not at all surprised when the porter came up to my room, and said he could not find my trunk any where.

I waited for it two days. No antiquary ever ransacked a city more thoroughly for curiosities than I Milan for that trunk. All the dark corners of the messageries and the post-office were turned topsy-turvy in the search. Waiters, commissioners, and porters were all under promise of reward if they should find it; and knowing one man could do more for himself than fifty for him, I deserted all pleasures after the first day, and relaxed no efforts to recover my lost property. Instead of admiring the columns and statues of the Duomo, or examining the pictures of the Brera, I spent the time in groping about dark store-rooms and the court-yards of stage-offices, till my loss and address were as well known in Milan as the Cathedral itself. On the morning of the third day I resolved to give it up entirely, and go. I paid my bill at the hotel, buckled on my knapsack, but at the last moment resolved to stay another day and try the telegraph, though with little hope of success, because the trunk should have been in Milan a week previous. However, I dispatched a message, and was waiting in my room two hours afterward for an answer, when enter the telegraphic messenger with my ten franc piece, saying *the wires were down!* Never was gold more unwelcome; but I swallowed my mortification, and a sound, practical lesson with it, which I give for the benefit of the reader, viz., *stick to your baggage if it is worth any thing;* and if you go on pedestrian excursions and carry a trunk, you should have nothing of much value in it. This principle, indeed, I had always acted on in traveling, and believe I would rather, in the beginning of the summer, have lost my trunk than my proposed foot tour. At the very end of it, it was a far different matter.

After this I took up a philosophical work to compose myself, and resolved to start in the evening. At two o'clock, when I had become quite calm and resigned —bless my eyes! for I could hardly believe them—tap, tap, at the door, and in walks my dear trunk, which I kissed and fondled as if it had been a lost wife. Never before was I so struck with the force of the parable of the lost sheep, which instantly recurred to my mind. The commissaire walked out of my room with my paletot, which I gave him rather spontaneously, as his reward, and the porters and others were also all well paid for their trouble; and if there was any happier man in the train for Venice that night than myself, I should much like to know what made him so.

But one accident or misfortune almost always draws on another, generally because few can act afterward exactly with their accustomed coolness. I have often observed that a terrible railway accident is followed by other minor ones. We become over-careful, and thus, while guarding against every possibility of danger at some one point, leave some other, where danger was never dreamed of, exposed.

Such was my case at Trieste. What care I took of that trunk! what marking, and watching, and chasing I gave it, till it was properly lodged in the position it would occupy till it arrived at Vienna! Then, having secured my place in the coupé of the malle-poste, I wandered leisurely about the city, and finally started for the diligence-office, so as to arrive fifteen minutes before the time. In sauntering thither, I met a malle-poste driving along at full speed, and I don't know why, but (though there are many malle-postes in Trieste) the thought instantly flashed across my mind that *I ought to be in that one!* It was a most villainously disagreeable thought, under the circumstances, and must have given my face an anxiety of expression that made the conductor halt under my fixed stare without my opening my lips. His first words were, "We waited a quarter of an hour for you, sir;" and, on comparing watches, I found *Vienna* time was half an hour ahead of my time! After traveling a distance of equal to three times the circumference of the globe, this was the *first* time that I ever came *near* being left behind. And I have never lost or forgotten the smallest article.

But misfortunes never come singly; and it seems my lessons were not all learned yet, for only a little while after this I had the chagrin of seeing a railway train start from one of the stations where I had descended a moment without me! It had gone but a little distance, however, when I heard the guide cry "Halt!" and the train stopped. It was for a lady and gentleman, who were in the same carriage that I had occupied, to get out. This enabled me to get in; but they were hardly out before they discovered they had mistaken the place, and immediately jumped back again, much to the rage of the conductor. And so their mistake, which, in all my railway traveling, was the only one of the kind I had ever seen, remedied mine, which was the only one of the kind that had ever happened to me; and that both these occurrences should happen at the same moment, in the middle of Austria, was certainly a most extraordinary coincidence. And thus I came near three (it is true, not very serious) accidents, but escaped from them all in so remarkable a manner that I thought them well worth relating, both as representing the curious freaks of travel, and as, perhaps, affording a useful, though not painful lesson (as most experience is) to some brother traveler, who may avoid putting himself in a like position. I feel truly thankful that, though my misfortunes did not come singly, I have never had to suffer from any thing worse in traveling than this trio of *almost accidents.*

I arrived at Venice just in time to share in the festivities consequent upon the birth of the Austrian princess. Fortunately, I had gone to the Hotel San Marco, which, overlooking the square of the same name, afforded me a fine coup d'œil of the animated scene below. From midday the piazza was full of people, who were amusing themselves variously, some by sitting in the doorways and vicinity of the cafés sipping ices (and the largest part of a Venetian café is the *outside* of it, where every body goes), some by promenading around the long galleries surrounding the square, some by looking at the curiosities in the shops, while others were going in or coming out of the Cathedral of San Marco. No one seemed particularly animated at the thought of a princess being born, but every one seemed enjoying himself in a "dolce far niente" and languid style that would be perfectly incomprehensible in America. The American is generally *resolved* not to enjoy himself; in the United States, pleasure is one of the lost arts. But if, on some extraordinary occasion, the free citizen does determine to be happy, he *goes at it* with such fury as to defeat his own ends; he rages over it, tears passion to bits,

> "from desire passes
> On to enjoyment, and, uneasy still,
> Even in enjoyment languishes for desire!"

Not so the Venetians. How easy seems their world! It looks like a different world from ours. How completely careless of all care they are! Truly, they *float* through life in more senses than one! They glide along down the stream of time gently, unthinkingly, unwatchingly, amid whatever pleasures offer themselves unsought, just as their gondolas are forever gliding noiselessly along between palaces and churches, almost without effort on the part of the skillful gondolier. See those fair Venetian ladies, with their dark, flashing eyes, sitting in the piazza San Marco, under no canopy but the stars, and clothed in the lightest flowing white robes; do they look a part of earth any more than their romantic city of the seventy isles?

As you hear those strains of music floating through the atmosphere, and feel that cooling breath of air from the bosom of the Adriatic, whence the full moonbeams are reflected back to heaven again, agitating many a raven lock and kissing many a Venetian cheek before it reaches you, do you not fancy yourself in some magic land, in some Calypso's isle, whence all the troubles of life are forever banished, and where the mere sense of existence is the highest pleasure the soul could crave? Such a spot must be the abode of love. Here Venus and Cupid have their homes; here they sail about in their passion-wafted gondolas, now mooring on the marble steps of the palace forever washed by the wave, and now floating into the more humble abode of the indolent plebeian.

What a contrast this scene formed with those I had just passed through! The snows of the Simplon were scarce melted from my shoes; the chill of its bleak, piercing air and cold fogs was still in my veins; the view of its barren rocks, and desolate wastes, and snow-covered heights was still present in memory before me; the sturdy forms and energetic movements of Swiss and German men glided rapidly by, or the broad back and large, unpoetic features of some hardy German girl planted themselves in pertinacious contiguity to some of the airy forms and passion-scorched features belonging to these pretty Venetian damsels.

The more the memory of the outer world, with its hardships, its practicalities, and its utilitarianisms, pressed upon me, the less could I resist the entrancing influences of the present moment. The braced-up muscles, hardened by hundreds of miles' walking, gradually relaxed under the mollifying atmosphere surrounding them. The limbs, lately bound by the heavy knapsack and cramped by warm clothing, now seemed to expand in their freedom, unconfined but by the light and easy-setting dress of the South. I yielded myself up to the voluptuousness of the moment, walking about the large piazza, now threading my way between the full white robes that flowed over upon the pavement in abundant folds from many a high-born dame, and now stopping a while to hear better the brilliant execution of an Austrian band—ay, and perhaps to see better the brilliant eyes of some other listener who was the real cause of my halting.

In sauntering about in this manner, I soon found myself on the borders of the *grand canal*, only a short distance from the piazza, and not beyond the usual promenade. In a moment I was lounging on the soft cushion of a gondola whose steel prow was turned toward the Rialto. A gondola is a sixth sense! One certainly feels a new and unknown sensation of luxury as he floats along in one of these carpeted barges, reclining on easy couches, and unconscious of the force that propels him. He frequently hears music from the window at either side, which, continually changing as he passes onward, seems more like the irregular strains of some new and unearthly Æolian than notes struck from the every-day harp, guitar, or piano. The illusion is not a little assisted by seeing these proud palaces springing white from the wave.

I was not without a pleasant adventure in Venice, commenced in rather a laughable way. At my hotel in the afternoon, in leaving my room, I became bewildered among the numerous passages, and not knowing which to select, followed the rule of a puzzled whist-player, who plays the card next his thumb. I seized the latch next my thumb, opened the door, and stood, full five feet ten, riveted to the spot before a young lady, in whose bed-room I found myself, and who was lying on the sofa. When I could sufficiently recover myself, I offered a thousand apologies, stating that I had mistaken my way (which, I confess, at that moment I secretly rejoiced to have done). The dark-eyed Italian, who was about seventeen or eighteen, with a frank courtesy which surprised me, arose and positively insisted on showing me the way down. How many seconds I gained in trying to dissuade her, and how many minutes were passed in her explanations about her being a poor guide herself, being in the hotel only to see the fête, and how delighted I was to see us both go wrong, and how altogether an acquaintanceship sprung up out of the adventure, you may readily imagine, but you can hardly fancy my surprise when, stepping into the gondola alluded to above, I saw her, not twenty feet distant, step into another. She bowed and waved her fan, which I was not backward in replying to, and it was not the last recognition that passed between the two gondolas as they swept toward the Rialto. Fortunately perhaps for me, she soon arrived at her home, and disappeared in one of the buildings lining the canal. Why are not *papas* easy to become acquainted with too? and why don't they come out of their houses and invite one in to tea? were questions that I vexatiously put to myself as my boat glided under the bridge of the Rialto.

Such is a glimpse of Venetian life—such is the way slaves are made!

VIENNA—A PEEP, NOT AT THE PICTURE-GALLERIES, BUT AT THE ENGLISH REVIEWS.

An Italian gentleman, the son of a former minister at Vienna, and myself were in possession of the malle-poste from Trieste to Laibach. We had plenty of room; the drivers drove rapidly; and when we were awakened at half past two in the morning, after an eleven hours' ride, we were surprised to find ourselves in Laibach so soon and with so little fatigue.

The train would not start till half past four, and it is not easy to kill two hours of time waiting in a dreary railway station at that hour of the night; consequently, we roamed all over the town, trying, by the flickering lamp-lights, to spell out the signs and to find out the handsome buildings, if there were any. We stumbled on deserted promenade grounds, and avenues of trees with benches under them, and large cafés and hotels, but all was darkness and silence. Not a sound was heard, not even the barking of a dog; not a moving thing was to be seen, not even a watchman—nothing but the waving of the bushes and trees, the rustling of whose leaves easily suggested thoughts of spectres. It was like a city of the dead. Disemboweled Pompeii could not be more quiet.

After prowling about in this way at midnight, in mid-Austria, for more than an hour, and being so lucky as not to be arrested as persons likely to overthrow the government, the dawn began to break, and we returned to the station, where, after a good washing with plenty of water and towels, we sat down in the open air to a bowl of delicious hot coffee and rolls. Whether that coffee was really very excellent, or whether our dark researches and the chilly morning prepared us to relish something inferior even, I will not pretend to say; but certainly we never relished coffee more than on that morning, and took our seats in the train afterward as fresh as if we had been sleeping soundly in our beds all night, and in a few minutes we were sweeping through plains, between and under mountains, up and down hills, and through tunnels toward Vienna.

The Semmering railway is among railways what the Simplon road is among roads. It is the most wonderful in the world. The train actually *climbs* over the Semmering Alps without any aid of "inclined planes," as they are called in America, but by mere force of its iron horse. One sees the road winding up the mountain, over most astonishing bridges, and skirting frightful precipices, and is at a loss to imagine how he will arrive at the top. But the train dashes up with apparent ease to a summit three thousand feet above the level of the sea, where there is a tunnel nearly a mile long.

My Italian friend had, unfortunately, taken a first-class ticket, so that we were separated; but his absence was very well supplied by a Styrian family, consisting of a gentleman, his wife, and daughter, who occupied, with myself, two seats facing one another (the cars being constructed on this road like those in America). We passed our time merrily, being not a little assisted by a young Hungarian dandy. This young fellow was as handsome as any man I have ever seen. He was by far too beautiful, for that is the word describing him, and was dressed ridiculously for a railway carriage, having on delicate straw-colored kid gloves, fitting tightly, a glossy black hat, glazed pumps, and every thing else to correspond. However, he was young, but a fine fellow for all that, and knew every inch of the road. Without him we should have missed much information.

We talked and laughed, ate cherries, smoked (not the ladies), compared guide-books, and, in short, did every thing our hands, tongues, and eyes could find to do in a railway carriage; and in parting, the young lady, with innocent simplicity, gave me a bouquet of flowers she had brought with her, and which I was compelled, after her departure, to thrust rather unceremoniously into my pocket, having but two hands, and as many packages to fill them.

At Vienna the Italian rejoined me, and said he would go to the same hotel. So, we jumped into a carriage and drove off, while his valet took care of our luggage.

In driving through the gates of the town, I was surprised at the perfect cleanness of the streets, and the good order prevailing every where. In this respect, no American city, excepting Philadelphia, can compare with Vienna proper—that is, the part within the walls, which is so small a part of the city, however, that one may walk around it in an hour. There was not a deformed person nor a beggar to be seen any where; there was nothing to affect the eye or the ear; on the contrary, what with the fine stores of the Graben, the palaces of the Herrngasse, Shenkenstrasse, and other streets, and the beautiful gardens, one might suppose he was in the model city of a model country instead of in the capital of a country associated with so much that is offensive to civilization.

This short ride to my hotel produced a long train of reflections in my mind. I could not help reading again a lesson I have read so often in Europe, viz., not to judge by the outside of things. It is human nature to be dazzled by fine raiment. *Dorure* is a better covering than the cloak of charity; you may never know what is under it. The *doré* plate may be all copper, but the superficial judge seizes it for solid gold instead of the solid silver one by its side. In the same way, people judge of cities and countries, and in this way Europeans compare and judge democracies and aristocracies.

There has never been a better opportunity of hearing these superficial judgments and comparisons than during the past summer, and, from what I have heard and seen, I am convinced that the grand struggle between democracy and aristocracy is now commencing in good earnest. The United States of America have grown to a power and importance that is causing the old monarchies of Europe, who have heretofore ignored her existence even, to tremble for the future, not because they fear the exertion on her part of any physical force, but the more powerful influence of her principles, which they know to be as universal as the pulsation of the human heart.

The tree of liberty is planted in America, but its roots extend to every soil, and their fibres receive nourishment from every heart. In the centre of France, in the middle of Austria, in the dungeons of Italy, in the wastes of Siberia, the pulse of freedom beats in unison with its great heart in America.

Tyrants look on and tremble, and hence the continued misrepresentations of the United States, generally purposely, but often unintentionally, by men who are blinded by the dazzling outsides of things.

Democracies always show their worst side, aristocracies their best. The evils in democracies rise healthily to the surface, and are thrown off; those of aristocracies are suppressed and hidden by the government, and rankle within. A democracy is like an over-hearty, healthy man, whose face looks somewhat coarse from pimples, which will cure themselves; an aristocracy is a fair-looking man, with face of roseate flush, in which the discerning judge sees the evidence of inward consumption, that is gradually but surely undermining the fabric. It is in the very nature of a republic that a few bad men will make more noise than a host of good men; they have a voice in the government; they are boisterous and rude, and enunciate even dangerous principles; but no one fears them, and, so long as they do not infringe upon their neighbor's rights, there is no army of bayonets or policemen to put them down and silence them. The grand majority, secure in their strength and virtue, deposit their votes quietly (for goodness is always quiet and unostentatious), until aroused by some great breach of order that unites them to a man, and shows their tremendous power.

In an aristocracy, the voice of the bad, who, from poverty and oppression, soon become the most numerous part of the community, is suppressed by the bayonet; but they forever machinate in secret, and hence are required large standing armies to prevent their outbreaks. The minority of an aristocracy becomes the majority of a democracy; it comprises the best citizens. If you doubt this, disband the standing armies of Europe for one day, and you will quickly see the difference between license and liberty, between a people who are quiet because they are forced to be so by the sword, and a people who are good citizens because they respect virtue.

Besides the inherent necessity in democracies of always showing their worst side, there is another reason why the United States should appear in a still worse light to Europe.

That republic is already regarded as a fair specimen of the working of its peculiar form of government, and by many is considered a failure. This is quite a mistake, although we have not the slightest objection to take it as it is. The example of a large nation existing as a republic under the same circumstances which govern European nations has not yet been seen. The most ardent Republican would hardly contend that man as he is, when loosened from a prison, or when suddenly freed from long generations of oppression, is capable at once of self-government. The limbs that have been long bound become useless. We have every year an immense number of such people thrown upon our shores to exert at first a bad influence. These, of course, produce blemishes and spots upon the system; but they are only temporary, and if the evil of too rapid immigration is not checked at once, its effects, at least, will be checked in course of time by a more than corresponding natural increase of population. But even the improvement operated on the worst of men who go to freedom's shores shows incontestably the advantages of a liberal government. The beggar becomes a donor; he who stole on account of poverty becomes a good member of society; the outcast learns that he is a human being, and that humanity is dignity, and hence follow self-respect and reform; the women learn modesty and virtue, so that what in Europe would have been a multiplying family of thieves or debauchees, becomes in America a respectable part of a good community—a family whose sons may be an honor instead of an expense and disgrace to the state.

Such examples may be seen every day in the United States, and one may also daily see there the manner in which a noisy few create that racket and apparent disturbance that is so pleasing to Europeans as an evidence of the speedy downfall of Republicanism. Take any village of the States containing 3000 persons, and you will find ten men make noise enough for the whole town, while the remainder are scarcely heard. In the large cities the proportion may be greater, but still it is a few only that brawl and fight as if they were going to upset the world.

But never has there been a time in the history of the United States when such an unfortunate combination of trivial circumstances has tended to make them look badly just at the moment they wished to look well as during the past summer. For a long time the only news from thirty-one states and thirty millions of people that the London journals could find worthy of copying were the price of cotton and a murder. Europe was distracted by war, and even when she was not she was occupied with intrigues, and cabals, and plots, and untruths, so that she has had but little time to bestow on a country that has been growing so quietly, blessed with all the arts of peace, as the United States.

But suddenly the Crampton affair comes up. The eyes of all Europe are turned to America. It is just at that leisure moment between the closing of one war and the intrigues and deceits that prepare another; consequently, there is an uncommon interest taken in American affairs. The Continental papers are full of articles from the London journals; and, *mark! America is on the Continent what she is represented to be by England, and principally as the London Times chooses to paint her.* I have seen extracts from that journal on the American difficulty copied into four languages (probably they were into twenty—I speak of what I saw), and I have rarely, in conversing with different persons on the Crampton question, found one who did not acknowledge that he had formed his opinions from the leading articles of the Times, and not from the merits of the question—an example of the immense influence of that able journal.

Gladstone, D'Israeli, Derby, and others of the noblest men of England acknowledge that America is in the right; but their voices are drowned, while the abuse and sophistries of the press speak trumpet-toned, and gain the too willing ear of all Europe. Then opportunely occurs that series of trivialities that is so eagerly seized by the newspapers to support a weak cause. Herbert kills a waiter in a fight, therefore Crampton is not guilty. Brooks strikes Sumner. Càn Crampton be guilty in a country where one legislator strikes another? Then a commotion breaks out in Kansas. Crampton's innocence begins to shine; and, finally, a buff vest appears at the doors of royalty —and Crampton is a martyr! Worthy climax!

I do not say that the killing of a man in a fight, the blow of a senator, a civil commotion, or even the wearing of a buff vest, are trivial things in themselves, but they are trivial when compared with the magnitude of the question with which they were unjustly connected. They are trivial when, for the sake of biasing men's minds, they are held up as the faults of a system of government; and they are trivial even when compared with the crimes committed in England during the very period these occurred in America. Therefore, under the circumstances, they were trivial in every sense of the word.

But this is not all. The reviews come to the aid of the journals, and with more conspicuous injustice, because more premeditated, rake the criminal calendar in order to blacken the character of the United States; and all this amid a profusion of endearing-looking sentences, such as "Our cousins across the water," "Our brothers in America," "Our child," etc.; so that now, when meeting such loving expressions in English articles, like the gentleman in one of Bulwer's novels when his wife began to say "My dear," I always feel sure that a storm is coming.

I open the July number of Tait's Magazine, with its meaningless motto, "Fiat Justitia," and turn to an article entitled "The United States Controversy," expecting, as I had been for some time deprived of both English and American books and journals, to find something to enlighten me on that controversy. The very first thing upon which my eye lights in that article is an account of a *legislator shooting a waiter*, then of Brooks shooting Sumner, and, finally, of a street-fight in Memphis—all in a short article on the *United States Controversy!*

I turn to Bentley's Miscellany for the same month, to an article entitled "The American Difficulty," hoping to find there at least some information on the question itself, and I copy verbatim what I found.

"Thursday, March 8 (in an American hotel).—A little boy of six or seven (whether feet long or years of age the Miscellany does not say) came in alone and sat gravely down, ordered, with the greatest self-possession, beefsteaks and potatoes, and awaited their coming with dignity!!" Oh for the lungs of a Dominie Sampson to exclaim *Prodigious!*

But that was not all of the *American difficulty.* In the same article, the Miscellany relates how a railway train tried to run over a negro in a cart! Naughty train! Logical Miscellany!

Next I came to Colburn's New Monthly Magazine for the same month—article, "American Presidential Morality." This relates the burning of a slave by a mob!

Nothing daunted, I take up Blackwood, always for the same month—article, "Dispute with America," where I again find the Brooks-Sumner affair and the civil war in Kansas rehashed.

And thus *four English magazines in one month* poison their readers' minds by artfully connecting a difficulty, in which their own nation is the one to blame, with all the crimes and peccadilloes they can scrape together from one end of the Union to the other. It must be a weak cause that needs such an unmanly defense.

Give your articles their proper names, gentlemen—"Crime in the United States in 1856."

What would the gentlemen of England say—nay, what would the gentlemen of America say even, if, in essays on the English difficulty published in the United States, we were to depict a Palmer respected in society, yet standing daily by the bedside of his poor sick wife, and killing her by slow torture? If to that we add a Dove murdering his wife in the same manner, and on the same day that Dove is hanged for the murder of his wife a woman is also hanged for the murder of her husband, and a mother imprisoned for starving and forcing dung down the throat of her child? There is not a magazine in America that could embody such things in an article of that kind on England. And yet all these things and a great many more happened in England during the very season that those July writers discover that "a boy of six or seven" calls for beefsteaks in America, and that a waiter is killed by a senator.

Whether is it worse for one man to strike another man down in hot blood, or for a man to stand quietly, like a fiend, and day by day pour death into the veins of his own wife? And heaven only knows how many have been slain in the same manner. But I blush to cite such things, and my only object is to show that in America such events are not made use of to convince the people that England is a nation of poisoners, or that, because the crime of poisoning is committed there, therefore she would be guilty of enlisting men in America.

Blackwood, waxing wroth, goes on to say,

"If England be forced to go to war with the United States, she need not go alone. The overbearing spirit of American diplomacy has become intolerable to *many* of the European states" (viz., to England); "and France and the *Western powers*" (viz., England) "especially recognize in its policy toward the weak states of Central America a perfect parallel to the recent aggressions of Russia upon Turkey, which Europe" (induced by England) "found necessary to resist by a general coalition. *A similar coalition will, in due time, if its arrogant policy be not discontinued, be formed against the American Union.*" "We have been insulted, and we know it, and woe betide Brother Jonathan if his hand ever seem again to approach our collar!"

Whoever—dare—this—*chip*—displace,—must—meet—John—Bull-dog—face—to—face!

But, seriously, the meaning of Blackwood is better and more elegantly expressed in the following language, which was used twenty-four centuries ago, and for which the words of Blackwood, "the overbearing spirit of American diplomacy has become intolerable," will serve as a text. "They are innovators, prompt to conceive, prompt to execute what they have conceived; you, on the contrary, you like to preserve that which is, without striving for that which is beyond, and without action, even where necessary. They are enterprising, even beyond their powers, audacious even to rashness, full of confidence in danger; with you, the deed always falls short of the power; what reflection makes most sure, leaves you without confidence; every difficulty seems to you insurmountable. They are energetic, you are temporizers; their love of travel equals your attachment to home. In their eyes, voyages are means of enriching one's self; you fear to compromise by absence that which you possess. Conquerors of their enemies, they push as far as possible their advantages; in defeat, none suffer less. They devote their body to their country, as if it did not belong to them; their thoughts are theirs only to be consecrated to its service. Not to attain the object of their pursuit is for them to be despoiled of what they possess; to attain it is to have done nothing in comparison with what remains to be done. Does one of their expectations fail, it is replaced by another, and the measure of them is none the less full. For them alone there is no difference between desire and possession, so rapid is the execution of their designs, and it is to that end they devote their whole life, in the midst of labors, fatigues, and dangers. Occupied unceasingly in acquiring, they hardly enjoy what they possess. They know of no enjoyment but the performance of duty, and consider idleness rather than laborious activity a misfortune. They are well painted at a stroke by saying that *they are born to know no repose, and to leave none to others.*

"And with such a people in front of you" (O Europeans!), "will you longer temporize?"

Such was the language used by the Corinthians more than 2000 years ago, when they wanted to stir up the Lacedemonians and other Grecian states to form a general coalition against the Athenians, and such is the substance of the declamations in the press of England to excite the enmity of the other European states against America. No art of eloquence is left untried, no sophistry is wanting, no means are spared to poison the minds of Europeans, and instigate them to an armed coalition against the United States. To-day they dwell on their increasing power and rapid growth, and the necessity of checking it; to-morrow they represent them as being on the point of anarchy and extinction.

In America, at least, you always know the worst. But what is the position of Europe—of this people who are boasting of their good government and excellent laws, while gravely and hypocritically compassionating the miserable state of America? Why, the assassination of one man would throw the whole Continent in a blaze! A revolution in one state would be followed by revolutions in half a dozen. But in America, the President, and Vice-president, and cabinet, and both houses of Congress might all be slain in one day, and the machinery of government would not be deranged; Kansas might slide into the Mississippi, but that would not necessarily disturb the Union. The laws exist the same without as with rulers; the people made them, are satisfied with them, and are not anxious to throw them off. In Europe the bayonet is law; take away the bayonet, and there is no law. Alas! it is a sad thing to see human nature reduced so low. The political condition of the Continent is pitiful in every respect. Spain is in a state of civil war, and ready to fall a prey to the first power that chooses to take her. Turkey, rotten to the core, virtually belongs to England and France, who have plucked her from Russia, and who will eventually quarrel over her. All Italy is ripe for insurrection. The Marianne Society, numbering thousands of members, every one sworn to devote himself to revolution, permeates every province of France. Germany, owing to her situation, is forced to draw the sword when others draw it. Hungary, Poland, and Greece, the unavenged wronged, lie sulky, but wakeful, and prepared for a spring. They say Ireland is quiet. What will they not say in Europe to gain an end? And in front of all these elements of weakness lies the great Russian Bear, tranquil in barbaric might, but eager for the moment to arrive when he may dart upon the prey.

So much we know, and such is the awful state of Europe; how much more is concealed we can not tell, for there the truth is ever hidden. Every thing goes on smoothly until the last moment, when the thoughtless and unheeding, who are admiring the *doré* outside of things, are suddenly startled by the explosion of revolution.

Such are the states who are to form a coalition against America! It is as amusing as the idea of King Bomba blowing the English fleet out of the water! Europeans have enough to do to take care of themselves. They should open their ears to hear the truth, and try to remedy their fearful position. They should not muzzle their press, and imprison those who preach wholesome verities. If France, a hundred years ago, had listened to the hints of some of her wise men, and made friends and counselors of them instead of enemies by banishing and imprisoning them, she might have avoided immense troubles and bloodshed. It has been reserved for one of those truth-tellers to have a glorious vengeance, which I can not help noticing in connection with this subject, as I have not seen it remarked upon. The author of the "*Contrat Social*" spoke in that work of the Corsicans "as a new people, and the only one in Europe who were not injured by legislation," and what hope there was in the future of such a people. French troops were immediately after this dispatched to the island of Corsica under the *doré* plea of protection, and the author regretted having written what he did, thus drawing, as he supposed, this people down with him in his own ruin. But the poor exile little imagined that the depth of his observation amounted to a prediction, which has since met with a most wonderful fulfillment. Five years after he penned that sentence Napoleon Bonaparte was born, and a *Corsican* ruled Europe! and on this day a Corsican dynasty is the most powerful in Europe for good or bad!

No, the threat of a coalition against the Union is idle. Sad will be the day for Europe on which she attempts such a thing! Many will be the chains loosened on that day! America has nearly as many friends in the Old World as she has citizens in the New, and misguided Europe, instead of having one Union to deal with, would find that Argus with his hundred eyes, and Briareus with his hundred hands, would be in her midst. There is only one nation that could instigate such a thing; it is she that dippeth her hand with us in the dish—that calleth us "brother" and "cousin." From the rancor *she* has lately shown, it is impossible to know what she may not attempt; for

"Quem vult perdere Deus, prius dementat!"

A STROLL ABOUT VIENNA.

It was pleasant to get away from the tergiversations of journals and reviews, not only too unmanly to acknowledge an error, but abusing their position as a medium of communication between Europe and America by inciting the enmity of the whole family of nations against the one they had already injured; it was pleasant to find one's self again in the pure and truthful air, for the air in the heart of Austria, although breathed by diplomatists, is pure and honest.

It was an Italio-Californian day, and more can not be said of weather; the heavens were of the deepest blue, and the air of a cool *crispness* that cracked in the breathing. I sauntered about mechanically until my ear caught the enlivening strains of music, which drew me in front of the Palace. The military band were playing, as usual, at midday. I should say it were worth a trip from Paris to Vienna merely to hear the soul-stirring music of an Austrian band. Paris has nothing to compare with it. It is *sui generis*—the

Jenny Lind of military music. There is an elasticity of touch about it that is perfectly electrical, and makes one's heart bound in a bounding body. It is to all other music what certain days in Italy and San Francisco are to all other days of all other places in the world. Every one that hears it is inspirited: the soldier looks martial, the citizen looks like a soldier, and even the little vagabond bristles up at the sound, and almost shows the blood of a gentleman.

A wealthy young American at my side, carried away by his enthusiasm, which, after being nourished for a week amid pictures, palaces, gardens, and music, had now reached its climax, exclaimed suddenly,

"Oh, how delightful! I would like to pass my whole life in Vienna. Look, there is not a rowdy to be found; every thing is decent and orderly, and, *between you and me*, how different this is from our country!"

His words were set to music; for, like magic, or as Moses struck water from the rock, the stately drum-major struck out of the elastic air one of the most inspiriting polkas I had ever heard. At the same instant, casting up my eyes, I beheld, in large letters, over a magnificent arch, the inscription,

JUSTITIA REGNORUM FUNDAMENTUM.

The flashing bayonets and brilliant accoutrements of the manly-looking regiment at my side dazzled my eyes as I threw them upon the motto, and, by a natural illusion, caused each word to glow like fire, as such a motto should. They burnt themselves into my forehead; and as I thought of a poor Calvi, a pious

Pellico, a heroic Orsini, and of the thousands of good men and true patriots at that moment languishing in Austrian prisons—as I thought of San Giorgio and of a hundred other dungeons in Italy and in this *decent, orderly-looking* country, I felt the letters burn to my heart, and wondered they did not set fire to the arch, the Palace, and tyranny's capital!

"Yes," said I to my friend, "*it is* different from our country; it is beautiful, but, alas! all a sham—only gilt, gilt, gilt."

Echo, rebounding against the walls of the palace itself, answered solemnly from that noble arch,

"GUILT! GUILT! GUILT!"

The people of Vienna are not much behind the Parisians in love of enjoyment; and if there is not such an appearance of refinement in an open-air crowd of Viennese as in the same kind of company in Paris, still there is quite as much decorum and good behavior. Indeed, it is surprising to observe how much better a large crowd behaves any where in Europe than in America. Assemblies in the United States would be benefited by the presence of a few more truncheons.

After an early dinner, I took a stroll round the fortifications which surround the city proper. These are now turned into delightful promenades, and a leisurely walk of an hour is sufficient to complete the circuit. On arriving at the Wasser Glacis, I was just in time for a grand open-air concert, given by Josef Gung'l. It commenced at five o'clock in the afternoon, and lasted till ten, and during that period there was not one moment of cessation in the music. Besides the band of Gung'l, there were two military bands, and the three played alternately. When Josef drew the bow he drew the crowd, for playing waltzes his is to other Austrian bands what all Austrian are to French bands. He was generally compelled to play each piece twice, and on one occasion was forced to play a favorite air four times in succession. I was not sorry. The garden, brilliantly illuminated, was thronged with ladies and gentlemen, while five times the number that were inside crowded around the inclosure outside. Ices, lemonades, orgeats, coffee, etc., were plentifully provided, and all seemed to enjoy themselves more than they would if they had traveled off five hundred miles to a fashionable bath, where they would pay dearly for being crushed and starved.

The five hours passed away so rapidly that I was sorry to hear the clock strike ten. I heard the music, however, all night in my dreams.

The next morning I went to Daum's, in the Kohlmarkt. It is the principal café in Vienna. The principal café in Vienna is about equal in style to a third class one in Paris. Cafés or restaurants are good places to see life. "Tell me what you eat," says Savarin, "and I will tell you what you are." Show me *how* you eat it, and I will tell you what you have been.

The only breakfast taken in Viennese cafés is dry bread or toast and coffee. The latter is always taken in a small tumbler or goblet instead of in a cup. No one takes butter. I ordered some, and the waiter was obliged to go out into the street to buy it. Not one waiter in fifty in Vienna understands French. They generally take two or three French newspapers. I found English papers only in one café: they were the Times and Galignani. American papers are rarely seen on the Continent in public places; they are more numerous in Switzerland than elsewhere. These café breakfasts being light, the dinner-hour is early, say at one or two o'clock. It surprised me to see how every one followed the general rule about breakfast. There was no exception to the bread and coffee meal. The lean man and the fat man, the hungry man and surfeited man, all took the same thing. These old countries are like a Macadamized road out of repair—every vehicle runs in the same rut. Routine is the rut of nations. Locke speaks in praise of indifference; routine is just the reverse of this. Custom makes us in love with *opinions* without examination. Perhaps the Viennese have discovered the very best breakfast; but I like better the independence of the Yankee, who *doubts*, and therefore will try sausages and buckwheats with the thermometer at 70°. He may get an indigestion, and discover by painful experience that he has not made a healthful breakfast, but the same bold inquisitiveness has led him to discover clipper ships instead of tubs. Poor man! he grows thin and dies young, a martyr to science and sausages! but succeeding generations bless his memory. They will discard his sausages and buckwheats, and keep his clipper ships.

On the other hand, perhaps the Viennese have *not* discovered the very best breakfast; then it is certain they never will, because they are wedded to an opinion.

For this very reason the Cuban and Mexican retain their clumsy wooden plows. For this reason many people will still sail in tubs instead of clippers, because they will hold more, forgetting that speed is tonnage; and for this reason the Chinese, unwarned by the fate of Absalom, still wear their tails on their heads.

During the summer season, the poor of Vienna and those who can not leave the city may enjoy all the privileges of a large watering-place. These pleasure-loving people, instead of going to the baths, bring the baths to the city, so that every morning early you may go to the Wasser Glacis, and there, in the cool morning air, while sipping whatever spring water you prefer, listen to a better band of music than is to be heard at Baden-Baden.

After several days spent in examining the curiosities of Vienna, I took the night train for Dresden, and was unfortunate enough to get into a car full of nurses and babies; however, we all managed to sleep in a heap, and more quietly than I expected. There was a Russian lady next to me, who offered a good example of the extraordinary facility with which people of that nation learn languages. She spoke English so well at first that I asked her how long since she left that country; to my surprise, she answered that she *had never been there.* French, Italian, and German she rattled off with equal facility.

It is singular with what a secure feeling one can confide himself to a railway carriage on the Continent or in England, while in America it is really an alarming undertaking. The carelessness of life on our roads, their bad management, and their bad construction, are a disgrace to our country, and a constant object of remark throughout Europe. Instead of double tracks, barriers across roads, and a sufficiency of guards, we seem to court danger, and rush our trains in opposite directions, at the same moment, on a single track, right through villages, across streets, and over exposed turnpikes, as if the bodies of five hundred human beings were not in momentary danger of being hurled into a common mass by a runaway horse, a careless driver, or even a stray cow! There is one very good way to remedy this thing, and bring directors to their senses, and that is to desert the railways as far as possible. Take stages and steam-boats, avoid pleasure-trips by rail, stay at home, do any thing to make these reckless men more careful of human life. But the best way of all would be to pass stringent laws upon the subject, as is the case in Europe.

I shall spend some days in Dresden and other cities before returning to France, but will only write next from Paris. I expected letters at Vienna, but got nothing. Merchants and lovers are the only faithful correspondents.

PARIS AGAIN.

I ARRIVED at home late last night, after more than three months' absence. Truly there is but one Paris, and that is the essence of all France. It is the queen of cities. It was made in a peculiar mould, and the mould was made of peculiar materials, and the materials do not exist out of France, and will not bear transportation. Only French heads and French tastes in France could concoct Paris; they would fail any where else. In Paris there is perfect reciprocity between city and people; they were made for one another, and are part of one another, and each is ever ornamenting the other; separated, they both pine and fade. The Parisian in a foreign land is but a melancholy shade, just what Paris is in mid-summer without its Parisians—lifeless and dull.

Most cities are a mere collection of houses, where people agree to live near one another. Two millions of people come together on the banks of the Thames, and decide to build all their dwellings on one spot and call it London. They also determine to do all those things that are absolutely necessary to do as a body, viz., to build sewers to drain off their water; to make side-walks and streets to walk through; and to light their streets at night. But if every family lived alone in the woods, they would do nearly the same thing on a small scale, only their streets would be foot-paths, their sewers would be gutters, and their gas-lights lanterns. A stranger, in either case, looking merely at the outside, would say these people do not enjoy themselves; and whatever happiness there might be within the dwellings, he would certainly be very right in supposing that they added but little to their enjoyment by building a city, in spite of their increased facilities for it. In Paris the case is just the reverse: a million of men get together on the banks of the Seine for the purpose of seeing and being with one another, and of contributing each his portion toward the enjoyment of the whole. One brings his music, another his painting, another his wit, another his architecture, another his science; and all this skill, instead of being hoarded by in the dwelling, is thrown into the common stock, and improved and refined by cultivation and attention. And thus the peculiar excellences which distinguish Paris and Parisians above all the world have their foundation in their eminent sociability. This is the touchstone of their elegance, refinement, and taste.

Driving down through the Boulevards, I could not help remarking, in contrast with all the cities of Europe, the fine, broad streets, the beautiful buildings, the noonday blaze of gas, the polish of the shop windows, and of the articles so temptingly arranged within them; the matchless brilliancy of the cafés, sparkling with mirrors, and gold and white enamel, and jets of fire; the well-dressed crowds moving with Parisian skill, quietly and unjostlingly, yet with animation; the carriages, coupés, fiacres, and omnibuses; the restaurants, with their trios of ladies seated high above the guests, and superintending, with careless, easy mien, yet watchful eyes, the movements of the black-coated waiters; the theatres, belching forth crowds of persons to spend the interlude in taking an ice, a *demi tasse*, or *petite verre*—all made a scene of life and gayety more resembling a fair in the open air than the everyday appearance of a great city.

Yet this is the dull season at Paris, and the bewildered stranger might well wonder how Paris looked in the gay season.

As I reached my house in the Rue de Rivoli, it really seemed like home again to meet the cordial welcome of the Concierge and his family, and afterward of my kind landlady, who had my room and bed all preserved exactly as I left it. Mons. Jean Jacques, too, the student "en droit," who had but recently passed his *Baccalaureat-es-lettres*, was still there preparing to surprise his confiding parents *en province*, not by what he had, but by what he had not learned of the law; still, to make amends for his ignorance in one branch of education, he will more than excel in another, which comprises a thorough knowledge of the "town." My neighbor, the smoker of bad cigars, has gone, but has actually left a mark above the keyhole, where his noxious smoke has blown through into my room, resembling the powder-stains around the vent-hole of a cannon. His company is agreeably replaced by a pretty mignonne Parisian, whose husband is traveling—poor thing! The two *bonnes* who were employed in the *mansarde* opposite my window, and who never used to look up from their work while I was dressing, though they found a great deal to laugh at in the shape of the stitches they were making just at the very moment I was shaving myself at the window, are gone too, and their place is occupied by a pair of mustaches and his lady, who for curtains have substituted white paint on the window-panes. I can always tell when he is at home, because the windows are then always shut. During his absence his lady sometimes takes a little air, and I am sure she knows all my movements from morn till night, my hours for rising and retiring, my hour for taking coffee, for going out and coming in, and whether I clean my teeth before putting on my boots, or put on my boots before cleaning my teeth. Narrow streets are apologies for all errors committed on both sides of them; one can't always be watching one's eyes on the one side, and one can't always be guarding one's movements on the other. But my *vis-a-vis* is not at all curious. She never appears with a bouquet in her hands, and has never addressed me one sentence after which could be properly added that Yankee character—?

Paris presents a very different aspect in summer from what it wears in winter. There is just as much gas in the streets during the former season as during the latter, and a good deal more in the Champs Elysées. And there are just as many people to be seen on the Boulevards in one season as in the other; perhaps there are a great many more in summer than in winter. There are certainly a great many more seated in front of the various cafés; and as for the shady side of the colonnade of the Palais Royal, the bases of the columns present a most motley array of shapes and colors when viewed from one end, and far exceed in novelty the columns of the old archbishop's palace of Liege, every one of which is of a different style of architecture from the preceding one. Here may be seen a turbaned head, there the scarlet frock-like pants of the Zouave; next the flowing robe of a grisette, supported by a pretty little toe, elevated rather higher than the line of beauty usually runs in sculpture. A slippered old gentleman follows next, who probably has a room over the spot where he sits, and who has not moved out of the precincts of the Palais Royal for a twelvemonth, perhaps. The glazed boot of the dandy, the blouse of the workman, and the calico of the *bonne*, all help to complete this singular-looking row, which may be seen from morn till midnight every day from June till October in the court-yard of this palace. There, in the evening, the fountain and the band play together; and once the sun has retired beyond the walls of the old home of Richelieu, the crowd thickens, filling the long, broad promenades, and the thousand chairs arranged under the trees, and completely besieging the popular Café de la Rotonde at one end of the garden, surrounding it with a compact mass of petticoats—that is, compact as the uncommon dimensions of those articles will admit.

But the *élite*, the haut ton of Paris, are all gone to the springs, or, if not gone, are closely barred within their houses; for a Parisian who was known to remain in Paris during the month of August would forever lose caste.

The summer excursions of the middling and poorer classes in Paris consist of little trips to the Bois de Boulogne, to Versailles, to St. Cloud, etc.; and at the latter place, when the *grandes eaux* play, you may see thousands of persons scattered over the beautiful grounds of the park, some in parties of two or three, and some in families of half a dozen, while sometimes two or three families are united in one large picnic party, and may be seen upon a grass-plat, under the shade of the overhanging trees, eating their simple refreshments, and talking and laughing as loudly and unconcernedly as if there were not five hundred people within a few hundred yards of them; hundreds of others will be found lying along the slope of the hill, occupied in reading or conversing, while the children are amusing themselves playing ball, hide-and-go-seek, or other games. The decorum and good order which prevail are truly astonishing. No one is boisterous, and never is any one seen under the effects of liquor. The refreshments used are of the simplest kind, such as *plaisirs* (a very light kind of cake) and other such infantile nourishment; or, if they go to the cafés, of which there are many on the ground, it is to take a glass of orgeat, lemonade, beer, wine, or coffee, with frequently a thimbleful of cognac. Thus a portion, although a small portion, of the Parisians, in comparison with the whole population, pass their Sabbaths; and this portion seems lately to be viewed by certain English statesmen as if it composed all Paris, and might be cited as an example of the good effects resulting from doing what one likes on the Sabbath.

It is a most surprising thing, that when the world is six thousand years old, and after mankind has enjoyed some thirty thousand Sabbaths, the most enlightened men of one of the most enlightened nations on earth are still debating as to what is the proper observance of that day. This shows, at least, that the Almighty has left us some little latitude in that respect, and that while we know it is positively wrong to work on the seventh day, it is not so certain that we may not indulge in a few quiet amusements. It is also a very curious freak that a few thousands of the British public have suddenly discovered that they *must—absolutely must*—have music on Sunday afternoon, or go down to perdition through a gin shop! That band is going to wash away all the sins of London, to close the gin palaces, to feed and clothe the poor, to make them industrious, virtuous, and temperate, and, finally, to refine and elevate their tastes! It's a wonderful invention, only it is a great pity that this modern reformer, this military Luther, can not be applied to the millions of mankind at once, instead of to a few Kensington Square people, who are over-greedy for the kingdom of Heaven.

Well, we will go all the way to London to look at the first man that is converted by fife and drum, pipe and hautboy!

The Continental mode of observing the Sabbath has had very little to do with keeping the French, Spanish, and Italians temperate. They have not the inclination to drink or to other coarse sensualities which distinguishes the lower classes of English and Americans. This is partly owing to their abundance of light wines, and partly, perhaps, to their less masculine organization. Without any Puritanic notions in the matter, I do not like to see *public amusements* provided for the people on the Sabbath. Every body has a right to that day as one of rest, and if public entertainments of any kind are held, a large number of people must be employed as officers to manage and conduct them. People are prone enough to amuse themselves without being legislated into it; and if there are some who can not get into the country, for instance, once in a week, why, it is a misfortune of their position in life, just as there are some who can not leave their beds *any* day in the week, others who can never ride in carriages, and others who can barely get sufficient nourishment. A band of music will not help a single one of these people, but there are other philanthropic measures that may. The man that spends his money on Sunday in gin, depend upon it, will, if he can, have the trombone and gin too. If he can not get to the country, it is his own fault—he prefers his Tom & Jerry! As a general rule, from individuals up to families, communities, cities, and countries, the better the Sabbath is observed, the better, happier, and more moral the people.

CONCLUSION—IN WHICH, LIKE THE LAST CHAPTER OF RASSELAS, ALL MY CONCLUSIONS REMAIN STILL UNCONCLUDED.

Having undertaken to prove nothing, nothing is proven. After much observation, however, the writer thinks he has never seen any people so agreeable as the French, none so honest and genuine-hearted as the Germans, none more refined than the Italians. There are no people who are so virile, spirited, and witty as the Irish, nor whose nationality is more strongly marked; and he believes that perhaps an eighth of the English are superior, morally, physically, and intellectually, to a picked eighth of any other nation on earth; and, finally, there is no country where there is so much liberty as in the United States.

But whether the sociability of the French would compensate for being a Frenchman; whether German honesty, sobriety, and steadiness would compensate for an ambitionless life; Italian refinement for Italian effeminacy; the superiority of a minority of the English for the arrogance, brutality, and dullness of the masses; whether it were worth the honor of being an

Irishman for the sake of *desiring to be* an Englishman, as so many Irish appear to do; or whether American liberty is a fair equivalent for American license and rowdyism, are questions I leave each to decide for himself; and while pondering these and collateral subjects, I think we shall all conclude it were better to consider more our own, and less the faults of our neighbors.

THE END.

Vagabond Life in Mexico.

By Gabriel Ferry, for Seven Years Resident in that Country. 12mo, Muslin, 87½ cents.

Madeira, Portugal, &c.

Sketches and Adventures in Madeira, Portugal, and the Andalusias of Spain. By the Author of "Daniel Webster and his Contempories." With Illustrations. 12mo, Muslin, $1 25.

Life and Travels of Herodotus.

The Life and Travels of Herodotus in the Fifth Century before Christ: an imaginary Biography founded on Fact, illustrative of the History, Manners, Religion, Literature, Arts, and Social Condition of the Greeks, Egyptians, Persians, Babylonians, Hebrews, Scythians, and other Ancient Nations, in the Days of Pericles and Nehemiah. By J. Talboys Wheeler, F.R.G.S. Map. 2 vols. 12mo, Muslin, $2 00.

Ewbank's Brazil.

Life in Brazil; or, a Journal of a Visit to the Land of the Cocoa and the Palm. With an Appendix, containing Illustrations of Ancient South American Arts, in recently discovered Implements and Products of Domestic Industry, and Works in Stone, Pottery, Gold, Silver, Bronze, &c. By Thomas Ewbank. With over 100 Illustrations. 8vo, Muslin, $2 00.

Squier's Central America.

Notes on Central America; particularly the States of Honduras, and San Salvador: their Geography, Topography, Climate, Population, Resources, Productions, &c., &c., and the proposed Interoceanic Railway. By E. G. Squier, formerly Chargé d'Affaires of the United States to the Republics of Central America. With original Maps and Illustrations. 8vo, Muslin, $2 00.

Ross Browne's Yusef.

Yusef; or, the Journey of the Frangi. A Crusade in the East. A new Edition. By J. Ross Browne. With numerous Illustrations. 12mo, Muslin, $1 25.

Waikna;

Or, Adventures on the Mosquito Shore. By Samuel A. Bard. With a Map of the Mosquito Shore, and upward of 60 original Illustrations. 12mo, Muslin, $1 25.

Kendall's Santa Fé Expedition.

Narrative of the Texan Santa Fé Expedition: comprising a Description of a Tour through Texas, and across the great Southwestern Prairies, the Camanche and Caygüa Hunting-grounds, &c. A new Edition. By G. W. Kendall. With a Map and Illustrations. 2 vols. 12mo, Muslin, $2 50.